Juvenile Rights, Child Rights and Women Rights

Lalita Verma

AMIGA PRESS INC.
Delhi: - 110051 (India)

AMIGA PRESS INC.
H.O:- 28-A, Indra Park, St.No-9
Chander Nagar, Krishna Nagar
Delhi: - 110051 (India)
Tel: - 011-22504028, +91-98736-57000
Email: - amigapress@gmail.com
info@amigapress.co.in
amigaeditorial@gmail.com
amigapub@gmail.com

Website: - www.amigapress.co.in

This edition is published by Amiga Press Inc.

ISBN: 978-93-84533-73-1

First Published 2020

Printed and bound by Amiga Press Inc.

PREFACE

The juvenile justice system has grown and changed substantially since 1899. Originally, the court process was informal—often nothing more than a conversation between the youth and the judge—and the defendant lacked legal representation. Proceedings were conducted behind closed doors with little public or community awareness of how the juvenile court operated or what happened to the children who appeared before it. Rather than confine young people in jails with adults, the early juvenile courts created a probation system and separate rehabilitation and treatment facilities to provide minors with supervision, guidance, and education.

The lack of formal process and constitutional due process in the juvenile justice system – and potential for substantial deprivations of children's liberty through extensive periods of incarceration even in juvenile facilities — came to light in the landmark 1967 U.S. Supreme Court decision *In re Gault*. In *Gault*, the U.S. Supreme Court determined that the Constitution requires that youth charged with delinquency in juvenile court have many of the same due process rights guaranteed to adults accused of crimes, including the right to an attorney and the right to confront witnesses against them. Following *Gault*, the Supreme Court extended additional constitutional rights to youth, including the right to have the charges against them proven beyond a reasonable doubt and the right against double jeopardy. In 1971, the Supreme Court ruled that youth were not entitled to jury trials in juvenile court, but several states have judicially or legislatively elected to provide youth a right to jury trial.

—Author

CONTENTS

CHAPTER - 1

INTRODUCTION OF JUVENILE

Children are the precious asset of our country and it is the responsibility of everyone to ensure that they have a safe environment to live in. But the last decade has seen a huge leap in the rate of Juvenile crime in a developing country like India. Today, Juvenile crime is like a disease to oursociety. The criminal justice system of India treats everyone differently for different crimes and also gives some exceptions and leniency to some classes of people. These exceptions are mentioned in the Indian Penal Code. "Juvenile" has been defined differently in different Acts, but as per the latest Act i.e. The Juvenile Justice (Care and Protection) Act, juveniles are those who have not attained the age of 18 years. There is a juvenile justice system that treats juveniles differently than adults, because our society believes that former is different from the latter, both in terms of responsibility and potential for rehabilitation.

Although there is concern with public safety and holding juvenile offenders accountable for their actions, there is greater emphasis on rehabilitation than on punishment in the juvenile justice system. "Rehabilitation" means to restore someone to a useful life through therapy and education. For example, a juvenile who commits an offense may be required to participate in counseling or a program to help him make better decisions in the future. But in the light of the present scenario does the "rehabilitation" really lead to a reformation in the child? In spite of the presence of the welfare laws for juveniles, there is a rise in the number of Juvenile offenders across the country. Juveniles are sent to the rehabilitation centers in order to make their future better. For this purpose, rehabilitation centers are made so that special care and protection can be given to these children and it is assumed that they will return back as a reformed person. So, a pertinent question arises here is that whether rehabilitation centre are playing their role at their best or not?

In this paper, the focus has been done on the functioning of the rehabilitation centre and rights of the juvenile. This paper starts with a historical background of legislation made on juveniles and covers all the current legislations along with the role of NGOs and the current scenario of juveniles in India and ends with the result of research.

ROLE OF SOCIAL WORKERS AND NGOS

The primary role of NGO is to offer a framework of operation in the child welfare sector, ensuring every child if ever enter the system, is treated with care and compassion with all its rights acknowledged and protected. Though since the 1980s there has been a shift from welfare to the justice approach, social workers continue to play a crucial role in the treatment of juvenile offenders. As earlier mentioned the JJB consists of a metropolitan magistrate or a judicial magistrate of the first class and two social workers. The social workers should have "been actively involved in health, education, or welfare activities pertaining to children for at least seven years". The Model Rules has prescribed the criterion necessary for appointment as a social worker on the board, "the social worker to be appointed as a member of the board shall be a person not less than 35 years of age, who has a postgraduate degree in social work, health, education, psychology, child development or any other social science discipline and has been actively involved and engaged in planning, implementing and administering measures relating to child welfare for at least seven years.

The two social workers are to "be appointed by the state government on the recommendation of the selection committee". The selection committee has its members, amongst others, "two representatives of reputed non-governmental organizations working in the area of child welfare". The social worker members on the JJB must be assertive, and not get overwhelmed by the magistrate, as they have an important role to play in the rehabilitation of the juvenile.

Under Section 5(4) of JJA 2000, the social worker members can overrule the magistrate. They should familiarize themselves with the provisions of juvenile legislation as also with the papers and proceeding of each case pending before the JJB to ensure that justice is done to the juvenile. It is for the social worker members to gain the confidence of the juvenile, whilst at the same time to portray to him that though his best interest is on their minds, he is going to be dealt with sternly. It is under the orders of the JJB that the juvenile is placed in an institution. Hence, it is imperative that the JJB, especially the social worker members, regularly visit the observation homes, the special homes and other institutions where juveniles are referred to ensure that the objective of reformation and rehabilitation is satisfied. The 1986 Act also recognized the importance of social workers whilst dispensing justice to juveniles. The Juvenile Court was to be assisted by a panel of two honorary social workers possessing such qualifications as may be prescribed, of whom at least one shall be a woman, and such panel shall be appointed by the state government. The 2000 Act elevated the social worker to being part of the bench that constitutes the JJB, instead of merely assisting the magistrate. Despite, social work intervention playing an important role, the same is always voiced alongside words such as "honorary", "voluntary", "charitable". Not only under the 1986 Act were "two honorary social workers" assisting the Juvenile Court, but a similar trend continues under the 2000 Act. The social worker members on the JJB are to be paid "travel and sitting allowances" as may be fixed by the state government. It is high time that the government recognizes that social workers are professionals, playing a crucial role, and the importance of whose work requires to be accepted and appreciated.

Pos are qualified social workers. The Superintendents of child-care institutions are also academically trained social workers, as is also the other senior staff employed in the homes. Pos and the staff attached to institutions have several critical parts to play in the lives of juveniles. Their role has a great significance as delinquents often indicate that their families are not concerned about their welfare.

Firstly, that of a friend so that the child feels comfortable to speak freely with him. Secondly, that of an advisor and guide so that the child has the confidence to approach him when in need. Thirdly, that of a reformer so that the child understands that what he did was wrong. Fourthly, that of a healer who helps the child accomplish his full potential, and directs him towards his future. The setting-up of a child guidance clinic in an institution is vital as repeated sessions with the juveniles are crucial to bringing about a change in his attitude. It is a qualified and trained child psychologist or psychotherapist in a child guidance clinic who can bring about positive change in the juvenile's future.

NGOs too play a pivotal role. They under JJA 2000, can seek a charge of juveniles pending or on completion of inquiry in the capacity of a "fit person" or "fit institution". The 2000 Act has empowered voluntary organizations under an agreement with state governments to establish and maintain observation homes and special homes. Moreover, voluntary organizations need to provide services within institutions established and maintained by the state government, such as counseling, imparting education and vocational training etc. to secure the juvenile his comprehensive rehabilitation.

Reformations in act

The Government of India enacted the Juvenile Justice Act in 1986. In 1989, the General Assembly of the United Nations adopted the Convention on the Rights of a Child. India ratified the UNCRC in 1992. The convention outlines the right of the child to reintegrate into the society without judicial proceedings, wherever avoidable. Hence, the Government, to fulfill the standards of the convention, felt a need to re-write the law. Hence in 2000, the old law was replaced by the Juvenile Justice (Care and Protection of Children) Act.

Current scenario

In spite of the presence of careful child Acts, the last decade has seen a huge leap in the rate of juvenile offenders in India. One of the six men involved in the Nirbhaya gang-rape case (in Delhi) was a juvenile at the time of committing the crime. The juvenile will walk free after three years at a reformatory home as per the Juvenile Justice Act. Members of the All India Mahila Sanskritik Sangathan staged a demonstration in the city to protest against an order passed by the JJB in New Delhi directing a 17-year old convict in the gang-rape of a 23-year old physiotherapy student to undergo three years, the maximum tenure prescribed under the JJ Act, in a Correctional Home.

The protestors called for more stringent punishment to the offender. There were demands from some in India to reduce the upper age limit for juveniles from 18 to 16, in light of the Delhi gangrape case. However, child rights activists said that changing this section of the law in response to a public outcry over a few cases would be a regressive step. In July, the Supreme Court dismissed eight petitions brought by the public asking the Court to rule that crimes of rape and murder committed by juveniles should be punished under adult laws and that the upper age limit for juveniles be lowered to 16. But a subsequent petition, currently being considered by the Supreme Court, asks judges to consider the mental maturity of the juvenile delinquents instead of his or her age in cases where a young person is accused of involvement in a particularly serious crime. Juvenility is mainly a state of mind, and not only a state of body.

Even as the nation pushes and the government debates lowering the age limit in juvenile crimes in the light of the Delhi gang rape, National Crime Records Bureau (NCRB) data shows that most juvenile crimes are committed by those in the age group of 16-18 years. Notably, the minor accused in the Delhi gang rape, who was allegedly the most brutal among the six accused, is 17 and a half years old The NCRB data also shows rapes committed by juveniles have jumped by 188%. The only categories of crimes involving juveniles for which growth figures are higher are theft and robbery which recorded a growth rate of around 200% and abduction of women which recorded an exponential rise of 660%.

Again, while the debate on the issue of revisiting age limit in juvenile crimes has focused on the juvenile justice act being a reformatory tool, the NCRB data is not very encouraging, especially in case of Delhi. Close to 22%, out of all juvenile criminals in Delhi, were repetitive offenders in contrast to the national average of 11.5%. Sources say even this data gives a very conservative figure as only those convicted earlier are called repetitive offenders. Also, those who have turned adults and continued in crime are not included. The grim picture this paints is a reflection of the failure of remand homes to reform juveniles. Even the argument that broken families and children without parents lead to more juveniles taking to crime falls flat if the NCRB data is any indication. It shows that in 2011, only 5.7% of all juveniles arrested were found to be homeless. The rest either stayed with their parents (81.3%) or relatives.

However, socio-economic conditions have been a factor. A large chunk of the offenders come from extremely poor families making for close to 57% of all juvenile criminals. Lack of education is another important factor with over 55% juvenile criminals being with illiterate or limited to primary education. Across the country, Madhya Pradesh, Maharashtra, Chhattisgarh, Andhra Pradesh, Rajasthan, and Gujarat accounted for close to 70% of all juvenile crimes registered in 2011. Madhya Pradesh led the pack in rape cases with 271 cases, followed UP (146) and Maharashtra (125). Delhi recorded 47 cases of rapes by juveniles. All together make for over 50% of all rape cases by juveniles.

It is widely proved that early-phase intervention represents the best approach to preventing juvenile delinquency. In order to prevent juvenile crimes, we have to deal not only with maladjusted children whose difficulties bring them before Law, but also with those who while not violating laws are disturbing others in school and other places. First of all, we should identify such juveniles and give them treatment. Prevention requires individual, group, organizational efforts that aim at keeping juveniles from breaking the law.

Juvenile crimes cannot be stopped only through the proper implementation and amendments of the Juvenile Justice Act. It is vital to make aware of civil society about this disease that exists in our sick society. Juveniles involved in crimes are not criminals, in fact, they are victims of society. Juvenile delinquency can be stopped at an early stage, provided special care is taken both at home and in school. Parents and teachers play a significant role in nurturing the mind of a child. Instead of labeling them as "criminals" or "delinquents," steps need to be taken to give them a scope of rectification and it would be better if the errors in their lives (involving social and psychological) are brought to their notice. The problem of child crime like many other social evils is linked up with the imperfections and maladjustment of our society. The idea is gradually gaining wider acceptance that juvenile delinquent needs the sympathy and understanding of our society and not the heavy hand of the law.

Minors in juvenile court delinquency proceedings do not have the same constitutional rights as those given to adults in regular criminal court cases. In fact, prior to the 1960s juveniles had few due process rights at all. But as juvenile court proceedings have become more formal, states and courts have strengthened juveniles' constitutional rights. Below is a summary of the due process rights that do and do not apply to juveniles in delinquency proceedings. Some of these rights derive from U.S. Supreme Court cases — and therefore apply to all states — while other rights vary by state. Probable cause needed to search a minor. Police officers must have probable cause to search and arrest a minor who is suspected of violating a criminal statute. However, public officials in quasi-parental relationships with minors — like school personnel — need only "reasonable suspicion" of wrongdoing rather than probable cause to temporarily detain and search minors.

Right to a phone call. Usually, a minor is allowed to make at least one phone call if they are in custody and not likely to be released quickly. The minor can call a parent or guardian, who in turn can contact an attorney. Or the minor can contact an attorney directly. By asking to speak with a parent or attorney, the minor invokes his or her Miranda rights. So, if police ignore the minor's request to consult a parent or attorney, anything the minor says to the police after that will likely be inadmissible in juvenile court. No right to bail. Juveniles do not have a constitutional right to seek bail. But many juveniles are released to their parents or guardians prior to arraignment in juvenile court. The right to counsel. In 1967, the U.S. Supreme Court ruled that minors have the right to an attorney in juvenile proceedings. If a minor cannot afford an attorney, he or she has the right to be represented by a state-appointed attorney.

The right to notice of the charges. In re Gault also requires that a juvenile be provided with notice of the delinquency charges he or she faces. The right to confront and cross-examine witnesses. Even though a juvenile adjudication hearing is not a formal criminal trial, a minor has the right to confront and cross-examine witnesses — meaning the minor gets a chance to question (through an attorney) the people called to testify by the state, and to challenge their testimony. The privilege against self-incrimination. Minors in juvenile court proceedings have a right to assert their Fifth Amendment privilege against self-incrimination. This means that a minor cannot be forced to testify against him or herself. No (or limited) right to a jury trial. Most states do not allow jury trials in juvenile delinquency cases. The few states that do allow jury trials often limit them to only certain types of juvenile cases.) The right to have charges proved beyond a reasonable doubt. The U.S. Supreme Court has ruled that if a juvenile faces incarceration or adjudication as "delinquent" as a result of juvenile court proceedings, then the state must prove the charges against the juvenile "beyond a reasonable doubt." If those penalties are not at issue, the state need only prove the charges by a "preponderance of evidence" standard.

Juvenile Justice (Care and Protection of Children) Act, 2015

Juvenile Justice (Care and Protection of Children) Act, 2015 has been passed by Parliament of India amidst intense controversy, debate and protest on many of its provisions by Child Rights fraternity. It replaced the Indian juvenile delinquency law, Juvenile Justice (Care and Protection of Children) Act, 2000, and allows for juveniles in conflict with Law in the age group of 16–18, involved in Heinous Offences, to be tried as adults. The Act came into force from 15 January 2016. It was passed on 7 May 2015 by the Lok Sabha amid intense protest by several Members of Parliament. It was passed on 22 December 2015 by the Rajya Sabha. To streamline adoption procedures for orphan, abandoned and surrendered children, the existing Central Adoption Resource Authority (CARA) has been given the status of a statutory body to enable it to perform its function more effectively. A separate chapter on Adoption provides detailed provisions relating to adoption and punishments for non compliance. Processes have been streamlined with timelines for both in-country and inter-country adoption including declaring a child legally free for adoption. As of 2018, Ministry of Women & Child Development of Government of India is working towards bringing an amendment, primarily to remove courts from adoption process and to handover it to Executive Magistrates/ District Magistrates, despite nationwide protest against such a move.

History

The Ministry of Women and Child Development began contemplating several desired amendments in 2011 and a process of consultation with various stake holders was initiated. The Delhi gang rape case in December 2012 had tremendous impact on public perception of the Act. One of the accused in the 2012 Delhi gang rape was a few months younger than 18 years of age. He was tried in a juvenile court. One of the convicts was found to be juvenile and sentenced to 3 years in a reform home. Eight writ petitionsalleging the Act and its several provisions to be unconstitutional were heard by the Supreme Court of India in the second week of July 2013 and were dismissed, holding the Act to be constitutional. Demands for a reduction of the age of juveniles from 18 to 16 years were also turned down by the Supreme Court, when the Union of India stated that there is no proposal to reduce the age of a juvenile.

On 31 July 2013, Subramanian Swamy, a BJP politician filed a Public Interest Litigation in the Supreme Court of India seeking that the boy be tried as an adult in a court. The Court asked the juvenile court to delay its verdict. After the Supreme Court allowed the juvenile court to give its verdict, the boy was sentenced to 3 years in a reform home on 31 August 2013. The victim's mother criticized the verdict and said that by not punishing the juvenile the court was encouraging other teenagers to commit similar crimes. In July 2014, Minister of Women and Child Development, Maneka Gandhi said that they were preparing a new law which will allow 16-year-olds to be tried as adult. She said that 50% of juvenile crimes were committed by teens who thought that they get away with it. She added that changing the law, which will allow them to be tried for murder and rape as adults, would scare them. The bill was introduced in the Parliament by Maneka Gandhi on 12 August 2014. On 22 April 2015, the Cabinet cleared the final version after some changes. A revamped Juvenile Justice Bill was passed in the Lok Sabha on 7 May 2015. The new bill will allow minors in the age group of 16-18 to be tried as adults if they commit heinous crimes. The crime will be examined by the Juvenile Justice Board to ascertain if the crime was committed as a 'child' or an 'adult'.

Summary

The bill will allow a Juvenile Justice Board, which would include psychologists and sociologists, to decide whether a juvenile criminal in the age group of 16–18 should be tried as an adult or not. The bill introduced concepts from the Hague Convention on Protection of Children and Cooperation in Respect of Inter-Country Adoption, 1993 which were missing in the previous act. The bill also seeks to make the adoption process of orphaned, abandoned and surrendered children more streamlined. The bill introduces foster care in India. Families will sign up for foster care and abandoned, orphaned children, or those in conflict with the law will be sent to them. Such families will be monitored and shall receive financial aid from the state. In adoption, disabled children and children who are physically and financially incapable will be given priority. Parents giving up their child for adoption will get 3 months to reconsider, compared to the earlier provision of 1 month.

A person giving alcohol or drugs to a child shall be punished with 7 years imprison and/or ^{1} 100,000 fine. Corporal punishment will be punishable by ^{1} 50,000 or 3 years of imprisonment. A person selling a child will be fined with ^{1} 100,000 and imprisoned for 5 years. One of the most criticized step in the new JJ Bill 2015 is introduction of "Judicial Waiver System" which allows treatment of juveniles, in certain conditions,in the adult criminal justice system and to punish them as adults. This is for the first time in India's history that such a provision has been prescribed. Given to the severe criticism, Bill was referred to a Standing Committee of Parliament which also rejected such provisions. Since recommendations of Parliament's Standing Committee are not binding, Government has moved ahead and introduced the Bill in Lok Sabha, where it stands passed. Bill is also criticized for prescribing an opaque Age Determination System and its poor draft. There are numerous drafting errors which have been coming to notice after the Bill has been rolled out for implementation on 15 January 2016. Now Government to working on an amendment to sure such errors.

The bill now stands Passed in Rajya-Sabha on Tuesday 22 December 2015, after the Nirbhaya case accused juvenile was released. From the above discussion, we can say that serious crimes like rape and murder also go unpunished with the offender wearing the grab of juvenility. Juvenile crimes cannot be stopped only through the proper implementation and amendments of the Juvenile Justice Act. In order to reform the juvenile in conflict with Law, the juvenile system as a whole needs to be reformed first. The ramshackle conditions of observation homes and juvenile justice boards need to be addressed immediately. The nation must strike to provide education, health care, sanitation and housing to every child. Apart from multiple laws governing children, there exist many other problems at the grassroots level. Government-sponsored children's homes are often unable to accommodate neglected children. Children are sometimes even kept in jail. Thus, there is a problem in the execution of laws pertaining to children and the maintenance of children's homes due to both a lack of awareness of child rights and India's burgeoning child population.

Criticism

Child Rights Activists and Women Rights Activists have called the bill a regressive step and have criticized the Bill. Many experts and activists viewed post December 2012 Delhi Gang Rape responses as creation of media sensationalisation of the issue, and cautioned against any regressive move to disturb the momentum of Juvenile Justice Legislation in the Country. During the debate in the Lok Sabha in May 2015, Shashi Tharoor, an INC Member the Parliament (MP), argued that the law was in contradiction with international standards and that most children who break the law come from poor and illiterate families. He said that they should be educated instead of being punished.

However some sections in the society felt that in view of terrorism and other serious offences, Juvenile Justice Act of 2000 needed to be amended to include punitive approaches in the existing Juvenile Justice Law, which so far is purely rehabilitative and reformative. Some argued that there is no need of tampering with Juvenile Justice Act for putting up effective deterrent against terrorism. Retired Judge of Delhi High Court, Justice RS Sodhi on 8 August 2015 told Hindustan Times, "We are a civilised nation and if we become barbaric by twisting our own laws, then the enemy will succeed in destroying our social structure. We should not allow that but we must condemn this move of sending children to fight their war"

Chapter - 2

Juvenile Delinquency

Juvenile delinquency, also known "juvenile offending", is the act of participating in unlawful behavior as minors (juveniles, i.e. individuals younger than the statutory age of majority). Most legal systems prescribe specific procedures for dealing with juveniles, such as juvenile detention centers and courts, with it being common that juvenile systems are treated as civil cases instead of criminal, or a hybrid thereof to avoid certain requirements required for criminal cases (typically the rights to a public trial or to a jury trial). A juvenile delinquent in the United States is a person who is typically below 18 years of age and commits an act that otherwise would have been charged as a crime if they were an adult. Depending on the type and severity of the offense committed, it is possible for people under 18 to be charged and treated as adults.

In recent years a higher proportion of youth have experienced arrests by their early 20s than in the past. Some scholars have concluded that this may reflect more aggressive criminal justice and zero-tolerance policies rather than changes in youth behavior.Juvenile crimes can range from status offenses (such as underage smoking/ drinking), to property crimes and violent crimes. Youth violence rates in the United States have dropped to approximately 12% of peak rates in 1993 according to official US government statistics, suggesting that most juvenile offending is non-violent.

However, juvenile offending can be considered to be normative adolescent behavior. This is because most teens tend to offend by committing non-violent crimes, only once or a few times, and only during adolescence. Repeated and/or violent offending is likely to lead to later and more violent offenses. When this happens, the offender often displays antisocial behavior even before reaching adolescence.Types Juvenile delinquency, or offending, is often separated into three categories:

- delinquency, crimes committed by minors, which are dealt with by the juvenile courts and justice system;
- criminal behavior, crimes dealt with by the criminal justice system;
- status offenses, offenses that are only classified as such because one is a minor, such as truancy, also dealt with by the juvenile courts.

According to the developmental research of Moffitt (2006), there are two different types of offenders that emerge in adolescence. One is the repeat offender, referred to as the life-course-persistent offender, who begins offending or showing antisocial/aggressive behavior in adolescence (or even in childhood) and continues into adulthood; and the age specific offender, referred to as the adolescence-limited offender, for whom juvenile offending or delinquency begins and ends during their period of adolescence. Considering that most teenagers tend to show some form of antisocial or delinquent behavior during adolescence, it is important to account for these behaviors in childhood in order to determine whether they will be life-course-persistent offenders or adolescence-limited offenders. Although adolescence-limited offenders tend to drop all criminal activity once they enter adulthood and show less pathology than life-course-persistent offenders, they still show more mental health, substance abuse, and financial problems, both in adolescence and adulthood, than those who were never delinquent.

The two largest predictors of juvenile delinquency are:

- parenting style, with the two styles most likely to predict delinquency being:
- "permissive" parenting, characterized by a lack of consequence-based discipline and encompassing two subtypes known as:
- "neglectful" parenting, characterized by a lack of monitoring and thus of knowledge of the child's activities; and
- "indulgent" parenting, characterized by affirmative enablement of misbehavior;
- "authoritarian" parenting, characterized by harsh discipline and refusal to justify discipline on any basis other than "because I said so";
- peer group association, particularly with antisocial peer groups, as is more likely when adolescents are left unsupervised.

Other factors that may lead a teenager into juvenile delinquency include poor or low socioeconomic status, poor school readiness/performance and/or failure, peer rejection, or attention deficit hyperactivity disorder (ADHD). There may also be biological factors, such as high levels of serotonin, giving them a difficult temper and poor self-regulation, and a lower resting heart rate, which may lead to fearlessness. Delinquent activity, particularly the involvement in youth gangs, may also be caused by a desire for protection against violence or financial hardship, as the offenders view delinquent activity as a means of surrounding themselves with resources to protect against these threats. Most of these influences tend to be caused by a mix of both genetic and environmental factors. Some research indicates that changes in the weather can increase the likelihood of children exhibiting deviant behavior.

Individual risk factors

Individual psychological or behavioral risk factors that may make offending more likely include low intelligence, impulsiveness or the inability to delay gratification, aggression, lack of empathy, and restlessness. Other risk factors that may be evident during childhood and adolescence include, aggressive or troublesome behavior, language delays or impairments, lack of emotional control (learning to control one's anger), and cruelty to animals. Children with low intelligence are more likely to do badly in school. This may increase the chances of offending because low educational attainment, a low attachment to school, and low educational aspirations are all risk factors for offending in themselves Children who perform poorly at school are also more likely to be truant, and the status offense of truancy is linked to further offending. Impulsiveness is seen by some as the key aspect of a child's personality that predicts offending. However, it is not clear whether these aspects of personality are a result of "deficits in the executive functions of the brain" or a result of parental influences or other social factors. In any event, studies of adolescent development show that teenagers are more prone to risk-taking, which may explain the high disproportionate rate of offending among adolescents.

Family environment and peer influence

Family factors that may have an influence on offending include: the level of parental supervision, the way parents discipline a child, particularly harsh punishment, parental conflict or separation, criminal parents or siblings, parental abuse or neglect, and the quality of the parent-child relationship. Children who develop behavioral problems early in life are at greater risk for continual life long antisocial behavior, criminal activity and violence. Some have suggested that having a lifelong partner leads to less offending Juvenile Delinquency, which basically is the rebellious or unlawful activities by kids in their teens or pre-teens, is caused by four main risk factors namely; personality, background, state of mind and drugs. These factors may lead to the child having low IQ and may increase the rate of illiteracy. Children brought up by single parents are more likely to start offending than those who live with both parents. It is also more likely that children of single parents may live in poverty, which is strongly associated with juvenile delinquency. However once the attachment a child feels towards their parent(s) and the level of parental supervision are taken into account, children in single parent families are no more likely to offend than others. Conflict between a child's parents is also much more closely linked to offending than being raised by a lone parent.

If a child has low parental supervision they are much more likely to offend. Many studies have found a strong correlation between a lack of supervision and offending, and it appears to be the most important family influence on offending. When parents commonly do not know where their children are, what their activities are, or who their friends are, children are more likely to truant from school and have delinquent friends, each of which are linked to offending. A lack of supervision is also connected to poor relationships between children and parents. Children who are often in conflict with their parents may be less willing to discuss their activities with them. Adolescents with criminal siblings are only more likely to be influenced by their siblings, and also become delinquent; the sibling is older, of the same sex/gender, and warm.Cases where a younger criminal sibling influences an older one are rare. An aggressive, non-loving/warm sibling is less likely to influence a younger sibling in the direction of delinquency, if anything, the more strained the relationship between the siblings, the less they will want to be like, and/or influence each other.

Peer rejection in childhood is also a large predictor of juvenile delinquency. Although children are rejected by peers for many reasons, it is often the case that they are rejected due to violent or aggressive behavior. This rejections affects the child's ability to be socialized properly, which can reduce their aggressive tendencies, and often leads them to gravitate towards anti-social peer groups. This association often leads to the promotion of violent, aggressive and deviant behavior. "The impact of deviant peer group influences on the crystallization of an antisocial developmental trajectory has been solidly documented." Aggressive adolescents who have been rejected by peers are also more likely to have a "hostile attribution bias", which leads people to interpret the actions of others (whether they be hostile or not) as purposefully hostile and aggressive towards them. This often leads to an impulsive and aggressive reaction. Hostile attribution bias however, can appear at any age during development and often lasts throughout a persons life. Children resulting from unintended pregnancies are more likely to exhibit delinquent behavior. They also have lower mother-child relationship quality.

Applicable crime theories

There are a multitude of different theories on the causes of crime; most, if not all, of are applicable to the causes of juvenile delinquency.

Rational choice

Classical criminology stresses that the causes of crime lie within the individual offender, rather than in their external environment. For classicists, offenders are motivated by rationalself-interest, and the importance of free will and personal responsibility is emphasized. Rational choice theory is the clearest example of this idea. Delinquency is one of the major factors motivated by rational choice.

Social disorganization

Current positivist approaches generally focus on the culture. A type of criminological theory attributing variation in crime and delinquency over time and among territories to the absence or breakdown of communal institutions (e.g. family, school, church and social groups.) and communal relationships that traditionally encouraged cooperative relationships among people.

Strain

Strain theory is associated mainly with the work of Robert Merton. He felt that there are institutionalized paths to success in society. Strain theory holds that crime is caused by the difficulty those in poverty have in achieving socially valued goals by legitimate means. As those with, for instance, poor educational attainment have difficulty achieving wealth and status by securing well paid employment, they are more likely to use criminal means to obtain these goals. Merton's suggests five adaptations to this dilemma:

1. Innovation: individuals who accept socially approved goals, but not necessarily the socially approved means.
2. Retreatism: those who reject socially approved goals and the means for acquiring them.
3. Ritualism: those who buy into a system of socially approved means, but lose sight of the goals. Merton believed that drug users are in this category.
4. Conformity: those who conform to the system's means and goals.
5. Rebellion: people who negate socially approved goals and means by creating a new system of acceptable goals and means.

A difficulty with strain theory is that it does not explore why children of low-income families would have poor educational attainment in the first place. More importantly is the fact that much youth crime does not have an economic motivation. Strain theory fails to explain violent crime, the type of youth crime that causes most anxiety to the public.

Differential association

The theory of Differential association also deals with young people in a group context, and looks at how peer pressure and the existence of gangs could lead them into crime. It suggests young people are motivated to commit crimes by delinquent peers, and learn criminal skills from them. The diminished influence of peers after men marry has also been cited as a factor in desisting from offending. There is strong evidence that young people with criminal friends are more likely to commit crimes themselves. However it may be the case that offenders prefer to associate with one another, rather than delinquent peers causing someone to start offending. Furthermore there is the question of how the delinquent peer group became delinquent initially.

Labeling

Labeling theory is a concept within Criminology that aims to explain deviant behavior from the social context rather than looking at the individual themselves. It is part of Interactionism criminology that states that once young people have been labeled as criminal they are more likely to offend. The idea is that once labelled as deviant a young person may accept that role, and be more likely to associate with others who have been similarly labelled. Labelling theorists say that male children from poor families are more likely to be labelled deviant, and that this may partially explain why there are more working class young male offenders.

Social control

Social control theory proposes that exploiting the process of socialization and social learning builds self-control and can reduce the inclination to indulge in behavior recognized as antisocial. The four types of control can help prevent juvenile delinquency are: Direct: by which punishment is threatened or applied for wrongful behavior, and compliance is rewarded by parents, family, and authority figures. Internal: by which a youth refrains from delinquency through the conscience or superego. Indirect: by identification with those who influence behavior, say because his or her delinquent act might cause pain and disappointment to parents and others with whom he or she has close relationships. Control through needs satisfaction, i.e. if all an individual's needs are met, there is no point in criminal activity.

Mental/conduct disorders

Juvenile delinquents are often diagnosed with different disorders. Around six to sixteen percent of male teens and two to nine percent of female teens have a conduct disorder. These can vary from oppositional-defiant disorder, which is not necessarily aggressive, to antisocial personality disorder, often diagnosed among psychopaths. A conduct disorder can develop during childhood and then manifest itself during adolescence. Juvenile delinquents who have recurring encounters with the criminal justice system, or in other words those who are life-course-persistent offenders, are sometimes diagnosed with conduct disorders because they show a continuous disregard for their own and others safety and/or property. Once the juvenile continues to exhibit the same behavioral patterns and turns eighteen he is then at risk of being diagnosed with antisocial personality disorder and much more prone to become a serious criminal offender. One of the main components used in diagnosing an adult with antisocial personality disorder consists of presenting documented history of conduct disorder before the age of 15. These two personality disorders are analogous in their erratic and aggressive behavior. This is why habitual juvenile offenders diagnosed with conduct disorder are likely to exhibit signs of antisocial personality disorder early in life and then as they mature. Some times these juveniles reach maturation and they develop into career criminals, or life-course-persistent offenders. "Career criminals begin committing antisocial behavior before entering grade school and are versatile in that they engage in an array of destructive behaviors, offend at exceedingly high rates, and are less likely to quit committing crime as they age."

Quantitative research was completed on 9,945 juvenile male offenders between the ages of 10 and 18 in Philadelphia, Pennsylvania in the 1970s. The longitudinal birth cohort was used to examine a trend among a small percentage of career criminals who accounted for the largest percentage of crime activity. The trend exhibited a new phenomenon among habitual offenders. The phenomenon indicated that only 6% of the youth qualified under their definition of a habitual offender (known today as life-course persistent offenders, or career criminals) and yet were responsible for 52% of the delinquency within the entire study. The same 6% of chronic offenders accounted for 71% of the murders and 69% of the aggravated assaults. This phenomenon was later researched among an adult population in 1977 and resulted in similar findings. S. A. Mednick did a birth cohort of 30,000 males and found that 1% of the males were responsible for more than half of the criminal activity. The habitual crime behavior found among juveniles is similar to that of adults. As stated before most life-course persistent offenders begin exhibiting antisocial, violent, and/or delinquent behavior, prior to adolescence. Therefore, while there is a high rate of juvenile delinquency, it is the small percentage of life-course persistent, career criminals that are responsible for most of the violent crimes.

Prevention

Delinquency prevention is the broad term for all efforts aimed at preventing youth from becoming involved in criminal, or other antisocial, activity. Because the development of delinquency in youth is influenced by numerous factors, prevention efforts need to be comprehensive in scope. Prevention services may include activities such as substance abuse education and treatment, family counseling, youth mentoring, parenting education, educational support, and youth sheltering. Increasing availability and use of family planning services, including education and contraceptives helps to reduce unintended pregnancy and unwanted births, which are risk factors for delinquency. Education is the great equalizer, opening doors to lift themselves out of poverty.... Education also promotes economic growth, national productivity and innovation, and values of democracy and social cohesion. Prevention through education aides the young people to interact more effectively in social contexts, therefore diminishing need for delinquency.

It has been noted that often interventions may leave at-risk children worse off then if there had never been an intervention. This is due primarily to the fact that placing large groups of at risk children together only propagates delinquent or violent behavior. "Bad" teens get together to talk about the "bad" things they've done, and it is received by their peers in a positive reinforcing light, promoting the behavior among them. A well-known intervention treatment that has not increased the prevention of juvenile delinquency is the Scared Straight Treatment. "The harmful effects of Scared Straight and boot-camp programs may be attributable to juvenile offenders' vicarious exposure to criminal role models, to the increased resentment engendered in them by confrontational interactions, or both".

This suggests that exposure to criminals could create a sense of idealization and defeat the entire purpose of scared straight treatment. Also, this treatment doesn't acknowledge the psychological troubles that the teenager may be experiencing. As mentioned before, peer groups, particularly an association with antisocial peer groups, is one of the biggest predictors of delinquency, and of life-course-persistent delinquency. The most efficient interventions are those that not only separate at-risk teens from anti-social peers, and place them instead with pro-social ones, but also simultaneously improve their home environment by training parents with appropriate parenting styles, parenting style being the other large predictor of juvenile delinquency. Two UK academics, Stephen Case and Kevin Haines, among others, criticized risk factor research in their academic papers and a comprehensive polemic text, The robustness and validity of much risk factor research is criticized for:

- Determinism, e.g., characterising young people as passive victims of risk experiences with no ability to construct, negotiate or resist risk.
- Imputation, e.g., assuming that risk factors and definitions of offending are homogenous across countries and cultures, assuming that statistical correlations between risk factors and offending actually represent causal relationships, and assuming that risk factors apply to individuals on the basis of aggregated data.
- Reductionism, e.g., over-simplfying complex experiences and circumstances by converting them to simple quantities, relying on a psychosocial focus while neglecting potential socio-structural and political influences.

Juvenile sex crimes

Juveniles who commit sexual crimes refer to individuals adjudicated in a criminal court for a sexual crime. Sex crimes are defined as sexually abusive behavior committed by a person under the age of 18 that is perpetrated "against the victim's will, without consent, and in an aggressive, exploitative, manipulative, and/or threatening manner". It is important to utilize appropriate terminology for juvenile sex offenders. Harsh and inappropriate expressions include terms such as "pedophile, child molester, predator, perpetrator, and mini-perp" These terms have often been associated with this group, regardless of the youth's age, diagnosis, cognitive abilities, or developmental stage. Using appropriate expressions can facilitate a more accurate depiction of juvenile sex offenders and may decrease the subsequent aversive psychological affects from using such labels. In the Arab Gulf states [sic], homosexual acts are classified as an offense, and constitute one of the primary crimes for which juvenile males are charged.

Examining prevalence data and the characteristics of juvenile sex offenders is a fundamental component to obtain a precise understanding of this heterogeneous group. With mandatory reporting laws in place, it became a necessity for providers to report any incidents of disclosed sexual abuse. Longo and Prescott indicate that juveniles commit approximately 30-60% of all child sexual abuse. The Federal Bureau of Investigation Uniform Crime Reports indicate that in 2008 youth under the age of 18 accounted for 16.7% of forcible rapes and 20.61% of other sexual offenses. Center for Sex Offender Management indicates that approximately one-fifth of all rapes and one-half of all sexual child molestation can be accounted for by juveniles.

Barbaree and Marshall indicate that juvenile males contribute to the majority of sex crimes, with 2–4% of adolescent males having reported committing sexually assaultive behavior, and 20% of all rapes and 30–50% of all child molestation are perpetrated by adolescent males. It is clear that males are over-represented in this population. This is consistent with Ryan and Lane's research indicating that males account for 91-93% of the reported juvenile sex offenses. Righthand and Welch reported that females account for an estimated 2–11% of incidents of sexual offending. In addition, it reported by The Office of Juvenile Justice and Delinquency Prevention that in the juvenile arrests during 2006, African American male youth were disproportionately arrested (34%) for forcible rape. In one case in a foster home a 13-year-old boy raped a 9-year-old boy by having forced anal sex with him, in a court hearing the 9-year-old boy said he has done this multiple times, that the 13-year-old boy was charged for sexual assault.

Juvenile sex crimes internationally

Sexual crimes committed by juveniles are not just an issue in the United States. Studies from the Netherlands show that out of 3200 sex offenders recorded by police in 2009, 672 of those were juveniles, approximately 21 percent of sexual offenders. The study also points out the male to female ratio of sexual predators. In 2009, a U.S. congressman proposed legislature that would create an International Sex Offender Registry. The bill was introduced due to the fact that because laws differ in different countries someone who is on the sex offender registry in the U.S. who may be barred from living certain places and doing certain activities has free range in other less developed countries. This can lead to child sex tourism, when a sexual predator will go to less developed countries and prey on young boys and girls. Karne Newburn in his article, The Prospect of an International Sex Offender Registry, pointed out some serious flaws in the proposed bill, such as creating safety issues within the communities for the sex offenders placed on the registry. Newburn suggested instead of creating an International Sex Offender Registry from the U.S. model the U.S. join other countries in a dialogue on creating an effective model. As of now no registry exists. Despite this there is still interest in creating some sort of international registry.Juvenile Law: a child must not be tried as an adult

Juvenile law, also known as justice for minors, is the law which deals with children. In order for children's rights to be respected, such laws must be specially adapted to their specific needs. Justice for minors, as the name indicates, is reserved for those who have not yet attained legal majority. In many countries, however, not all births are officially registered, and children themselves can ignore their own age. It can be very difficult to know for sure if certain adolescents are truly younger than 18, or if the child to be tried has instead attained the age of criminal responsibility. Criminal responsibility occurs at a certain age when national law considers children to have attained adequate emotional, psychological, and intellection maturity to take responsibility for committing a crime. For younger children, their parents or guardians are considered responsible for their actions. Most countries have a fixed threshold of criminal responsibility, but it is often placed too young, far lower than the internationally recommended 15 years old. It differs greatly among cultures and areas, ranging from 7 to 18 years old. The justice system must be adapted to the age of the accused or the victim, whether they are an adult, a criminally responsible adolescent, or a child.

Rights of Children in the Justice System

A child who is involved in the justice system has many rights.

- The right of information: An invicted child has the right to ask questions about anything they do not understand. They must know what they are accused of and have the right to know their rights.
- The right to defense: This is a fundamental right. Children have the right to disagree with those who have accused them. They must also be able to express their opinions and concerns and have those be heard.

- The right to assistance: Children must have access to an informed lawyer because they are not often knowledgeable about the law or how justice systems function. Any conversations they have with the lawyer must be private and held in the native language of the child. Other assistance can include financial, social, linguistic, or of health services, especially for victims. Aid is particularly required for sick or handicapped children.
- The right to protection: All children must be allowed to function in the justice system without feeling pressure or intimidation, or fearing for their own life or the lives of their families, especially as witnesses. Direct contact between a victim and the accused party should be avoided as much as possible throughout the investigation and trial. This also means that children have the right to protection against further injury.
- The right to compensation: These can right wrongs do and help a child to heal. They can include financial aid, health care, or social services. This compensation can come from the one who committed the crime or even from the government.
- The right to remain silent.
- The right to have a parent or guardian present.
- The right to privacy: This is the right to keep certain things private, such as personal information (including identity, in certain situations), to speak to people without others listening in, and to be left alone, out of sight of others. This also means that no information which can be used to identify a juvenile delinquent may be published in the media.

Special Treatment for Children

A Child's Best Interest

This must be the most important thing for any child who appears in court. This means that legal actors must be cognizant of the consequences that their decisions have on such children. Anything which affects a child should neither harm them nor destroy their future. Each child's dignity must be respected, whether they are the accused, a victim, or a witness. Victimized children in particular must be treated with compassion. Children must also be ensured protection against violence and negligence, and their needs must be fulfilled, including those of water, food, safety, and hygiene. A minor's well-being and best interests must be important determining factors in investigations.

A Fast and Fair Trial, With Commensurate Decisions

It is important for trials to be fast when they involve children, so that accused children do not remain in prison for too long and victimized children can quickly receive reparations. Justice must also be completely neutral and impartial. This includes presumption of innocence as well as the principle of nondiscrimination. The same rules must apply to all minors, without any receiving different treatment because of their race, color, sex, age, language, religion, nationality, opinions, religious beliefs, cultural practices, wealth, class, birth, family situation, or ethnic or social origin. Trials must always be fair and equal. Finally, all decisions from judicial authorities and members of the court must be commensurate with the severity of the infraction. This means that they must choose appropriate punitive sanctions. Children must not be punished in the same manner for stealing an apple as they would be for stealing a car. The justice system must also take into account the personal circumstances of the child, including their social position, family situation, and the intention and circumstances of the crime.

A Specialized Service

In order for children to receive this specialized treatment, justice for children should be a separate service from justice for adults. In countries which do not have this specialization, usually for political reasons or a lack of resources, children are largely treated as adults. This does not support appropriate reparations for victims or a correct rehabilitation for delinquents into society. There are various titles and processes that governments put in place to deal with children. Some create children's courts, others have special processes for children in normal courts. Some large cities also create special police forces. It is important that these services are always easily accessible. Reporting processes also allow any victimized or detained child to call attention to any rights violations and improve the efficiency of the judicial system.

Involved Personnel

Many people are involved with judicial processes for minors, including everyone charged with protecting the law, of course, but also many people in civil services, as social services and judicial systems often work hand in hand. In the judicial system: police; armed forces; detectives; judges and court members; ministers of justice and child mediators; personnel from juvenile prisons, adult prisons, temporary detention camps, labor camps and military camps; probation officers; regulatory agencies. Throughout society: community judicial officers; chiefs in villages; workers in child protection services; minors' council's members; personnel from reformatories and sealed youth shelters; social aid officers.

Adequate Training to protect children and fulfill their needs.

In order for everyone to best carry out their functions, they must receive specific training and learn the best way to protect children and fulfill their needs. This makes judicial processes fairer and more efficient. People who work solely with children often use surveillance solutions which avoid the judicial system and is often better for children. These techniques must be learned – arresting and detaining juvenile delinquents and interrogations of witnesses – especially for police and prison guards, as they are responsible for the majority of children's rights violations in the judicial system. In some countries, abuse and torture are common practices in the police force.

Sentencing Children

When children in conflict with the law are found guilty, they usually receive a sentence. This can vary greatly depending on the nature and circumstances of the crime, as well as the country in which the trial occurred, as not all countries apply the same punishments. Ideally, separating a child from its family and placing them in prison should be avoided. While in prison, a child's needs and the actual reasons for their conflict with the law are often ignored. Detention should only be used when no other solutions are available, and should always last for as little time as possible. The best sentences support a child's reintegration into society, while treating the root causes of the crime. They allow the child to develop normally, and decrease the rate of criminal occurrences.

Such measures can be as follows:

- Fine, indemnity, and/or return of goods
- Participating in orientation groups or community activities
- Community service
- Placement in a family
- Placement in an education center
- Probation
- Arrangement of semi-freedom

Unfortunately, punishments which deprive people of their freedom are the most used measures in justice systems for adults as well as children. Some countries send children to prison for the most minor infractions. In Sierra Leone, for example, a youth of 15 was condemned to three years in prison for breaking a car window.

Certain countries still use corporal punishments (beatings, mutilations) as judicial punishments for children, even though international conventions prohibit them. In Tonga, for example, the justice system authorizes flogging (whipping) for a child above 7 years old. Also, in spite of the international community's protests, some countries still sentence children to death. It is especially problematic in Iran, Mauritania, Sudan, Saudi Arabia, the United Arab Emirates, Nigeria, and Yemen. The issue of justice for children within armed conflicts poses two special problems: the absence of justice for victims and trials for child soldiers.

Lack of National Justice

During an armed conflict, many children are witnesses or victims of horrific violent acts which deeply affect them. They are often manipulated, abused, or raped. They also often lose family members and lack a proper education and childhood. Most of the time, a country's justice systems do not function during a conflict and take a long time to restart after peace has returned. This prevents victims from accessing their rightful reparations and witnesses from securely reporting what they have seen. Fortunately, the international community has put new processes into place in the last twenty years to help States fight impunity after conflicts, such as formal judicial or non-judiciary courts and tribunals. The most common are the International Court of Justice and Truth and Reconciliation Commissions which attempt to reunite divided populations.

Victimized children are playing a more and more important role in these processes. However, many are not actually heard as witnesses, because the processes are often so long that the children have become adults before the trials' end, or because judicial authorities have a hard time believing what the children say, especially if the events have happened a long time before the trial. Child soldiers present a delicate issue. In modern wars, hundreds of thousands of children have been enlisted into military service, sometimes as young as eight years old, even though it is a serious crime in the eyes of the law. Most of them did not voluntarily present themselves for service and were forced by adults to commit terrible crimes. It is important to acknowledge their responsibility for their actions, but coming before justice systems and being imprisoned are not necessarily the best solutions to the problem. They prevent these children, who are also victims themselves, from moving on from their very difficult past. Unfortunately, in most cases, these children are arrested under the pretext of presenting a menace to society. Also, communities do not welcome these former child soldiers. They are often thrown out of their families and their village. In Uganda, for example, many villages believe that former soldiers possess the "cen," an evil spirit. These children are not reintegrated back into society and often suffer from poverty and shame, without the ability to put their past behind them.

CHAPTER - 3

CHILDREN'S RIGHTS

Children's rights are the human rights of children with particular attention to the rights of special protection and care afforded to minors. The 1989 Convention on the Rights of the Child (CRC) defines a child as "any human being below the age of eighteen years, unless under the law applicable to the child, majority is attained earlier." Children's rights includes their right to association with both parents, human identity as well as the basic needs for physical protection, food, universal state-paid education, health care, and criminal laws appropriate for the age and development of the child, equal protection of the child's civil rights, and freedom from discrimination on the basis of the child's race, gender, sexual orientation, gender identity, national origin, religion, disability, color, ethnicity, or other characteristics. Interpretations of children's rights range from allowing children the capacity for autonomous action to the enforcement of children being physically, mentally and emotionally free from abuse, though what constitutes "abuse" is a matter of debate. Other definitions include the rights to care and nurturing. There are no definitions of other terms used to describe young people such as "adolescents", "teenagers", or "youth" in international law, but the children's rights movement is considered distinct from the youth rights movement. The field of children's rights spans the fields of law, politics, religion, and morality.

There is a mass of human rights law, both treaty and 'soft law', both general and child-specific, which recognises the distinct status and particular requirements of children. Children, owing to their particular vulnerability and their significance as the future generation, are entitled to special treatment generally, and, in situations of danger, to priority in the receipt of assistance and protection. As minors by law, children do not have autonomy or the right to make decisions on their own for themselves in any known jurisdiction of the world. Instead their adult caregivers, including parents, social workers, teachers, youth workers, and others, are vested with that authority, depending on the circumstances. Some believe that this state of affairs gives children insufficient control over their own lives and causes them to be vulnerable. Louis Althusser has gone so far as to describe this legal machinery, as it applies to children, as "repressive state apparatuses".

Structures such as government policy have been held by some commentators to mask the ways adults abuse and exploit children, resulting in child poverty, lack of educational opportunities, and child labour. On this view, children are to be regarded as a minority group towards whom society needs to reconsider the way it behaves. Researchers have identified children as needing to be recognized as participants in society whose rights and responsibilities need to be recognized at all ages.

Historic definitions of children's rights

Sir William Blackstone recognized three parental duties to the child: maintenance, protection, and education. In modern language, the child has a right to receive these from the parent. The League of Nations adopted the Geneva Declaration of the Rights of the Child , which enunciated the child's right to receive the requirements for normal development, the right of the hungry child to be fed, the right of the sick child to receive health care, the right of the backward child to be reclaimed, the right of orphans to shelter, and the right to protection from exploitation. The United Nations Universal Declaration of Human Rights (1948) in Article 25(2) recognized the need of motherhood and childhood to "special protection and assistance" and the right of all children to "social protection." The United Nations General Assembly adopted the United Nations Declaration of the Rights of the Child (1959), which enunciated ten principles for the protection of children's rights, including the universality of rights, the right to special protection, and the right to protection from discrimination, among other rights.

Consensus on defining children's rights has become clearer in the last fifty years. A 1973 publication by Hillary Clinton (then an attorney) stated that children's rights were a "slogan in need of a definition". According to some researchers, the notion of children's rights is still not well defined, with at least one proposing that there is no singularly accepted definition or theory of the rights held by children. Children's rights law is defined as the point where the law intersects with a child's life. That includes juvenile delinquency, due process for children involved in the criminal justice system, appropriate representation, and effective rehabilitative services; care and protection for children in state care; ensuring education for all children regardless of their race, gender, sexual orientation, gender identity, national origin, religion, disability, color, ethnicity, or other characteristics, and; health care and advocacy.

Children have two types of human rights under international human rights law. They have the same fundamental general human rights as adults, although some human rights, such as the right to marry, are dormant until they are of age, Secondly, they have special human rights that are necessary to protect them during their minority. General rights operative in childhood include the right to security of the person, to freedom from inhuman, cruel, or degrading treatment, and the right to special protection during childhood. Particular human rights of children include, among other rights, the right to life, the right to a name, the right to express his views in matters concerning the child, the right to freedom of thought, conscience and religion, the right to health care, the right to protection from economic and sexual exploitation, and the right to education. Children's rights are defined in numerous ways, including a wide spectrum of civil, political, economic, social and cultural rights. Rights tend to be of two general types: those advocating for children as autonomous persons under the law and those placing a claim on society for protection from harms perpetrated on children because of their dependency. These have been labeled as the right of empowerment and as the right to protection. United Nations educational guides for children classify the rights outlined in the Convention on the Rights of the Child as the "3 Ps": Provision, Protection, and Participation. They may be elaborated as follows:

- Provision: Children have the right to an adequate standard of living, health care, education and services, and to play and recreation. These include a balanced diet, a warm bed to sleep in, and access to schooling.
- Protection: Children have the right to protection from abuse, neglect, exploitation and discrimination. This includes the right to safe places for children to play; constructive child rearing behavior, and acknowledgment of the evolving capacities of children.
- Participation: Children have the right to participate in communities and have programs and services for themselves. This includes children's involvement in libraries and community programs, youth voice activities, and involving children as decision-makers.

In a similar fashion, the Child Rights International Network (CRIN) categorizes rights into two groups:

- Economic, social and cultural rights, related to the conditions necessary to meet basic human needs such as food, shelter, education, health care, and gainful employment. Included are rights to education, adequate housing, food, water, the highest attainable standard of health, the right to work and rights at work, as well as the cultural rights of minorities and indigenous peoples.
- Environmental, cultural and developmental rights, which are sometimes called "third generation rights," and including the right

to live in safe and healthy environments and that groups of people have the right to cultural, political, and economic development.

Amnesty International openly advocates four particular children's rights, including the end to juvenile incarceration without parole, an end to the recruitment of military use of children, ending the death penalty for people under 21, and raising awareness of human rights in the classroom. Human Rights Watch, an international advocacy organization, includes child labor, juvenile justice, orphans and abandoned children, refugees, street children and corporal punishment. Scholarly study generally focuses children's rights by identifying individual rights. The following rights "allow children to grow up healthy and free

Physical rights

A report by the Committee on Social Affairs, Health, and Sustainable Development of the Parliamentary Assembly of the Council of Europe identified several areas the Committee was concerned about, including procedures such as "female genital mutilation, the circumcision of young boys for religious reasons, early childhood medical interventions in the case of intersex children and the submission to or coercion of children into piercings, tattoos or plastic surgery". The Assembly adopted a non-binding resolution in 2013 that calls on its 47 member-states to take numerous actions to promote the physical integrity of children. Article 19 of the Convention on the Rights of the Child enjoins parties to "take all appropriate legislative, administrative, social and educational measures to protect the child from all forms of physical or mental violence, injury or abuse, neglect or negligent treatment, maltreatment or exploitation".

The Committee on the Rights of the Child interprets article 19 as prohibiting corporal punishment, commenting on the "obligation of all States Party to move quickly to prohibit and eliminate all corporal punishment." The United Nations Human Rights Committee has also interpreted Article 7 of the International Covenant on Civil and Political Rights prohibiting "cruel, inhuman or degrading treatment or punishment" to extend to children, including corporal punishment of children. Newell (1993) argued that "...pressure for protection of children's physical integrity should be an integral part of pressure for all children's rights." The Committee on Bioethics of the American Academy of Pediatrics (AAP) (1997), citing the Convention on the Rights of the Child (1989), asserts that "every child should have the opportunity to grow and develop free from preventable illness or injury."

Military use of children : Children in the military

Children in the military are children (defined by the Convention on the Rights of the Child as people under the age of 18) who are associated with military organisations, such as state armed forces and non-state armed groups. Throughout history and in many cultures, children have been involved in military campaigns. For example, thousands of children participated on all sides of the First World War and the Second World War Children may be trained and used for combat, assigned to support roles such as porters or messengers, or used for tactical advantage as human shields or for political advantage in propaganda.

Children are easy targets for military recruitment due to their greater susceptibility to influence compared to adults. Some are recruited by force while others choose to join up, often to escape poverty or because they expect military life to offer a rite of passage to maturity. Child recruits who survive armed conflict frequently suffer psychiatric illness, poor literacy and numeracy, and behavioural problems such as heightened aggression, leading to a high risk of poverty and unemployment in adulthood. Research in the UK and US has also found that the enlistment of adolescent children, even when they are not sent to war, is accompanied by a higher risk of attempted suicide, stress-related mental disorders, alcohol misuse, and violent behaviour. A number of treaties have sought to curb the participation of children in armed conflicts. According to Child Soldiers International these agreements have helped to reduce child recruitment, but the practice remains widespread and children continue to participate in hostilities around the world. Some economically powerful nations continue to rely on military recruits aged 16 or 17, and the use of younger children in armed conflict has increased in recent years as militant Islamist movements and the groups fighting them recruited children in large numbers.

History is filled with children who have been trained and used for fighting, assigned to support roles such as porters or messengers, used as sex slaves, or recruited for tactical advantage as human shields or for political advantage in propaganda. In 1814, for example, Napoleon conscripted many teenagers for his armies. Thousands of children participated on all sides of the First World War and the Second World War. Children continued to be used throughout the 20th and early 21st century on every continent, with concentrations in parts of Africa, Latin America, and the Middle East. Only since the turn of the millennium have international efforts begun to limit and reduce the military use of children.

Current situation2

State armed forces

Since the adoption in 2000 of the Optional Protocol on the involvement of children in armed conflict (OPAC) the global trend has been towards restricting armed forces recruitment to adults aged 18 or over, known as the Straight-18 standard. Most states with armed forces have opted in to OPAC, which also prohibits states that still recruit children from using them in armed conflict. Nonetheless, Child Soldiers International reported in 2018 that children under the age of 18 were still being recruited and trained for military purposes in 46 countries; of these, most recruit from age 17, fewer than 20 recruit from age 16, and an unknown, smaller number, recruit younger children. States that still rely on children to staff their armed forces include the world's three most populous countries (China, India, and the United States) and the most economically powerful (all G7 countries apart from Italy and Japan).The United Nations Committee on the Rights of the Child and others have called for an end to the recruitment of children by state armed forces, arguing that military training, the military environment, and a binding contract of service are not compatible with children's rights and jeopardise healthy development during adolescence Saudi Arabia and the United Arab Emirates hired child soldiers from Sudan Darfur to fight against Houthis during thYemeni Civil War (2015-present).

Non-state armed groups

These include non-state armed paramilitary organisations, using children such as militias, insurgents, terrorist organizations, guerrilla movements, ideologically or religiously-driven groups, armed liberation movements, and other types of quasi-military organisation. In 2017 the United Nations identified 14 countries where children were widely used by such groups: Afghanistan, Colombia, Central African Republic, Democratic Republic of the Congo, Iraq, Mali, Myanmar, Nigeria, Philippines, Somalia, South Sudan, Sudan, Syria, and Yemen. Not all armed groups use children and approximately 60 have entered agreements to reduce or end the practice since 1999. For example, by 2017, the Moro Islamic Liberation Front (MILF) in the Philippines had released nearly 2,000 children from its ranks, and in 2016, the FARC-EP guerrilla movement in Colombia agreed to stop recruiting children.Other countries have seen the reverse trend, particularly Afghanistan, Iraq, Nigeria and Syria, where Islamist militants and groups opposing them have intensified their recruitment, training, and use of children.

Global estimate

In 2003 P. W. Singer of the Brookings Institution estimated that child soldiers participate in about three-quarters of ongoing conflicts. In the same year the UN Office for the Coordination of Humanitarian Affairs (UNOCHA) estimated that most of these children were aged over 15, although some were younger. Today, due to the widespread military use of children in areas where armed conflict and insecurity prevent access by UN officials and other third parties, it is difficult to estimate how many children are affected. In 2017 Child Soldiers International estimated that several tens of thousands of children, possibly more than 100,000, were in state- and non-state military organisations around the world, and in 2018 the organisation reported that children were being used to participate in at least 18 armed conflicts.

Rationale for the use of children

Despite children's physical and psychological underdevelopment relative to adults, there are many reasons why state- and non-state military organisations seek them out. Cited examples include:

- Peter W. Singer has suggested that the global proliferation of light automatic weapons, which children can easily handle, has made the use of children as direct combatants more viable.
- Roméo Dallaire has pointed to the role of overpopulation in making children a cheap and accessible resource for military organisations.
- Roger Rosenblatt has suggested that children are more willing than adults to fight for non-monetary incentives such as religion, honour, prestige, revenge and duty.
- Several commentators, including Bernd Beber, Christopher Blattman, Dave Grossman, Michael Wessels, and McGurk and colleagues, have argued that since children are more obedient and malleable than adults, they are easier to control, deceive and indoctrinate.
- David Gee and Rachel Taylor have found that in the UK, the army finds it easier to attract child recruits starting from age 16 than adults from age 18.
- Some leaders of armed groups have claimed that children, despite their underdevelopment, bring their own qualities as combatants to a fighting unit, often being remarkably fearless, agile and hardy.

While some children are forcibly recruited, deceived, or bribed into joining military organisations, others join of their own volition. There are many reasons for this. In a 2004 study of children in military organisations around the world, Rachel Brett and Irma Specht pointed to a complex of factors that incentivise enlisting, particularly:

- Background poverty including a lack of civilian education or employment opportunities
- The cultural normalisation of war
- Seeking new friends
- Revenge (for example, after seeing friends and relatives killed)
- Expectations that a "warrior" role provides a rite of passage to maturity

The following testimony from a child recruited by the Cambodian armed forces in the 1990s is typical of many children's motivations for joining up: I joined because my parents lacked food and I had no school... I was worried about mines but what can we do—it's an order [to go to the front line]. Once somebody stepped on a mine in front of me—he was wounded and died... I was with the radio at the time, about 60 metres away. I was sitting in my hammock and saw him die... I see young children in every unit... I'm sure I'll be a soldier for at least a couple of more years. If I stop being a soldier I won't have a job to do because I don't have any skills. I don't know what I'll do...

Impact on children

The scale of the impact on children was first acknowledged by the international community in a major report commissioned by the UN General Assembly, Impact of Armed Conflict on Children (1996), which was produced by the human rights expert Graça Machel. The report was particularly concerned with the use of younger children, presenting evidence that many thousands of children were being killed, maimed, and psychiatrically injured around the world every year.

Since the Machel Report further research has shown that child recruits who survive armed conflict face a markedly elevated risk of debilitating psychiatric illness, poor literacy and numeracy, and behavioural problems. Research in Palestine and Uganda, for example, has found that more than half of former child soldiers showed symptoms of post-traumatic stress disorder and nearly nine in ten in Uganda screened positive for depressed mood. Researchers in Palestine also found that children exposed to high levels of violence in armed conflict were substantially more likely than other children to exhibit aggression and anti-social behaviour. The combined impact of these effects typically includes a high risk of poverty and lasting unemployment in adulthood. Further harm is caused when child recruits are detained by armed forces and groups, according to Human Rights Watch. Children are often detained without sufficient food, medical care, or under other inhumane conditions, and some experience physical and sexual torture. Some are captured with their families, or detained due to the activity of one of their family members. Lawyers and relatives are frequently banned from any court hearing.

Other research has found that the enlistment of children, including older children, has a detrimental impact even when they are not used in armed conflict until they reach adulthood. Military academics in the US have characterised military training (at all ages) as "intense indoctrination" in conditions of sustained stress, the primary purpose of which is to establish the unconditional and immediate obedience of recruits. The academic literature has found that adolescents are more vulnerable than adults to a high-stress environment, such as that of initial military training, particularly those from a background of childhood adversity. Enlistment, even before recruits are sent to war, is accompanied by a higher risk of attempted suicide in the US, higher risk of mental disorders in the US and the UK, higher risk of alcohol misuse and higher risk of violent behaviour, relative to recruits' pre-enlistment background. Military settings are also characterised by elevated rates of bullying and sexual harassment Military recruitment practices have also been found to exploit the vulnerabilities of children in mid-adolescence. Specifically, evidence from Germany, the UK and the US has shown that recruiters disproportionately target children from poorer backgrounds using marketing that omits the risks and restrictions of military life. Some academics have argued that marketing of this kind capitalises on the psychological susceptibility in mid-adolescence to emotionally-driven decision-making

International law

Recruitment and use of children

The Convention on the Rights of the Child defines a child as any person under the age of 18. The Paris Principles define a child associated with an armed force or group as: ...any person below 18 years of age who is or who has been recruited or used by an armed force or armed group in any capacity, including but not limited to children, boys and girls, used as fighters, cooks, porters, messengers, spies or for sexual purposes. The document is approved by the United Nations General Assembly. It does not only refer to a child who is taking or has taken a direct part in hostilities.

Children aged under 15

The Additional Protocols to the 1949 Geneva Conventions (1977, Art. 77.2), the Convention on the Rights of the Child (1989), and the Rome Statute of the International Criminal Court (2002) all forbid state armed forces and non-state armed groups from using children under the age of 15 directly in armed conflict (technically "hostilities"). This is now recognised as a war crime.

Children aged under 18

Most states with armed forces are also bound by the higher standards of the Optional Protocol on the Involvement of Children in Armed Conflict (OPAC) (2000) and the Worst Forms of Child Labour Convention (1999), which forbid the compulsory recruitment of those under the age of 18. OPAC also requires governments that still recruit children (from age 16) to "take all feasible measures to ensure that persons below the age of 18 do not take a direct part in hostilities". In addition, OPAC forbids non-state armed groups from recruiting children under any circumstances, although the legal force of this is uncertain. The highest standard in the world is set by the African Charter on the Rights and Welfare of the Child, which forbids state armed forces from recruiting children under the age of 18 under any circumstances. Most African states have ratified the Charter.

Limitations and loopholes

States that are not a party to OPAC are subject to the lower standards set by Protocol I of the Geneva Conventions, which allows armed forces to use children over the age of fifteen in hostilities, and possibly to use younger children who have volunteered as spotters, observers, and message-carriers: The Parties to the conflict shall take all feasible measures in order that children who have not attained the age of fifteen years do not take a direct part in hostilities and, in particular, they shall refrain from recruiting them into their armed forces. In recruiting among those persons who have attained the age of fifteen years but who have not attained the age of eighteen years, the Parties to the conflict shall endeavor to give priority to those who are oldest.

The International Committee of the Red Cross had proposed that the Parties to the conflict should "take all necessary measures", which became in the final text, "take all feasiblemeasures", which is not a total prohibition because feasible is understood as meaning "capable of being done, accomplished or carried out, possible or practicable". During the negotiations over the clause "take a part in hostilities" the word "direct" was added to it, opening up the possibility that child volunteers could be involved indirectly in hostilities, such as by gathering and transmitting military information, helping in the transportation of arms and munitions, provision of supplies, etc. However, Article 4.3.c of Protocol II, additional to the Geneva Conventions of 12 August 1949, and relating to the Protection of Victims of Non-International Armed Conflicts, adopted in 1977, states "children who have not attained the age of fifteen years shall neither be recruited in the armed forces or groups nor allowed to take part in hostilities".

Standards for the release and reintegration of children

OPAC requires governments to demobilise children within their jurisdiction who have been recruited or used in hostilities and to provide assistance for their physical and psychological recovery and social reintegration. Under war, civil unrest, armed conflict and other emergency situations, children and youths are also offered protection under the United Nations Declaration on the Protection of Women and Children in Emergency and Armed Conflict. To accommodate the proper disarmament, demobilisation and reintegration of former members of armed groups, the United Nations started the Integrated DDR Standards in 2006.

War crimes

Opinion is currently divided over whether children should be prosecuted for war crimes. International law does not prohibit the prosecution of children who commit war crimes, but Article 37 of the Convention on the Rights of the Child limits the punishment that a child can receive: "Neither capital punishment nor life imprisonment without possibility of release shall be imposed for offenses committed by persons below eighteen years of age."

Example: Sierra Leone

In the wake of the Sierra Leone Civil War, the UN mandated the Special Court for Sierra Leone (SCSL) to try former combatants aged 15 and older for breaches of humanitarian law, including war crimes. However, the Paris Principles state that children who participate in armed conflict should be regarded first as victims, even if they may also be perpetrators:... [those] who are accused of crimes under international law allegedly committed while they were associated with armed forces or armed groups should be considered primarily as victims of offenses against international law; not only as perpetrators. They must be treated by international law in a framework of restorative justice and social rehabilitation, consistent with international law which offers children special protection through numerous agreements and principles. This principle was reflected in the Court's statute, which did not rule out prosecution but emphasised the need to rehabilitate and reintegrate former child soldiers. David Crane, the first Chief Prosecutor of the Sierra Leone tribunal, interpreted the statute in favour of prosecuting those who had recruited children, rather than the children themselves, no matter how heinous the crimes they had committed.

Example: Omar Khadr

In the USA, prosecutors charged Omar Khadr, a Canadian, for offences they allege he committed in Afghanistan while under the age of 16 and fighting for the Taliban against US forces. These crimes carry a maximum penalty of life imprisonment under US law. In 2010, while under torture and duress, Khadr pleaded guilty to murder in violation of the laws of war, attempted murder in violation of the laws of war, conspiracy, two counts of providing material support for terrorism, and spying. The plea was offered as part of a plea bargain, which would see Khadr deported to Canada after one year of imprisonment to serve seven further years there. Omar Khadr remained in Guantanamo Bay and the Canadian government faced international criticism for delaying his repatriation. Khadr was eventually transferred to the Canadian prison system in September 2012 and was freed on bail by a judge in Alberta in May 2015. As of 2016, Khadr was appealing his US conviction as a war criminal.

Before sentencing the Special Representative to the UN Secretary-General for Children and Armed Conflict wrote to the US military commission at Guantanamo appealing unsuccessfully for Khadr's release into a rehabilitation program. In her letter she said that Khadr represented the "classic child soldier narrative: recruited by unscrupulous groups to undertake actions at the bidding of adults to fight battles they barely understand".

The role of the UN Commission on Human Rights

Children's rights advocates were left frustrated after the final text of the Convention on the Rights of the Child (1989) did not prohibit the military recruitment of all children under the age of 18, and they began to call for a new treaty to achieve this goal. As a consequence the newly formed Committee on the Rights of the Child made two recommendations: first, to request a major UN study into the impact of armed conflict on children; and second, to establish a working group of the UN Commission on Human Rights to negotiate a supplementary protocol to the Convention. Both proposals were accepted.

Responding to the Committee on the Rights of the Child, the UN General Assembly acknowledged "the grievous deterioration in the situation of children in many parts of the world as a result of armed conflicts" and commissioned the human rights expert Graça Machel to conduct a major fact-finding study. The Machel Report, Impact of armed conflict on children, was published in 1996. The report noted: Clearly one of the most urgent priorities is to remove everyone under 18 years of age from armed forces. Meanwhile, the UN Commission on Human Rights established a working group to negotiate a treaty to raise standards with regard to the use of children for military purposes.

After complex negotiations and a global campaign, the new treaty was agreed in 2000 as the Optional Protocol to the Convention on the Rights of the Child on the Involvement of Children in Armed Conflict. The treaty prohibits the direct participation of children in armed conflict, but not their recruitment by state armed forces from age 16. Special Representative of the Secretary-General for Children and Armed Conflict The Machel Report led to a new mandate for a Special Representative of the Secretary-General for Children and Armed Conflict (SRSG-CAAC). Among the tasks of the SRSG is to draft the Secretary-General's annual report on children and armed conflict, which lists and describes the worst situations of child recruitment and use from around the world.

Security Council

The United Nations Security Council convenes regularly to debate, receive reports, and pass resolutions under the heading "Children in armed conflict". The first resolution on the issue, Resolution 1261, was passed in 1999. In 2004 Resolution 1539 was passed unanimously, condemning the use of child soldiers and mandating the UN Secretary-General to establish a means of tracking and reporting on the practice, known as the Monitoring and Reporting Mechanism.

United Nations Secretary-General

The Secretary-General publishes an annual report on children and armed conflict. The 2017 report identified 14 countries where children were widely used by armed groups during 2016 (Afghanistan, Colombia, Central African Republic, Democratic Republic of the Congo, Iraq, Mali, Myanmar, Nigeria, Philippines, Somalia, South Sudan, Sudan, Syria, and Yemen) and six countries where state armed forces were using children in hostilities (Afghanistan, Myanmar, Somalia, Sudan, South Sudan, and Syria).

Children in the military today—by region and country

Africa

In 2003, the UN Office for the Coordination of Humanitarian Affairs estimated that up to half of children involved with state armed forces and non-state armed groups worldwide were in Africa. In 2004, Child Soldiers International estimated that 100,000 children were being used in state and non-state armed forces on the continent; and in 2008 an estimate put the total at 120,000 children, or 40 percent of the global total. The African Charter on the Rights and Welfare of the Child (1990), which has been ratified by most African states, prohibits all military recruitment of children aged under 18. Nonetheless, according to the UN, in 2016 children were being used by armed groups in seven African countries (Central African Republic, Democratic Republic of the Congo, Mali, Nigeria, Somalia, South Sudan, Sudan) and by state armed forces in three (Somalia, Sudan, South Sudan).

International efforts to reduce the number of children in military organisations in Africa began with the Cape Town Principles and Best Practices, developed in 1997. The Principles proposed that African governments commit to OPAC, which was being negotiated at the time, and raise the minimum age for military recruitment from 15 to 18. The Principles also defined a child soldier to include any person under the age of 18 who is "part of any kind of regular or irregular armed force or group in any capacity ... including girls recruited for sexual purposes ..." In 2007, the Free Children from War Conference in Paris produced the Paris Principles, which refined and updated the Cape Town Principles, applied them globally, and outlined a practical approach to reintegrating current child soldiers.

Central African Republic

The use of children by armed groups in the Central African Republic has historically been common. Between 2012 and 2015 as many as 10,000 children were used by armed groups in the nationwide armed conflict and as of 2016 children were still being used. The mainly Muslim Séléka coalition of armed groups and the predominantly Christian Anti-Balaka militias have both used children in this way; some are as young as eight. In May 2015 at the Forum de Bangui (a meeting of government, parliament, armed groups, civil society and religious leaders), a number of armed groups agreed to demobilise thousands of children. In 2016 a measure of stability returned to the Central African Republic and, according to the United Nations, 2,691 boys and 1,206 girls were officially separated from armed groups. Despite this, the recruitment and use of children for military purposes increased by approximately 50 percent over that year, mostly attributed to the Lord's Resistance Army.

Democratic Republic of the Congo

Thousands of children serve in the military of the Democratic Republic of the Congo (DRC), as well as in various rebel militias. It has been estimated that at the height of the Second Congo War more than 30,000 children were fighting with various parties to the conflict. It was claimed in the film Kony 2012 that the Lord's Resistance Army recruited this number. Currently the DRC has one of the highest proportions of child soldiers in the world. The international court has passed judgment on these practices during the war. Thomas Lubanga Dyilo, one of the warlords in the DRC, has been sentenced to 14 years in prison because of his role in the recruitment of child soldiers between 2002 and 2003. Lubanga directed the Union of Congolese Patriots and its armed wing Patriotic Forces for the Liberation of Congo. The children were forced to fight in the armed conflict in Ituri.

Somalia

A report published by the Child Soldiers International in 2004 estimated that 200,000 children had been recruited into the country's militias against their will since 1991. In 2017 UN Secretary-General António Guterres commented on a UN report which estimated that over 50 percent of Al-Shabaab's membership in the country was under the age of 18, with some as young as nine being sent to fight. The report verified that 6,163 children had been recruited in Somalia between 1 April 2010 and 31 July 2016, of which 230 were girls. Al-Shabaab accounted for seventy percent of this recruitment, and the Somali National Army was also recruiting children.

Sudan

In 2004 approximately 17,000 children were being used by the state armed forces and non-state armed groups. As many as 5,000 children were part of the main armed opposite group at the time, the Sudan People's Liberation Army (SPLA). Some former child soldiers were sentenced to death for crimes committed while they were soldiers. In 2006, children were also recruited from refugee camps in Chad, and thousands were used in the conflict in Darfur. In 2005 the government ratified the OPAC treaty and by 2008 the military use of children had reduced in the country, but both state armed forces and the SPLA continued to recruit and use them. The use of children has continued to diminish, but in 2017 the UN was still receiving reports of children as young as 12 in government forces.

Zimbabwe

In 2003, the Guardian reported multiple human rights violations by the National Youth Service, a state-sponsored youth militia in Zimbabwe. Originally conceived as a patriotic youth organisation, it became a paramilitary group of youth aged between 10 and 30, and was used to suppress dissent in the country. The organisation was finally banned in January 2018.

Americas

Bolivia

In 2001 the government of Bolivia acknowledged that children as young as 14 may have been forcibly conscripted into the armed forces during recruitment sweeps. About 40% of the Bolivian army was believed to be under the age of 18, with half of those below the age of 16. As of 2018, Bolivia invites children to begin their adult conscription early, from age 17.

Canada

In Canada, people may join the reserve component of the Canadian Forces at age 16 with parental permission, and the regular component at 17 years of age, also with parental permission. They may not volunteer for a tour of duty until reaching age 18.

Colombia

In the Colombian armed conflict, from the mid-1960s to present, one fourth of non-state combatants have been and still are under 18 years old. In 2004 Colombia ranked fourth in the world for the greatest use of child soldiers. There are currently 11,000–14,000 children in armed groups in the country. In negotiations with the government, armed groups have offered to stop the recruitment of minors as a bargaining chip, but they have not honoured these offers. Bjørkhaug argues that most child soldiers were recruited through some combination of voluntary participation and coercion. In 1998 a Human Rights Watch press release indicated that 30 percent of some guerrilla units were made up of children and up to 85 percent of some of the militias, which are considered to serve as a "training ground for future guerrilla fighters", had child soldiers In the same press release it was estimated that some of the government-linked paramilitary units consisted of up to 50 percent children .

Legality of child pornography

The legality of child pornography is explicitly addressed in 94 of the 187 Interpol member states as of 2008, according to research performed by the International Centre for Missing & Exploited Children (ICMEC) Koons

Family Institute on International Law and Policy.Of those 94 countries, 58 criminalized possession of child pornography regardless of intent to distribute. This figure does not count legislation outlawing all pornography; figures that also include non-specific bans on all pornography would therefore be higher if available. The Special Rapporteur on the sale of children, child prostitution, and child pornography is one of the thematic special procedures overseen by the United Nations Human Rights Council. The mandate holder addresses the root causes of the sale of children, child prostitution, and child pornography and works to identify and promote the best practices for combatting these serious problems. The rehabilitation of child victims of sexual exploitation is an area of special focus for the Special Rapporteur, who relies on the Convention on the Rights of the Child and the Optional Protocol to the Convention on the Rights of the Child on the sale of children, child prostitution and child pornography for guidance in his or her work. The Special Rapporteur must apply a gender perspective throughout the work of his or her mandate.

Composition and working methods1

The mandate of the Special Rapporteur lasts for a period of three years. The mandate is filled by one highly-qualified individual. The UN Commission on Human Rights established the Special Rapporteurship in 1990 with Resolution 1990/68. The Human Rights Council extended its mandate in 2008 (Resolution 7/13), 2011 (Resolution 16/12), and 2014 (Resolution 25/6). In fulfilling the obligations of this special procedure, the mandate holder may: undertake country visits, consider individual complaints, submit allegation letters and urgent appeals to States concerning specific situations, and submit activity reports to the UN General Assembly and Human Rights Council.

Country Visits

The Special Rapporteur undertakes an average of two country visits per year, on the basis of an invitation from the country concerned. Past reports of the Working Group on its country visits can be viewed here. Country visits provide the Special Rapporteur an opportunity to engage governments, intergovernmental organizations, and civil society in constructive dialogue about the causes and strategies for elimination of the sexual exploitation of children. This dialogue enables the Special Rapporteur to identify best practices on measures to combat the sale of children, child prostitution, and child pornography. Following each country visit, the Special Rapporteur reports his or her findings, conclusions, and recommendations. More than 100 countries have extended standing invitations to country visits by all thematic special procedures..

Individual Complaints

The Special Rapporteur receives information from governments, UN bodies, specialized agencies, intergovernmental and nongovernmental organizations, and individuals about the alleged violation of children's rights through sexual exploitation. The Special Rapporteur generally takes action if the information relates to the sale of children, child prostitution, child pornography, trafficking and sexual abuse, and situations in which a child is at risk of becoming a victim of one of these offenses. Importantly, the Special Rapporteur does not issue decisions concerning individual complaints and cannot require the State to remedy any alleged violation; rather, the Special Rapporteur raises the issue of concern with the relevant State.

In response to complaints, the Special Rapporteur may contact the government concerned to invite comment, seek clarification, remind the government of its international obligations, or request information on steps being taken by the government to investigate redress the situation. He or she may also write to the government jointly with other special procedures mandate holders. Generally called "communications," these exchanges with the government can take a variety of forms of varying degrees of significance. Specifically, the Special Rapporteur contacts a government through either an allegation letter or an urgent appeal. In all of its communications, the Special Rapporteur is careful not to draw any conclusions about the facts of the case. Instead, the Special Rapporteur simply presses for the government to ensure that the rights of children are not violated.

Allegation Letters

Generally, the Special Rapporteur sends an allegation letter in circumstances where the alleged violation has already occurred, relates to a general pattern of violations, or is not so pressing as to warrant sending an urgent appeal. An allegation letter generally contains a request for the government to clarify the substance of the allegation and to forward any information related to the allegation to the Special Rapporteur.

Urgent Appeals

The urgent appeals procedure is reserved for cases in which there are sufficiently reliable allegations that the situation is time-sensitive in terms of loss of life, life-threatening situations, or imminent or ongoing damage of a grave nature. If it appears that the allegation letters procedure is unlikely to address the situation in a timely enough manner, the Special Rapporteur will send an urgent appeal to the government concerned.

Submitting a complaint

Complaints should be submitted via the online submission form. When submitting a complaint, it is important to include the information requested on the Special Rapporteur's information sheet questionnaire, including:

- general information about the incident, such as the number and nationality of the alleged victims and the country or countries in which the incident took place,
- identity of the persons concerned, such as their name, sex, age, nationality, and ethnic background (if relevant),
- description of the alleged violation, such as the alleged perpetrator(s) and the date, place, and time of the incident(s),
- steps taken by the victim(s) or on their behalf, steps taken by authorities, and any other steps that have been taken and their outcomes,
- identity and contact information of the person or institution submitting the complaint, and
- whether any information contained in the complaint should be kept confidential.

Bottom of Form

Child pornography is illegal in most jurisdictions of the world. Convictions for possessing child pornography also usually include prison sentences, but those sentences are often converted to probation for first-time offenders. Some nations such as Canada and Australia have laws banning cartoon, anime, manga or written child pornography and others require ISPs (Internet service providers) to monitor internet traffic to detect it. The United Nations Optional Protocol on the Rights of the Child requires states to outlaw the "producing, distributing, disseminating, importing, exporting, offering, selling or possessing for the above purposes" of child pornography. The Council of Europe's Cybercrime Convention, the Council of Europe Convention on the Protection of Children against Sexual Exploitation and Sexual Abuse, and the EU Framework Decision that became active in 2006 require signatory or member states to criminalize all aspects of child pornography. Article 34 of the United Nations Convention on the Rights of the Child (UNCRC) stated that all signatories shall take appropriate measures to prevent the exploitative use of children in pornographic performances and materials.

International treaties

International obligations to pass specific laws against child pornography "punishable by appropriate penalties that take into account their grave nature" as well as enable extradition, mutual assistance in investigation, and seizure of property were mandated by the Optional Protocol on the Sale of Children, Child Prostitution and Child Pornography. Some of the negotiations and reviews of the process took place at the World Congress against Commercial Sexual Exploitation of Children held in 1996 and 2001.

Debate

While laws criminalizing child sexual abuse now exist in all countries of the world, more diversity of views exists on questions like exactly how young those depicted in pornography should be allowed to be, whether the mere possession of child pornography should be a crime, or whether sentences for such possession should be modified.

In 1999, in the case of R. v. Sharpe, British Columbia's highest court struck down a law against possessing child pornography as unconstitutional. That opinion, written by Justice Duncan Shaw, held, "There is no evidence that demonstrates a significant increase in the danger to children caused by pornography", and "A person who is prone to act on his fantasies will likely do so irrespective of the availability of pornography." The Opposition in the Canadian Parliament considered invoking the notwithstanding clause to override the court's ruling. However, it was not necessary because the Canadian Supreme Court overturned the decision with several findings including that viewing such material makes it more likely that the viewer will abuse, that the existence of such materials further hurts the victims as they know of its existence, and that the demand for such images encourages the abuse.

In the United States, some federal judges have argued that the U.S. Sentencing Guidelines' recommended penalties for possessors of child pornography are too harsh. Judge Jack B. Weinstein of New York criticizes the mandatory sentence for possession of child pornography as often higher than the penalty for actually committing the act of child abuse it depicts. Furthermore, child pornography prosecutions have led to dozens of suicides, some of them among the innocently accused. The requirement that people convicted of possessing child pornography pay restitution has been criticized by some judges and law professors. This has been particularly controversial in cases involving millions of dollars of restitution, as in those pertaining to the Misty Series. But in 2010, the US Ninth Circuit Court of Appeals ruled that restitution directly to depicted minors was an appropriate penalty for possession of child pornography.

During the nomination process at the 2008 Libertarian National Convention, anarcho-capitalist and U.S. Presidential candidate Mary Ruwart came under fire for her comment in her 1998 book, Short answers to the tough questions, in which she stated her opposition not only to laws against possession of child pornography but even against its production, based on her belief that such laws actually encourage such behavior by increasing prices. Shane Cory, on behalf of the minarchist United States Libertarian Party in his role as executive director, issued a response saying, "We have an obligation to protect children from sexual exploitation and abuse, and we can do this by increasing communication between state and federal agencies to help combat this repulsive industry. While privacy rights should always be respected in the pursuit of child pornographers, more needs to be done to track down and prosecute the twisted individuals who exploit innocent children." Cory resigned after the party refused to vote on a resolution asking states to strongly enforce existing child porn laws.

Difference between children's rights and youth rights

"In the majority of jurisdictions, for instance, children are not allowed to vote, to marry, to buy alcohol, to have sex, or to engage in paid employment." Within the youth rights movement, it is believed that the key difference between children's rights and youth rights is that children's rights supporters generally advocate the establishment and enforcement of protection for children and youths, while youth rights (a far smaller movement) generally advocates the expansion of freedom for children and/ or youths and of rights such as suffrage.

Parental powers

Parent are given sufficient powers to fulfill their duties to the child.

Parents affect the lives of children in a unique way, and as such their role in children's rights has to be distinguished in a particular way. Particular issues in the child-parent relationship include child neglect, child abuse, freedom of choice, corporal punishment and child custody. There have been theories offered that provide parents with rights-based practices that resolve the tension between "commonsense parenting" and children's rights. The issue is particularly relevant in legal proceedings that affect the potential emancipation of minors, and in cases where children sue their parents. A child's rights to a relationship with both their parents is increasingly recognized as an important factor for determining the best interests of the child in divorce and child custodyproceedings. Some governments have enacted laws creating a rebuttable presumption that shared parenting is in the best interests of children.

Limitations of parental powers

Parents do not have absolute power over their children. Parents are subject to criminal laws against abandonment, abuse, and neglect of children. International human rights law provides that manifestation of one's religion may be limited in the interests of public safety, for the protection of public order, health or morals, or for the protection of the rights and freedoms of others. Courts have placed other limits on parental powers and acts. The United States Supreme Court, in the case of Prince v. Massachusetts, ruled that a parent's religion does not permit a child to be placed at risk. The Lords of Appeal in Ordinary ruled, in the case of Gillick v West Norfolk and Wisbech Area Health Authority and another, that parental rights diminish with the increasing age and competency of the child, but do not vanish completely until the child reaches majority. Parental rights are derived from the parent's duties to the child. In the absence of duty, no parental right exists. The Supreme Court of Canada ruled, in the case of E. (Mrs.) v. Eve, that parents may not grant surrogate consent for non-therapeutic sterilization. The Supreme Court of Canada has ruled, in the case of B. (R.) v. Children's Aid Society of Metropolitan Toronto. "While children undeniably benefit from the Charter, most notably in its protection of their rights to life and to the security of their person, they are unable to assert these rights, and our society accordingly presumes that parents will exercise their freedom of choice in a manner that does not offend the rights of their children." Adler (2013) argues that parents are not empowered to grant surrogate consent for non-therapeutic circumcision of children.

Movement

The 1796 publication of Thomas Spence's Rights of Infants is among the earliest English-language assertions of the rights of children. Throughout the 20th century, children's rights activists organized for homeless children's rights and public education. The 1927 publication of The Child's Right to Respect by Janusz Korczak strengthened the literature surrounding the field, and today dozens of international organizations are working around the world to promote children's rights.

In the UK the formation of a community of educationalists, teachers, youth justice workers, politicians and cultural contributors called the New Ideals in Education Conferences (1914–37) stood for the value of 'liberating the child' and helped to define the 'good' primary school in England until the 80s. Their conferences inspired the UNESCO organisation, the New Education Fellowship. A.S. Neill's 1915 book A Dominie's Log (1915), a diary of a headteacher changing his school to one based on the liberation and happiness of the child, can be seen as a cultural product that celebrates the heroes of this movement

Opposition

The opposition to children's rights long predates any current trend in society, with recorded statements against the rights of children dating to the 13th century and earlier.Opponents to children's rights believe that young people need to be protected from the adultcentric world, including the decisions and responsibilities of that world. In a dominantly adult society, childhood is idealized as a time of innocence, a time free of responsibility and conflict, and a time dominated by play. The majority of opposition stems from concerns related to national sovereignty, states' rights, the parent-child relationship. Financial constraints and the "undercurrent of traditional values in opposition to children's rights" are cited, as well. The concept of children's rights has received little attention in the United States.

International human rights law

The Universal Declaration of Human Rights is seen as a basis for all international legal standards for children's rights today. There are several conventions and laws that address children's rights around the world. A number of current and historical documents affect those rights, including the Declaration of the Rights of the Child, drafted by Eglantyne Jebbin 1923, endorsed by the League of Nations in 1924 and reaffirmed in 1934. A slightly expanded version was adopted by the United Nations in 1946, followed by a much expanded version adopted by the General Assembly in 1959. It later served as the basis for the Convention on the Rights of the Child.

International Covenant on Civil and Political Rights

The United Nations adopted the International Covenant on Civil and Political Rights (ICCPR) in 1966. The ICCPR is a multilateral international covenant that has been ratified or acceded to by nearly all nations on Earth. Nations which have become state-parties to the Covenant are required to honor and enforce the rights enunciated by the Covenant. The treaty came into effect on 23 March 1976. The rights codified by the ICCPR are universal, so they apply to everyone without exception and this includes children. Although children have all rights, some rights such as the right to marry and the right to vote come into effect only after the child reaches maturity.

Some general rights applicable to children include:

- the right to life
- the right to security of person
- the right to freedom from torture
- the right to freedom from cruel, inhuman or degrading treatment or punishment
- the right to be separated from adults when charged with a crime, the right to speedy adjudication, and the right to be accorded treatment appropriate to their age

Article 24 codifies the right of the child to special protection due to his minority, the right to a name, and the right to a nationality.

Convention on the Rights of the Child

The United Nations' 1989 Convention on the Rights of the Child, or CRC, is the first legally binding international instrument to incorporate the full range of human rights—civil, cultural, economic, political and social rights. Its implementation is monitored by the Committee on the Rights of the Child. National governments that ratify it commit themselves to protecting and ensuring children's rights, and agree to hold themselves accountable for this commitment before the international community. The CRC is the most widely ratified human rights treaty with 196 ratifications; the United States is the only country not to have ratified it. The CRC is based on four core principles: the principle of non-discrimination; the best interests of the child; the right to life, survival and development; and considering the views of the child in decisions that affect them, according to their age and maturity. The CRC, along with international criminal accountability mechanisms such as the International Criminal Court, the Yugoslavia and Rwanda Tribunals, and the Special Court for Sierra Leone, is said to have significantly increased the profile of children's rights worldwide.Vienna Declaration and Programme of Action.

The Vienna Declaration and Programme of Action urges, at Section II para 47, all nations to undertake measures to the maximum extent of their available resources, with the support of international cooperation, to achieve the goals in the World Summit Plan of Action. And calls on States to integrate the Convention on the Rights of the Child into their national action plans. By means of these national action plans and through international efforts, particular priority should be placed on reducing infant and maternal mortality rates, reducing malnutrition and illiteracy rates and providing access to safe drinking water and basic education.

Whenever so called for, national plans of action should be devised to combat devastating emergencies resulting from natural disasters and armed conflicts and the equally grave problem of children in extreme poverty. Further, para 48 urges all states, with the support of international cooperation, to address the acute problem of children under especially difficult circumstances. Exploitation and abuse of children should be actively combated, including by addressing their root causes. Effective measures are required against female infanticide, harmful child labour, sale of children and organs, child prostitution, child pornography, and other forms of sexual abuse. This influenced the adoptions of Optional Protocol on the Involvement of Children in Armed Conflict and Optional Protocol on the Sale of Children, Child Prostitution and Child Pornography.

Enforcement

A variety of enforcement organizations and mechanisms exist to ensure children's rights. They include the Child Rights Caucus for the United Nations General Assembly Special Session on Children. It was set up to promote full implementation and compliance with the Convention on the Rights of the Child, and to ensure that child rights were given priority during the UN General Assembly Special Session on Children and its Preparatory process. The United Nations Human Rights Council was created "with the hope that it could be more objective, credible and efficient in denouncing human rights violations worldwide than the highly politicized Commission on Human Rights." The NGO Group for the Convention on the Rights of the Child is a coalition of international non-governmental organisations originally formed in 1983 to facilitate the implementation of the United Nations Convention on the Rights of the Child.

National law

Many countries around the world have children's rights ombudspeople or children's commissioners whose official, governmental duty is to represent the interests of the public by investigating and addressing complaints reported by individual citizens regarding children's rights. Children's ombudspeople can also work for a corporation, a newspaper, an NGO, or even for the general public.

United States law

The United States has signed but not ratified the CRC. As a result, children's rights have not been systematically implemented in the U.S. Children are generally afforded the basic rights embodied by the Constitution, as enshrined by the Fourteenth Amendment to the United States Constitution. The Equal Protection Clause of that amendment is to apply to children, born within a marriage or not, but excludes children not yet born. This was reinforced by the landmark US Supreme Courtdecision of In re Gault (1967). In this trial 15-year-old Gerald Gault of Arizona was taken into custody by local police after being accused of making an obscene telephone call. He was detained and committed to the Arizona State Industrial School until he reached the age of 21 for making an obscene phone call to an adult neighbor. In an 8–1 decision, the Court ruled that in hearings which could result in commitment to an institution, people under the age of 18 have the right to notice and counsel, to question witnesses, and to protection against self-incrimination. The Court found that the procedures used in Gault's hearing met none of these requirements.

The United States Supreme Court ruled in the case of Tinker v. Des Moines Independent Community School District (1969) that students in school have Constitutional rights. The United States Supreme Court has ruled in the case of Roper v. Simmons that persons may not be executed for crimes committed when below the age of eighteen. It ruled that such executions are cruel and unusual punishment, so they are a violation of the Eighth Amendment to the United States Constitution. There are other concerns in the United States regarding children's rights. The American Academy of Adoption Attorneys is concerned with children's rights to a safe, supportive and stable family structure. Their position on children's rights in adoption cases states that, "children have a constitutionally based liberty interest in the protection of their established families, rights which are at least equal to, and we believe outweigh, the rights of others who would claim a 'possessory' interest in these children." Other issues raised in American children's rights advocacy include children's rights to inheritance in same-sex marriages and particular rights for youth.

German law

A report filed by the President of the INGO Conference of the Council of Europe, Annelise Oeschger finds that children and their parents are subject to United Nations, European Union and UNICEF human rights violations. Of particular concern is the German (and Austrian) agency, Jugendamt that often unfairly allows for unchecked government control of the parent-child relationship, which have resulted in harm including torture, degrading, cruel treatment and has led to children's death. The problem is complicated by the nearly "unlimited power" of the Jugendamt officers, with no processes to review or resolve inappropriate or harmful treatment. By German law, Jugendamt officers are protected against prosecution. Jugendamt (JA) officers span of control is seen in cases that go to family court where experts testimony may be overturned by lesser educated or experienced JA officers; In more than 90% of the cases the JA officer's recommendation is accepted by family court. Officers have also disregarded family court decisions, such as when to return children to their parents, without repercussions. Germany has not recognized related child-welfare decisions made by the European Parliamentary Court that have sought to protect or resolve children and parental rights violations.

Child Poverty Action Group

The persistence of child poverty in the United States and the pervasive health consequences it engenders present unique challenges to the health care system. Human capital theory and empirical observation suggest that the increased disease burden experienced by poor children originates from social conditions that provide suboptimal educational, nutritional, environmental, and parental inputs to good health. Faced with the resultant excess rates of pediatric morbidity, the US health care system has developed a variety of compensatory strategies. In the first instance, Medicaid, the federal-state governmental finance system designed to assure health insurance coverage for poor children, has increased its eligibility thresholds and expanded its benefits to allow greater access to health services for this vulnerable population.

A second arm of response involves a gradual reengineering of health care delivery at the practice level, including the dissemination of patient-centered medical homes, the use of team-based approaches to care, and the expansion of care management beyond the practice to reach deep into the community. Third is a series of recent experiments involving the federal government and state Medicaid programs that includes payment reforms of various kinds, enhanced reporting, concentration on high-risk populations, and intensive case management. Fourth, pediatric practices have begun to make use of specific tools that permit the identification and referral of children facing social stresses arising from poverty. Finally, constituencies within the health care system participate in enhanced advocacy efforts to raise awareness of poverty as a distinct threat to child health and to press for public policy responses such as minimum wage increases, expansion of tax credits, paid family leave, universal preschool education, and other priorities focused on child poverty. Childhood poverty is a widespread issue in the United States with one in five children living in need. Poverty has both immediate and lasting consequences that can follow a child into adulthood. Here are just ten ways poverty can impact the health and education of a child.

Health

There are identifiable side-effects of poverty such as hunger, but there are also long-term side-effects that can go unnoticed and follow a child into adulthood. Brain Development: Conditions that correspond with poverty (noise, substandard housing, family turmoil, etc.) can be toxic to a developing brain. Self Confidence: A healthy self-esteem is crucial to a child's health. Without strong levels of confidence, children may be susceptible to various other health problems or unhealthy habits. And since self-esteem tends to form in childhood and continue through adulthood, it's even more important to help kids feel good about themselves. Heart Disease: Studies have shown that growing up in poverty (less access to healthy meals, lack of proper attire, and insufficient health coverage) might put children at risk for heart disease in adulthood. "Learned Helplessness": Children feel as if they have no power to control their circumstances. This is a behavioral pattern that can be a result of prolonged poverty. Toxic Stress: Toxic stress is the prolonged activation of stress response systems in the body/brain. This can occur when a child experiences strong, frequent, and/or prolonged adversity—such as emotional abuse or the accumulated burdens of family economic hardship—without adequate adult support.

Education

Poverty can also impact a child's ability to succeed in school. Here are two shocking statistics from a study by the Urban Institute: Children who are poor from birth to age 2 are 30 percent less likely to complete high school than children who are poor for the first time later in their life. Nearly 30 percent of poor children do not complete high school, which limits future economic success and potential employability, leading to poverty as an adult. School Preparation: Students living above the poverty line are entering kindergarten more prepared than those below it. Higher income families are able to put more money towards their children's cognitive development than those living in poverty. Parents with low incomes, on average, have less time to read to their children, no-funds for pre-school, and less stable home environments. The difference in preparation tends to persist through elementary and high school.

School Attendance: Chronic absenteeism (missing more than 10 percent of school a year) occurs at rates three to four times higher in high-poverty areas. An overwhelming majority of chronically absent kids are impoverished, dealing with such daily stresses as caring for siblings, high rates of disease, violence in the community, and frequent familial moves to find employment. Educational Attainment: Early childhood poverty is related to lower educational achievement.Bullying: A study by the American Journal of Public Health found that kids and teens from poor families are more likely to be bullied than others and also concluded that schools with the largest economic inequality (or a big difference between how wealthy some families are and how poor other families are) had the highest rates of bullying.

School Behavior: Strong, secure relationships help stabilize children's behavior and provide the core guidance needed to build lifelong social skills. Children who grow up with such relationships learn healthy, appropriate emotional responses to everyday situations. But children raised in poor households often fail to learn these responses, to the detriment of their school performance.

History

The Group first met on 5 March 1965, at a meeting organised by Harriett C. Wilson. It followed the publication of Brian Abel-Smith and Peter Townsend's work Poor and the Poorest: both men were founding members of the Group. At the second meeting one of the points raised was "That although increased family allowance might be the simplest and most equitable way of overcoming the poverty of large families, there was likely to be considerable difficulties in bringing about a change of this kind, partly because of the fear that this would tend to encourage people to have large families." One of its first actions was to send a letter to the Prime Minister, on 22 December 1965, signed by a number of distinguished public figure, which stated: "The signatories of this letter would probably not all agree on the precise details of a scheme for reform: we are agreed, however, that action should be taken to achieve a radical improvement in the standard of living of families in poverty and we wish to bring this memorandum to your attention. We ask that the present arrangements for family allowances and the allowances for children be reconsidered and revised, and that bigger direct allowances be paid in respect of children in the poorest families."

Organisational aims

The stated aims of the CPAG are:

- Raise awareness of the causes, extent, nature and impact of poverty, and strategies for its eradication and prevention;
- Bring about positive policy changes for families with children in

poverty;

- Enable those eligible for income maintenance to have access to their full entitlement.

Activities

CPAG programmes include:

- Research and publish the latest facts and figures of family and child poverty in the UK
- Lobby the UK government, lead and support campaigns for effective policies to prevent, alleviate and abolish child and family poverty
- Provide up to date information and reliable advice on the UK social security and tax credits systems
- Conduct training courses in Welfare Rights, for both new and experienced advisers, to help them keep up to date with developments in social security and tax credits
- Undertake test-cases to extend the interpretation of law in favour of claimants in social security, tax credits and related law using, where appropriate the European Court of Justice and the European Court of Human Rights.

United Nations Convention on the Rights Of The Child

The most significant of all international laws for children is the UN Convention on the Rights of the Child, popularly referred to as the CRC. This, together with our Indian Constitution and Laws, determine what rights all children must have.

What is the UN Convention on the Rights of the Child?

Human rights belong to all people, regardless of their age, including children. However, because of their special status - whereby children need extra protection and guidance from adults - children also have some special rights of their own. These are called children's rights and they are laid out in the UN Convention on the Rights of the Child (CRC). Significant features of the UN Convention on the Rights of the Child (CRC)

- Applies equally to both girls and boys up to the age of 18, even if they are married or already have children of their own.
- The convention is guided by the principles of 'Best Interest of the Child' and 'Non-discrimination' and 'Respect for views of the child.'
- It emphasises the importance of the family and the need to create an environment that is conducive to the healthy growth and development of children.

- It obligates the state to respect and ensure that children get a fair and equitable deal in society.

It draws attention to four sets of civil, political, social, economic and cultural rights:

- Survival
- Protection
- Development
- Participation

Right to Survival includes

- Right to life.
- The highest attainable standard of health.
- Nutrition.
- Adequate standard of living.
- A name and a nationality.

Right to Development includes

- Right to education.
- Support for early childhood care and development.
- Social security.
- Right to leisure, recreation and cultural activities.

Right to Protection includes freedom from all forms of

- Exploitation.
- Abuse.
- Inhuman or degrading treatment.
- Neglect.
- Special protection in special circumstances such as situations of emergency and armed conflicts, in case of disability etc.

Right to Participation includes

- Respect for the views of the child.
- Freedom of expression.
- Access to appropriate information.
- Freedom of thought, conscience and religion.

All rights are dependent on each other and are indivisible. However, because of their nature all rights are divided into: Immediate Rights (Civil and Political Rights) which include such things as discrimination, punishment, right to a fair hearing in criminal cases and a separate system of juvenile justice. The full list of rights for children and young people under the age of 18 is set out in the United Nations Convention on the Rights of the Child, the most accepted standard on children's rights in the world. Ireland committed to promote children's rights when it signed up to the Convention in 1992. Children's rights include the right to health, education, family life, play and recreation, an adequate standard of living and to be protected from abuse and harm. Children's rights cover their developmental and age-appropriate needs that change over time as a child grows up.

There are four general principles that underpin all children's rights:

- Non-discrimination means that all children have the same right to develop their potential in all situations and at all times. For example, every child should have equal access to education regardless of the child's gender, race, ethnicity, nationality, religion, disability, parentage, sexual orientation or other status
- The best interests of the child must be "a primary consideration" in all actions and decisions concerning a child, and must be used to resolve conflicts between different rights. For example, when making national budgetary decisions affecting children, Government must consider how cuts will impact on the best interests of the child
- The right to survival and development underscores the vital importance of ensuring access to basic services and to equality of opportunity for children to achieve their full development. For example, a child with a disability should have effective access to education and health care to achieve their full potential
- The views of the child mean that the voice of the child must be heard and respected in all matters concerning his or her rights. For example, those in power should consult with children before making decisions that will affect them.
- Children and young people have the same general human rights as adults and also specific rights that recognize their special needs. Children are neither the property of their parents nor are they helpless objects of charity. They are human beings and are the subject of their own rights.
- The Convention on the Rights of the Child sets out the rights that must be realized for children to develop to their full potential.
- The Convention offers a vision of the child as an individual and as a member of a family and community, with rights and responsibilities appropriate to his or her age and stage of development. By recognizing children's rights in this way, the Convention firmly sets the focus on the whole child.
- The Convention recognizes the fundamental human dignity of all children and the urgency of ensuring their well-being and

development. It makes clear the idea that a basic quality of life should be the right of all children, rather than a privilege enjoyed by a few.

Interested in learning more about child rights? Take this short course to transform your understanding of child rights and a child rights approach, introduce you to UNICEF's mandate as it relates to child rights, and inspire you to apply a child rights lens to your everyday work and life.

The importance of children's rights

- There are many reasons for singling out children's rights in a separate human rights Convention:
- Children are individuals
- Children are neither the possessions of parents nor of the state, nor are they mere people-in-the-making; they have equal status as members of the human family.
- Children start life as totally dependent beings
- Children must rely on adults for the nurture and guidance they need to grow towards independence. Such nurture is ideally found from adults in children's families, but when primary adult caregivers cannot meet children's needs, it is up to the State as the primary duty bearer to find an alternative in the best interests of the child.
- The actions, or inactions, of government impact children more strongly than any other group in society
- Practically every area of government policy – from education to public health – affects children to some degree. Short-sighted policymaking that fails to take children into account has a negative impact on the future of all members of society.
- Children's views should be heard and considered in the political process
- Children generally do not vote and do not traditionally take part in political processes. Without special attention to the opinions of children – as expressed at home and in schools, in local communities and even in governments – children's views go unheard on the many important issues that affect them now or will affect them in the future.
- Many changes in society are having a disproportionate, and often negative, impact on children
- Transformation of the family structure, globalization, climate change, digitalization, mass migration, shifting employment patterns and a shrinking social welfare net in many countries all have strong impacts on children. The impact of these changes can be particularly devastating in situations of armed conflict and other emergencies.
- The healthy development of children is crucial to the future well-being of any society

- Because they are still developing, children are especially vulnerable – more so than adults – to poor living conditions such as poverty, inadequate health care, nutrition, safe water, housing and environmental pollution. The effects of disease, malnutrition and poverty threaten the future of children and therefore the future of the societies in which they live.
- The costs to society of failing its children are huge

Social research findings show that children's earliest experiences significantly influence their future development. The course of their development determines their contribution, or cost, to society over the course of their lives. A right is as an agreement or contract established between the persons who hold a right (often referred to as the "rights-holders") and the persons or institutions which then have obligations and responsibilities in relation to the realization of that right (often referred to as the "duty-bearers".) Child rights are specialized human rights that apply to all human beings below the age of 18.

Universally child rights are defined by the United Nations and United Nations Convention on the Rights of the Child (UNCRC). According to the UNCRC Child Rights are minimum entitlements and freedoms that should be afforded to all persons below the age of 18 regardless of race, colour, gender, language, religion, opinions, origins, wealth, birth status or ability and therefore apply to all people everywhere. The UN finds these rights interdependent and indivisible, meaning that a right can not be fulfilled at the expense of another right. The purpose of the UNCRC is to outline the basic human rights that should be afforded to children. There are four broad classifications of these rights. These four categories cover all civil, political, social, economic and cultural rights of every child.

- Right to Survival: A child's right to survival begins before a child is born. According to Government of India, a child life begins after twenty weeks of conception. Hence the right to survival is inclusive of the child rights to be born, right to minimum standards of food, shelter and clothing, and the right to live with dignity.
- Right to Protection: A child has the right to be protected from neglect, exploitation and abuse at home, and elsewhere.
- Right to Participation: A child has a right to participate in any decision making that involves him/her directly or indirectly. There are varying degrees of participation as per the age and maturity of the child.
- Right to Development: Children have the right to all forms of development: Emotional, Mental and Physical. Emotional development is fulfilled by proper care and love of a support system, mental development through education and learning and physical development through recreation, play and nutrition.

What is Child Protection?

UNICEF considers child protection as the prevention of or responding to the incidence of abuse, exploitation, violence and neglect of children. This includes commercial sexual exploitation, trafficking, child labour and harmful traditional practices, such as female genital mutilation/cutting and child marriage. Protection also allows children to have access to their other rights of survival, development, growth and participation. UNICEF maintains that when child protection fails or is absent children have a higher risk of death, poor physical and mental health, HIV/AIDS infection, educational problems, displacement, homelessness, vagrancy and poor parenting skills later in life. According to the Integrated Child Protection Scheme (ICPS) Child Protection is about keeping children safe from a risk or perceived risk to their lives or childhood. It is about recognizing that children are vulnerable and hence reducing their vulnerability by protecting them from harm and harmful situations. Child protection is about ensuring that children have a security net to depend on, and if they happen to fall through the holes in the system, the system has the responsibility to provide the child with the necessary care and rehabilitation to bring them back into the safety net.

Understanding the Difference

It is important to understand the difference between these two concepts. Child rights are a set of principles or ideals. They are entitlements and some of them are justifiable in a court of law, but they are not tangible. Protection is one of these rights. But Child Protection is more than a right. It is a framework or system by which the rights of a child can come to be. The framework consists of various duty bearers such as the departments of the government, police, school, civil society, who all have roles to play to ensure that a child's rights are met, and in the case that a child's rights are violated that the violator be brought to justice and care be provided to the child. Child protection is not only treatment, but should also be preventive. Risk management needs to take place to reduce the risk of violation of child rights in any given circumstance or space.

Child protection is hence the means through which all other rights of a child can be upheld. For example a child has a right to live a normal childhood in a family environment. The child protection framework need to first take steps to ensure families are able to survive by providing them when health, education, and food for free or at minimal cost. The next step is to address the needs of children who have fallen through the cracks such as destitute, abandoned, and orphan children. The framework includes the mechanisms to relocate these children into caring families either through adoption or foster care and provide these children with access to health and education services. Hence the framework is not a single ministry or single government body it is the interlinking functions of all ministries and sectors

Violation of Child Rights in Indian Society

Any research or grassroots activism in the field of child rights will reveal that child rights violation isn't a phenomenon triggered by a single factor but in fact interplay of multiple catalysts. These factors are interlinked, which means that a substantial defence of child rights will require not only comprehensive policy reforms but unprecedented attempts at changing people's psyche towards the right of the child. The world's best NGO for charity in the field of child rights, Save the Children, has given a new hope to generations of children. The simplest thing you can do today is to support an NGO - every single rupee counts.

Here is how child rights violation happens in India

1. Trafficking of children, particularly for sexual exploitation

With instances where children just "disappear" overnight in some parts of India, as many as 1 every 8 minutes, the sordid horror of child trafficking is very apparent. Children are today traded like objects, but the nature of this crime makes it hard to track in India. This is why India is not only a hub but simultaneously a transit point for child trafficking, via Nepal and Bangladesh. At last count, 200,000 Nepalese girls under the age of 16 were found to be actively involved in prostitution in India.

There are 3 reasons behind India's child trafficking problem

i. Rampant poverty and lack of opportunities: parents sell their children for merely a handful of rupees

ii. Child trafficking as a highly profitable, albeit illegal business which has buyers from across the world. It is the third most profitable organised crime business, generating billion dollar revenues annually.

iii. Vulnerability of the child, and lack of enforcement of child rights

Save the Children, a pioneer in the field of child rights, fights the menace of child trafficking through a 3Ps strategy of Prevention, Protection, and Prosecution. The NGO uses a community-based approach to empowering children with education, job skills, and grassroots activism that frees children from labour and other forms of exploitation. India's most oppressed demographic, marginalized children, therefore, receive a new lease of life.

Violence against children, including sexual violence

One of the biggest reasons for unreported and therefore largely unaddressed incidence of violence against children, especially sexual violence, is a social stigma. 2012 saw 9500 child and adolescent murders, making India the third largest contributor to child homicide (WHO 2014, Global Health Estimates), while 1 in 3 adolescent girls between 15 to 19 years experience violence (physical, sexual or emotional), from their significant others. Child abuse is often unreported when it involves family members or by people in institutions such as schools or government homes, due to the classic family structure practiced in rural India. According to the 'UN Special Rapporteur On Violence Against Women', there has been a 336% increase of child rape cases from 2001 to 2011. Neglect is an important component of emotional violence, and it occurs when children are not given enough attention, food, or recreation time.

Child labour, including working in hazardous conditions

According to a 2015 report by the U.S. Department of Labour, a list of goods produced by child labour or forced labour featured India among 74 countries with "significant incidence of critical working conditions". Recent legislation regarding child labour has been unfavourable, with permission to children below 14 years of age to work in family enterprises or entertainment industry. This still includes scope for abuse, especially considering that India is home to the largest child labour population in the world. It is not rare to find thousands of children toiling in the fields for 14-16 hours a day, in labour intensive professions like farming, stone cutting sector, mining industry, and zari and embroidery.

This is being worsened by the entry of multinational companies into India, to exploit the lack of accountability in labour law and cheap labour. Child labour is reportedly highest among scheduled tribes, Muslims, schedule castes and OBC children, despite aggressive reservation policies favouring this demographic. Forced displacement, caused by 'development' projects (including Special Economic Zones) migration to urban areas, farmer suicides, and armed conflict is also another cause of child labour. This often results in children being exploited into bonded child labour, a form of slavery. These children become psychologically and mentally disturbed, they thus become dependent on their 'owners'.

Discrimination against girls in education and in access to food

There is a saying in Andhra Pradesh "Bringing up a daughter is like watering a plant in another's courtyard." While there is extensive research about the socio-economic impact of gender discrimination, the biggest effect is on the mind of tomorrow's women, Indian girls, who are deeply influenced by the myth of female inferiority. This translates to a generation of women unaware of their rights and capabilities. Even at birth, India's masses prefer a boy over a girl. Girls in India are given less food (including access to breastfeeding), fewer healthcare consultations, making anaemia and mineral deficiency common. Despite high female literacy, Delhi, Gujarat and Rajasthan still show discrimination against girls. This is seen in the high dropout rate of girls, who are expected to help with household work and taking care of younger siblings. This worsens the rural gender gap in female and male equality, as girls underperform in school. Depriving a child of their basic rights, just because they are a girl, is a gross violation of child rights. Discrimination against children on the basis of caste, tribe or indigenous background People belonging to scheduled castes (SCs) and scheduled tribes (STs) have faced discrimination throughout generations, and this trend is prevalent even to this day. According to Parliamentary findings, violence against the SC/ST community has increased over the years. An upward graph emerges when seeing the number of cases lodged under the SCs/STs Prevention of Atrocities Act in 1999 (34,799), and 2001 (39,157 cases) a large number of cases of violence against SC/ST are reported in Rajasthan and Madhya Pradesh has the largest number of atrocities against Scheduled Tribes. Many of these cases are unregistered. Child abuse is prevalent in Dalit and other tribal communities, and anecdotes of violence, rape, and torture are common. These acts are executed not only by high caste Hindus but also separatists and insurgents. This has resulted in systematic oppression of the community; Literacy among SC/ST population is incredibly low, and states like Rajasthan, Uttar Pradesh, and West Bengal have the lowest SC enrolment and attendance figures.

Conclusion

With the span of child rights violation in India, it is clear that this is an issue which needs to be addressed at many levels, via a comprehensive programme. The role of both NGOs and Government bodies is imperative. A policy reform can 'give teeth' to police action on those who participate in this heinous crime, only if corruption doesn't enable cover-ups, and hence erasure of these experiences. Grassroots activism by NGOs like Save the Children is, therefore, vital to be the guiding light to expose this crime, educate both children and adults, and liberate children from a life of suffering. With great tax benefits of donating to charity, a small investment can yield a huge reward when it comes to child rights. All children deserve a chance at a happy childhood and together we can help them get one.

CHAPTER - 4

WOMEN'S RIGHTS

RIGHT TO HEALTH

The right to health is the economic, social, and cultural right to a universal minimum standard of health to which all individuals are entitled. The concept of a right to health has been enumerated in international agreements which include the Universal Declaration of Human Rights, International Covenant on Economic, Social and Cultural Rights, and the Convention on the Rights of Persons with Disabilities. There is debate on the interpretation and application of the right to health due to considerations such as how health is defined, what minimum entitlements are encompassed in a right to health, and which institutions are responsible for ensuring a right to health.

India is a party to the International Covenant on Civil and Political Rights and the International Covenant on Economic, Social and Cultural Rights. The Supreme Court held that Article 21 of the Constitution of India in relation to human rights has to be interpreted in conformity with international law (1). Further, Article 25 [2] of the Universal Declaration of Human Rights and Article 7 (b) of the International Covenant on Economic, Social and Cultural Rights have been cited by the Supreme Court while upholding the right to health by a worker.

These covenants find statutory acceptance in the Statement of Objects and Reasons of The Protection of Human Rights Act, 1993. In addition, human rights commissions are empowered to study treaties and other international instruments on human rights and make recommendations for their effective implementation (3). In the recent past, many complaints of alleged medical negligence and deficient service by private and government hospitals and medical professionals have been filed with the national or state Human Rights Commissions.

The Constitution of India on the right to health care

The Constitution incorporates provisions guaranteeing everyone's right to the highest attainable standard of physical and mental health. Article 21 of the Constitution guarantees protection of life and personal liberty to every citizen. The Supreme Court has held that the right to live with human dignity, enshrined in Article 21, derives from the directive principles of state policy and therefore includes protection of health (4). Further, it has also been held that the right to health is integral to the right to life and the government has a constitutional obligation to provide health facilities (5). The Declaration of the Rights of the Child, sometimes known as the Geneva Declaration of the Rights of the Child, is an international document promoting child rights, drafted by Eglantyne Jebb and adopted by the League of Nations in 1924, and adopted in an extended form by the United Nations in 1959.

Declaration of the Rights of the Child (1924

The text of the document, as published by the International Save the Children Union in Geneva on 23 February 1923, is as follows:

1. The child must be given the means requisite for its normal development, both materially and spiritually.
2. The child that is hungry must be fed, the child that is sick must be nursed, the child that is backward must be helped, the delinquent child must be reclaimed, and the orphan and the waif must be sheltered and succoured.
3. The child must be the first to receive relief in times of distress.
4. The child must be put in a position to earn a livelihood, and must be protected against every form of exploitation.
5. The child must be brought up in the consciousness that its talents must be devoted to the service of its fellow men.

This text was endorsed by the League of Nations General Assembly on 26 November 1924 as the World Child Welfare Charter, and was the first human rights document approved by an inter-governmental institution. It was reaffirmed by the League in 1934. Heads of State and Government pledged to incorporate its principles in domestic legislation. In France, it was ordered to be displayed in every school. The original document, in the archives of the city of Geneva, carries the signatures of various international delegates, including Jebb, Janusz Korczak, and Gustave Ador, a former President of the Swiss Confederation.

History

After considering a number of options, including that of drafting an entirely new declaration, the United Nations resolved in 1946 to adopt the document, in a much expanded version, as its own statement of children's rights. Many different governments were involved in the drafting process. A slightly expanded version, with seven points in place of five, was adopted in 1948. Then on 20 November 1959 the United Nations General Assembly adopted a Declaration of the Rights of the Child, based on the structure and contents of the 1924 original, with ten principles. An accompanying resolution, proposed by the delegation of Afghanistan, called on governments to recognise these rights, strive for their acceptance, and publicise the document as widely as possible. This date has been adopted as the Universal Children's Day. This Declaration was followed in 1989 by the Convention on the Rights of the Child, adopted by the UN General Assembly, adopted and opened for signature, ratification and accession by General Assembly resolution 44/25 of 20 November 1989; entry into force 2 September 1990, in accordance with article 49.

In addition to the UK organisation, there are 29 other national Save the Children organisations who are members of the Save the Children Alliance, a global network of nonprofit organisations supporting local partners and Save the Children International in more than 120 countries around the world. Further, Save the Children has been involved in other initiatives through partners such as Bernard Arnault Africa Relief (BAAR International), which has operations in various parts of Kenya such as Elgeyo Marakwet, Kajiado, Homa Bay, Narok, Makueni and Machakos, as well as Southern Sudan. The organisation promotes policy changes in order to gain more rights for young people especially by enforcing the UN Declaration of the Rights of the Child. Alliance members co-ordinate emergency-relief efforts, helping to protect children from the effects of war and violence. Save the Children has general consultative status with the United Nations Economic and Social Council. In 2016, former Danish Prime Minister Helle Thorning-Schmidt was appointed Chief Executive.

Nations that ratify this convention are bound to it by international law. Compliance is monitored by the UN Committee on the Rights of the Child, which is composed of members from countries around the world. Once a year, the Committee submits a report to the Third Committee of the United Nations General Assembly, which also hears a statement from the CRC Chair, and the Assembly adopts a Resolution on the Rights of the Child.

Governments of countries that have ratified the Convention are required to report to, and appear before, the United Nations Committee on the Rights of the Child periodically to be examined on their progress with regards to the advancement of the implementation of the Convention and the status of child rights in their country. Their reports and the committee's written views an concerns are available on the committee's website. The UN General Assembly adopted the Convention and opened it for signature on 20 November 1989 (the 30th anniversary of its Declaration of the Rights of the Child). It came into force on 2 September 1990, after it was ratified by the required number of nations. Currently, 196 countries are party to it, including every member of the United Nations except the United States. Two optional protocols were adopted on 25 May 2000. The First Optional Protocol restricts the involvement of children in military conflicts, and the Second Optional Protocol prohibits the sale of children, child prostitution and child pornography. Both protocols have been ratified by more than 160 states. A third optional protocol relating to communication of complaints was adopted in December 2011 and opened for signature on 28 February 2012. It came into effect on 14 April 2014.

The Convention deals with the child-specific needs and rights. It requires that the "nations that ratify this convention are bound to it by international law". Ratifying states must act in the best interests of the child. In all jurisdictions implementing the Convention requires compliance with child custody and guardianship laws as that every child has basic rights, including the right to life, to their own name and identity, to be raised by their parents within a family or cultural grouping, and to have a relationship with both parents, even if they are separated. The Convention obliges states to allow parents to exercise their parental responsibilities. The Convention also acknowledges that children have the right to express their opinions and to have those opinions heard and acted upon when appropriate, to be protected from abuse or exploitation, and to have their privacy protected, and it requires that their lives not be subject to excessive interference. The Convention also obliges signatory states to provide separate legal representation for a child in any judicial dispute concerning their care and asks that the child's viewpoint be heard in such cases.

The Convention forbids capital punishment for children. In its General Comment 8 (2006) the Committee on the Rights of the Child stated that there was an "obligation of all state parties to move quickly to prohibit and eliminate all corporal punishment and all other cruel or degrading forms of punishment of children". Article 19 of the Convention states that state parties must "take all appropriate legislative, administrative, social and educational measures to protect the child from all forms of physical or mental violence", but it makes no reference to corporal punishment. The Committee's interpretation of this section to encompass a prohibition on corporal punishment has been rejected by several state parties to the Convention, including Australia, Canada and the United Kingdom.

States party and signatories

Currently 196 countries are parties to the treaty (some with stated reservations or interpretations). This includes every member of the United Nations (except the United States), plus the Cook Islands, Niue, the State of Palestine, and the Holy See. The United States has not ratified it. South Sudan did not sign the convention, however ratification was complete in January 2015. Somalia's domestic ratification finished in January 2015 and the instrument was deposited with the United Nations in October 2015. All successor states of Czechoslovakia and Yugoslavia (Bosnia and Herzegovina, Croatia, Czech Republic, Macedonia, Montenegro, Serbia, Slovenia, and Slovakia) made declarations of succession to the treaty and currently apply it.

Azerbaijan

Azerbaijan ratified Convention on the Rights of the Child on 21 July 1992. In terms of the ratification of the Convention on the Rights of the Child, a significant number of laws, decrees and resolutions were approved in Azerbaijan by the President and the Cabinet of Ministers focusing on the development of the child welfare system. In this regard, the Convention [1]182 on "Elimination of the worst forms of child labour" and Recommendation [1]190 of the International Labour Organization and the Hague Convention on International adoption of children were ratified by Milli Majlis in 2004.

There is a concern over the administration of juvenile justice in Azerbaijan, mostly regarding compliance with articles 37, 39 and 40 of the Convention on the Rights of the Child, as well as other relevant standards such as the Beijing Rules, the Riyadh Guidelines and the United Nations Rules for the Protection of Juveniles Deprived of their Liberty. Therefore, international organizations assisted Azerbaijan to improve the situation in the field of juvenile justice. Juvenile offenders have been added to the Presidential pardons on a regular basis. Azerbaijan has built cooperation with many international organizations, in particular with UNICEF in the field of child protection. In 1993, UNICEF began its activity in Azerbaijan. In 2005, Azerbaijan and UNICEF signed a 5-year country program. The country program for 2005-2009 was implemented in the field of child protection, children's health and nutrition, children's education and youth health, their development and participation. In addition, UNICEF supports Azerbaijan in developing juvenile justice system, establishing alternative care system and raising awareness among youth about HIV/AIDS.

Canada

Canada became a signatory to the Convention on 28 May 1990 and ratified in 1991. Youth criminal laws in Canada underwent major changes resulting in the Youth Criminal Justice Act (YCJA) which went into effect on 1 April 2003. The Act specifically refers to Canada's different commitments under the Convention..

India

India ratified UNCRC on 11 December 1992, agreeing in principles all articles except with certain reservations on issues relating to child labor. In India there is law that children under the age of 18 should not work, but there is no outright ban on child labor, and the practice is generally permitted in most industries except those deemed "hazardous".Although a law in October 2006 banned child labor in hotels, restaurants, and as domestic servants, there continues to be high demand for children as hired help in the home. Current estimates as to the number of child laborers in the country range from the government's conservative estimate of 4 million children under 14 years of age

Iran

Iran has adhered to the convention (except for alleged child slavery) since 1991 and ratified it in the Parliament in 1994. Upon ratification, Iran made the following reservation: "If the text of the Convention is or becomes incompatible with the domestic laws and Islamic standards at any time or in any case, the Government of the Islamic Republic shall not abide by it." Iran has also signed the both optional protocols which relate to the special protection of children against involvement in armed conflict and the sale of children and sexual exploitation. Although Iran is a state party to the Convention, international human rights organisations and foreign governments routinely denounced executions of Iranian child offenders as a violation of the treaty. But on 10 February 2012, Iran's parliament changed the controversial law of executing juveniles. In the new law, the age of 18 (solar year) would be for both genders considered the cut-off for adulthood and offenders under this age will be sentenced under a separate law. Based on the previous Islamic law, which was revised, girls at the age of 9 and boys at 15 (lunar year, 11 days shorter than a solar year) were fully responsible for their crimes. "According to Islamic sources, the criterion for criminal responsibility is reaching the age of maturity which, according to the Shi'ite School of the IRI, is 9 lunar years (8 years and 9 months) for girls and 15 lunar years (14 years and 7 months) for boys."

Ireland

Ireland signed the Convention on the Rights of the Child on 30 September 1990 and ratified it, without reservation, on 28 September 1992. In response to criticisms expressed in the 1998 review by the UN Committee on the Rights of the Child in Geneva, the Irish government established the office of Ombudsman for Children and drew up a national children's strategy. In 2006, following concerns expressed by the committee that the wording of the Irish Constitution does not allow the State to intervene in cases of abuse other than in very exceptional cases, the Irish government undertook to amend the constitution to make a more explicit commitment to children's rights.

Israel

Israel ratified the Convention in 1991. In 2010, UNICEF criticized Israel for its failure to create a government-appointed commission on children's rights or to adopt a national children's rights strategy or program in order to implement various Israeli laws addressing children's rights. The report criticizes Israel for holding that the Convention does not apply in the West Bank and for defining as Palestinians under the age of 16 in the occupied territories as children, even though Israeli law defines a child as being under 18, in line with the Convention. A contemporaneous report by the Organisation for Economic Co-operation and Development found that Israel's investment in children is below the international average and the actual investment had fallen between 1995 and 2006. In 2012, the United Nations Committee on the Rights of the Child criticized Israel for its bombing attacks on Palestinians in the Gaza Strip, stating, "Destruction of homes and damage to schools, streets and other public facilities gravely affect children" and called them "gross violations of the Convention on the Rights of the Child, its Optional Protocol on the involvement of children in armed conflict and international humanitarian law". It also criticized Palestinian rocket attacks from Gaza on southern Israel which traumatized Israeli children, calling on all parties to protect children.

Public interest petitions have been filed under Article 21 in response to violations of the right to health. They have been filed to provide special treatment to children in jail (8); on pollution hazards (9); against hazardous drugs (10); against inhuman conditions in after-care homes (11); on the health rights of mentally ill patients (12); on the rights of patients in cataract surgery camps (13); for immediate medical aid to injured persons (14); on conditions in tuberculosis hospitals (15); on occupational health hazards (16); on the regulation of blood banks and availability of blood products (17); on passive smoking in public places (18); and in an appeal filed by a person with HIV on the rights of HIV/AIDS patients (19).

Constitution of the World Health Organization (1946)

The preamble of the 1946 World Health Organization (WHO) Constitution defines health broadly as "a state of complete physical, mental and social well-being and not merely the absence of disease or infirmity." The Constitution defines the right to health as "the enjoyment of the highest attainable standard of health," and enumerates some principles of this right as healthy child development; equitable dissemination of medical knowledge and its benefits; and government-provided social measures to ensure adequate health. Frank P. Grad credits the WHO Constitution as "claiming ... the full area of contemporary international public health," establishing the right to health as a "fundamental, inalienable human right" that governments cannot abridge, and are rather obligated to protect and uphold. The WHO Constitution, notably, marks the first formal demarcation of a right to health in international law. International Convention on the Elimination of All Forms of Racial Discrimination (1965) Health is briefly addressed in the United Nations' International Convention on the Elimination of All Forms of Racial

Discrimination, which was adopted in 1965 and entered into effect in 1969. The Convention calls upon States to "Prohibit and to eliminate racial discrimination in all its forms and to guarantee the right of everyone, without distinction as to race, colour, or national or ethnic origin, to equality before the law," and references under this provision "The right to public health, medical care, social security and social services." International Covenant on Economic, Social and Cultural Rights (1966) The United Nations further defines the right to health in Article 12 of the 1966 International Covenant on Economic, Social and Cultural Rights, which states: The States Parties to the present Covenant recognize the right of everyone to the enjoyment of the highest attainable standard of physical and mental health. The steps to be taken by the States Parties to the present Covenant to achieve the full realization of this right shall include those necessary for: The reduction of the stillbirth-rate and of infant mortality and for the healthy development of the child; The improvement of all aspects of environmental and industrial hygiene; The prevention, treatment and control of epidemic, endemic, occupational and other diseases; The creation of conditions which would assure to all medical service and medical attention in the event of sickness.

General Comment No. 14 (2000)

In 2000, the United Nations' Committee on Economic, Social and Cultural Rights issued General Comment No. 14, which addresses "substantive issues arising in the implementation of the International Covenant on Economic, Social and Cultural Rights" with respect to Article 12 and "the right to the highest attainable standard of health." The General Comment provides more explicit, operational language on the freedoms and entitlements included under a right to health.

The General Comment makes the direct clarification that "the right to health is not to be understood as a right to be healthy." Instead, the right to health is articulated as a set of both freedoms and entitlements which accommodate the individual's biological and social conditions as well as the State's available resources, both of which may preclude a right to be healthy for reasons beyond the influence or control of the State. Article 12 tasks the State with recognizing that each individual holds an inherent right to the best feasible standard of health, and itemizes (at least in part) the 'freedoms from' and 'entitlements to' that accompany such a right; however, it does not charge the State with ensuring that all individuals, in fact, are fully healthy, nor that all individuals have made full recognition of the rights and opportunities enumerated in the right to health.

Relation to other rights

Like the Universal Declaration of Human Rights, the General Comment clarifies the interrelated nature of human rights, stating that, "the right to health is closely related to and dependent upon the realization of other human rights," and thereby underscoring the importance of advancements in other entitlements such as the rights to food, work, housing, life, non-discrimination, human dignity, and access to importance, among others, towards the recognition of the right to health. Similarly, the General Comment acknowledges that "the right to health embraces a wide range of socio-economic factors that promote conditions in which people can lead a healthy life, and extends to the underlying determinants of health." In this respect, the General Comment holds that the specific steps towards realizing the right to health enumerated in Article 12 are non-exhaustive and strictly illustrative in nature.

The inextricable link between health and human rights

Jonathan Mann was a Francois-Xavier Bagnoud Professor of Health and Human Rights and Professor of Epidemiology and International Health at the Harvard T. H. Chan School of Public Health. He was known for being a powerful pioneer and advocate for the promotion of health, ethics, and human rights, championing the theory that health and human rights were inextricably interlinked in a dynamic relationship. According to Mann, health and human rights are complementary approaches for defining and advancing human well-being. In 1994, Jonathan Mann and his colleagues started the "Health and Human Rights Journal" to underline the importance of this inextricable link between health and human rights. In the first volume of the "Health and Human Rights Journal," Jonathan Mann and his colleagues published a transformative article to explore the potential collaboration in health and human rights. In this article, Mann et al. describe a framework for connecting the two domains that are interlinked. This framework is broken into three broad relationships.

The first relationship between health and human rights is a political one. Mann and colleagues state that health policies, programs, and practices have an impact on human rights, especially when state power is considered in the realm of public health. Next, the article posits a reverse relationship: that human rights violations have health impacts. It also calls for health expertise to help understand how health and well-being can be impacted by human rights violations through measurement and assessment. The third segment of the framework linking health and human rights introduces the concept that the protection and promotion of human rights and health are linked fundamentally in a dynamic relationship.

While literature has largely supported the first two relationships, this third hypothesis has not been explored as substantially. The article supports this concept by stating that this link suggests there are dramatic practical consequences in the independent operations of, but also in the interaction in activities of, the practice of public health and the practice of human rights. There is what is deemed an interdependence that cannot be negated. Mann and his colleagues further posit that research, education, experience, and advocacy are all required to understand this intersection, in order to understand and advance human well-being globally. Ultimately, Mann and his colleague's mission is to convey that, while individual health has been much of the focus for medical and other health provision services, especially concerning physical illness and disability, public health's focus has more so evolved around how people can be healthy. According to this surprisingly simple definition, public health's mission is to promote positive health and prevention of health problems – disease, disability, premature death. That is, the traditional sense of individual health as understood and processed by health care services is "one essential condition for health," but does is not the sole qualifier or an exchangeable term with "health." In other words, health care services are not sufficient for health, as public health practitioners understand it – there are external factors that have both nuanced as well as pronounced positive and negative impact on health and well-being of the global human population.

Health equity

The General Comment also makes additional reference to the question of health equity, a concept not addressed in the initial International Covenant. The document notes, "The Covenant proscribes any discrimination in access to health care and underlying determinants of health, as well as to means and entitlements for their procurement." Moreover, responsibility for ameliorating discrimination and its effects with regards to health is delegated to the State: "States have a special obligation to provide those who do not have sufficient means with the necessary health insurance and health-care facilities, and to prevent any discrimination on internationally prohibited grounds in the provision of health care and health services." Additional emphasis is placed upon non-discrimination on the basis of gender, age, disability, or membership in indigenous communities.

Responsibilities of states and international organizations

Subsequent sections of the General Comment detail the obligations of nations and international organizations towards a right to health. The obligations of nations are placed into three categories: obligations to respect, obligations to protect, and obligations to fulfill the right to health. Examples of these (in non-exhaustive fashion) include preventing discrimination in access or delivery of care; refraining from limitations to contraceptive access or family planning; restricting denial of access to health information; reducing environmental pollution; restricting coercive and/or harmful culturally-based medical practices; ensuring equitable access to social determinants of health; and providing proper guidelines for the accreditation of medical facilities, personnel, and equipment. International obligations include allowing for the enjoyment of health in other countries; preventing violations of health in other countries; cooperating in the provision of humanitarian aid for disasters and emergencies; and refraining from use of embargoes on medical goods or personnel as an act of political or economic influence. Convention on the Elimination of All Forms of Discrimination Against Women Article 12 of the 1979 United Nations Convention on the Elimination of All Forms of Discrimination against Women outlines women's protection from gender discrimination when receiving health services and women's entitlement to specific gender-related healthcare provisions. The full text of Article 12 states:

Article 12:

1. States Parties shall take all appropriate measures to eliminate discrimination against women in the field of health care in order to ensure, on a basis of equality of men and women, access to health care services, including those related to family planning.
2. Notwithstanding the provisions of paragraph I of this article, States Parties shall ensure to women appropriate services in connection with pregnancy, confinement and the post-natal period, granting free services where necessary, as well as adequate nutrition during pregnancy and lactation.

Convention on the Rights of the Child

Health is mentioned on several instances in the Convention on the Rights of the Child (1989). Article 3 calls upon parties to ensure that institutions and facilities for the care of children adhere to health standards. Article 17 recognizes the child's right to access information that is pertinent to his/her physical and mental health and well-being. Article 23 makes specific reference to the rights of disabled children, in which it includes health services, rehabilitation, preventive care. Article 24 outlines child health in detail, and states, "Parties recognize the right of the child to the enjoyment of the highest attainable standard of health and to facilities for the treatment of illness and rehabilitation of health. States shall strive to ensure that no child is deprived of his or her right of access to such health care services." Towards implementation of this provision, the Convention enumerates the following measures:

- To diminish infant and child mortality;
- To ensure the provision of necessary medical assistance and health care to all children with emphasis on the development of primary health care;
- To combat disease and malnutrition, including within the framework of primary health care, through, inter alia, the application of readily available technology and through the provision of adequate nutritious foods and clean drinking-water, taking into consideration the dangers and risks of environmental pollution;

- To ensure appropriate pre-natal and post-natal health care for mothers;
- To ensure that all segments of society, in particular parents and children, are informed, have access to education and are supported in the use of basic knowledge of child health and nutrition, the advantages of breastfeeding, hygiene and environmental sanitation and the prevention of accidents;
- To develop preventive health care, guidance for parents and family planning education and services.

The World Health Organization website comments, "The CRC is the normative and legal framework for WHO's work across the broad spectrum of child and adolescent health."Goldhagen presents the CRC as a "template for child advocacy" and proposes its use as a framework for reducing disparities and improving outcomes in child health.

Convention on the Rights of Persons with Disabilities

Article 25 of the Convention on the Rights of Persons with Disabilities (2006) specifies that "persons with disabilities have the right to the enjoyment of the highest attainable standard of health without discrimination on the basis of disability." The sub-clauses of Article 25 state that States shall give the disabled the same "range, quality, and standard" of health care as it provides to other persons, as well as those services specifically required for prevention, identification, and management of disability. Further provisions specify that health care for the disabled should be made available in local communities and that care should be geographically equitable, with additional statements against the denial or unequal provision of health services (including "food and fluids" and "life insurance") on the basis of disability. Hendriks criticizes the failure of the Convention to define specifically the term "disability"; he contends further that "the absence of a clear description may prejudice the uniform interpretation, or at least place in jeopardy the consistent protection the Convention seeks to guarantee." He does, however, acknowledge that the lack of a clear definition for "disability" may benefit the disabled by limiting the State's ability to limit extension of the Convention's provisions to specific populations or those with certain conditions.

Definitions in academic literature

While most human rights are theoretically framed as negative rights, meaning that they are areas upon which society cannot interfere or restrict by political action, Mervyn Sussercontends that the right to health is a particularly unique and challenging right because it is often expressed as a positive right, where society bears an obligation to provide certain resources and opportunities to the general population. Susser further sets out four provisions that he sees as covered under a right to health: equitable access to health and medical services; a "good-faith" social effort to promote equal health among different social groups; means to measure and assess health equity; and equal sociopolitical systems to give all parties a unique voice in health advocacy and promotion. He is careful to note here that, while this likely entails some minimum standard of access to health resources, it does not guarantee or necessitate an equitable state of health for each person due to inherent biological differences in health status. This distinction is an important one, as some common critiques of a "right to health" are that it establishes a right to an unreachable standard and that it aspires to a state of health that is too subjectively variable from person to person or from one society to the next.

While Susser's discussion centers on healthcare as a positive right, Paul Hunt refutes this view and makes the argument that the right to health also encompasses certain negative rights such as a protection from discrimination and the right to not receive medical treatment without the recipient's voluntary consent. However, Hunt does concede that some positive rights, such as the responsibility of society to pay special attention to the health needs of the underserved and vulnerable, are included in the right to health. Paul Farmer addresses the issue of unequal access to health care in his article, "The Major Infectious Diseases in the World - To Treat or Not to Treat." He discusses the growing "outcome gap" between the populations receiving health interventions and the ones that are not. Poor people are not receiving the same treatment, if any at all, as the more financially fortunate. The high costs of medicine and treatment make it problematic for poor countries to receive equal care. He states, "Excellence without equity looms as the chief human-rights dilemma of health care in the 21st century."

The human right to health means that everyone has the right to the highest attainable standard of physical and mental health, which includes access to all medical services, sanitation, adequate food, decent housing, healthy working conditions, and a clean environment.

- The human right to health guarantees a system of health protection for all.
- Everyone has the right to the health care they need, and to living conditions that enable us to be healthy, such as adequate food, housing, and a healthy environment.
- Health care must be provided as a public good for all, financed publicly and equitably.

The human right to health care means that hospitals, clinics, medicines, and doctors' services must be accessible, available, acceptable, and of good quality for everyone, on an equitable basis, where and when needed. The design of a health care system must be guided by the following key human rights standards:

Universal Access: Access to health care must be universal, guaranteed for all on an equitable basis. Health care must be affordable and comprehensive for everyone, and physically accessible where and when needed. Availability: Adequate health care infrastructure (e.g. hospitals, community health facilities, trained health care professionals), goods (e.g. drugs, equipment), and services (e.g. primary care, mental health) must be available in all geographical areas and to all communities. Acceptability and Dignity: Health care institutions and providers must respect dignity, provide culturally appropriate care, be responsive to needs based on gender, age, culture, language, and different ways of life and abilities. They must respect medical ethics and protect confidentiality. Quality: All health care must be medically appropriate and of good quality, guided by quality standards and control mechanisms, and provided in a timely, safe, and patient-centered manner.

The human right to health also entails the following procedural principles, which apply to all human rights: Non-Discrimination: Health care must be accessible and provided without discrimination (in intent or effect) based on health status, race, ethnicity, age, sex, sexuality, disability, language, religion, national origin, income, or social status. Transparency: Health information must be easily accessible for everyone, enabling people to protect their health and claim quality health services. Institutions that organize, finance or deliver health care must operate in a transparent way.

Participation: Individuals and communities must be able to take an active role in decisions that affect their health, including in the organization and implementation of health care services. Accountability: Private companies and public agencies must be held accountable for protecting the right to health care through enforceable standards, regulations, and independent compliance monitoring. Healthcare Is a Human Right campaigns now exist in several U.S. states, inspired by the example of Vermont, which in 2011 became the first state to pass a law for a universal, publicly financed health care system. All of these campaigns have translated the human rights standards listed above into clear human rights principles that guide their actions and policy positions:

- Universality: Everyone must have access to equal high-quality and comprehensive health care.
- Equity: Resources and services must be distributed and accessed according to people's needs. We get what we need and give what we can.
- Accountability: The health care system must be accountable to the people it serves.
- Transparency: The health care system must be open with regard to information, decision-making, and management.
- Participation: The health care system must enable meaningful public participation in all decisions affecting people's right to health care.

Human right to health care

An alternative way to conceptualize one facet of the right to health is a "human right to health care." Notably, this encompasses both patient and provider rights in the delivery of healthcare services, the latter being similarly open to frequent abuse by the states. Patient rights in health care delivery include: the right to privacy, information, life, and quality care, as well as freedom from discrimination, torture, and cruel, inhumane, or degrading treatment. Marginalized groups, such as migrants and persons who have been displaced, racial and ethnic minorities, women, sexual minorities, and those living with HIV, are particularly vulnerable to violations of human rights in healthcare settings. For instance, racial and ethnic minorities may be segregated into poorer quality wards, disabled persons may be contained and forcibly medicated, drug users may be denied addiction treatment, women may be forced into vaginal examinations and may be denied life-saving abortions, suspected homosexual men may be forced into anal examinations, and women of marginalized groups and transgender persons may be forcibly sterilized.

Provider rights include: the right to quality standards of working conditions, the right to associate freely, and the right to refuse to perform a procedure based on their morals.Healthcare providers often experience violations of their rights. For instance, particularly in countries with weak rule of law, healthcare providers are often forced to perform procedures which negate their morals, deny marginalized groups the best possible standards of care, breach patient confidentiality, and conceal crimes against humanity and torture. Furthermore, providers who do not oblige these pressures are often persecuted. Currently, especially in the United States, much debate surrounds the issue of "provider consciousness", which retains the right of providers to abstain from performing procedures that do not align with their moral code, such as abortions. Legal reform as a mechanism to combat and prevent violations of patient and provider rights presents a promising approach. However, in transitional countries (newly formed countries undergoing reform), and other settings with weak rule of law, may be limited. Resources and tools for lawyers, providers, and patients interested in improving human rights in patient care have been formulated.

Criticism

Philip Barlow writes that health care should not be considered a human right because of the difficulty of defining what it entails and where the 'minimum standard' of entitlements under the right ought to be established. Additionally, Barlow contends that rights establish duties upon others to protect or guarantee them, and that it is unclear who holds the social responsibility for the right to health. John Berkeley, in agreement with Barlow, critiques further that the right to health does not consider adequately the responsibility that an individual has to uphold his or her own health. Richard D Lamm vehemently argues against making healthcare a right. He defines a right as one that is to be defended at all costs, and a concept that is defined and interpreted by the judicial system. Making healthcare a right would require governments to spend a large portion of its resources to provide its citizens with it. He asserts that the healthcare system is based on the erroneous assumption of unlimited resources. Limited resources inhibits governments from providing everyone with adequate healthcare, especially in the long term. Attempting to provide "beneficial" healthcare to all people utilizing limited resources could lead to economical collapse. Lamm asserts that access to healthcare but a small part in producing a healthy society, and to create a healthy society, resources should also be spent on social resources.

Another criticism of the right to health is that it is not feasible. Imre J.P. Loefler argues that the financial and logistical burdens of ensuring health care for all are unattainable, and that resource constraints make it unrealistic to justify a right towards prolonging life indefinitely. Instead, Loefler suggests that the goal of improving population health is better served through socioeconomic policy than a formal right to health.WHO

Key facts

- The WHO Constitution (1946) envisages "...the highest attainable standard of health as a fundamental right of every human being."
- Understanding health as a human right creates a legal obligation on states to ensure access to timely, acceptable, and affordable health care of appropriate quality as well as to providing for the underlying determinants of health, such as safe and potable water, sanitation, food, housing, health-related information and education, and gender equality.
- A States' obligation to support the right to health – including through the allocation of "maximum available resources" to progressively realise this goal - is reviewed through various international human rights mechanisms, such as the Universal Periodic Review, or the Committee on Economic, Social and Cultural Rights. In many cases, the right to health has been adopted into domestic law or Constitutional law.
- A rights-based approach to health requires that health policy and programmes must prioritize the needs of those furthest behind first towards greater equity, a principle that has been echoed in the recently adopted 2030 Agenda for Sustainable Development and Universal Health Coverage. (1)
- The right to health must be enjoyed without discrimination on the grounds of race, age, ethnicity or any other status. Non-discrimination

and equality requires states to take steps to redress any discriminatory law, practice or policy.

- Another feature of rights-based approaches is meaningful participation. Participation means ensuring that national stakeholders – including non-state actors such as non-governmental organizations – are meaningfully involved in all phases of programming: assessment, analysis, planning, implementation, monitoring and evaluation.

"The right to the highest attainable standard of health" implies a clear set of legal obligations on states to ensure appropriate conditions for the enjoyment of health for all people without discrimination. The right to health is one of a set of internationally agreed human rights standards, and is inseparable or 'indivisible' from these other rights. This means achieving the right to health is both central to, and dependent upon, the realisation of other human rights, to food, housing, work, education, information, and participation. The right to health, as with other rights, includes both freedoms and entitlements:

- Freedoms include the right to control one's health and body (for example, sexual and reproductive rights) and to be free from interference (for example, free from torture and non-consensual medical treatment and experimentation).
- Entitlements include the right to a system of health protection that gives everyone an equal opportunity to enjoy the highest attainable level of health.

Focus on disadvantaged populations

Disadvantage and marginalization serve to exclude certain populations in societies from enjoying good health. Three of the world's most fatal communicable diseases – malaria, HIV/AIDS and tuberculosis – disproportionately affect the world's poorest populations, and in many cases are compounded and exacerbated by other inequalities and inequities including gender, age, sexual orientation or gender identity and migration status. Conversely the burden of non-communicable diseases – often perceived as affecting high-income countries – is increasing disproportionately among lower-income countries and populations, and is largely associated with lifestyle and behaviour factors as well as environmental determinants, such as safe housing, water and sanitation that are inextricably linked to human rights.

A focus on disadvantage also reveals evidence of those who are exposed to greater rates of ill-health and face significant obstacles to accessing quality and affordable healthcare, including indigenous populations. While data collection systems are often ill-equipped to capture data on these groups, reports show that these populations have higher mortality and morbidity rates, due to noncommunicable diseases such as cancer, cardiovascular diseases, and chronic respiratory disease. These populations may also be the subject of laws and policies that further compound their marginalization and make it harder for them to access healthcare prevention, treatment, rehabilitation and care services.

Violations of human rights in health

Violations or lack of attention to human rights can have serious health consequences. Overt or implicit discrimination in the delivery of health services – both within the health workforce and between health workers and service users – acts as a powerful barrier to health services, and contributes to poor quality care. Mental ill-health often leads to a denial of dignity and autonomy, including forced treatment or institutionalization, and disregard of individual legal capacity to make decisions. Paradoxically, mental health is still given inadequate attention in public health, in spite of the high levels of violence, poverty and social exclusion that contribute to worse mental and physical health outcomes for people with mental health disorders. Violations of human rights not only contribute to and exacerbate poor health, but for many, including people with disabilities, indigenous populations, women living with HIV, sex workers, people who use drugs, transgender and intersex people, the health care setting presents a risk of heightened exposure to human rights abuses – including coercive or forced treatment and procedures.

Human rights-based approaches

A human rights-based approach to health provides a set of clear principles for setting and evaluating health policy and service delivery, targeting discriminatory practices and unjust power relations that are at the heart of inequitable health outcomes. In pursuing a rights-based approach, health policy, strategies and programmes should be designed explicitly to improve the enjoyment of all people to the right to health, with a focus on the furthest behind first. The core principles and standards of a rights-based approach are detailed below.

Core principles of human rights

Accountability

States and other duty-bearers are answerable for the observance of human rights. However, there is also a growing movement recognising the importance of other non-state actors such as businesses in the respect and protection of human rights. (2)

Equality and non-discrimination

The principle of non-discrimination seeks '...to guarantee that human rights are exercised without discrimination of any kind based on race, colour, sex, language, religion, political, or other opinion, national or social origin, property, birth or other status such as disability, age, marital and family status, sexual orientation and gender identity, health status, place of residence, economic and social situation'. Any discrimination, for example in access to health care, as well as in means and entitlements for achieving this access, is prohibited on the basis of race, colour, sex, language, religion, political or other opinion, national or social origin, property, birth, physical or mental disability, health status (including HIV/AIDS), sexual orientation ,and civil, political, social or other status, which has the intention or effect of impairing the equal enjoyment or exercise of the right to health.

The principle of non-discrimination and equality requires WHO to address discrimination in guidance, policies, and practices, such as relating to the distribution and provision of resources and health services. Non-discrimination and equality are key measures required to address the social determinants affecting the enjoyment of the right to health. Functioning national health information systems and availability of disaggregated data are essential to be able to identify the most vulnerable groups and diverse needs.

Participation

Participation requires ensuring that all concerned stakeholders including non-state actors have ownership and control over development processes in all phases of the programming cycle: assessment, analysis, planning, implementation, monitoring, and evaluation. Participation goes well beyond consultation or a technical addition to project design; it should include explicit strategies to empower citizens, especially the most marginalized, so that their expectations are recognised by the State. Participation is important to accountability as it provides "...checks and balances which do not allow unitary leadership to exercise power in an arbitrary manner".

Universal, indivisible and interdependent

Human rights are universal and inalienable. They apply equally, to all people, everywhere, without distinction. Human Rights standards – to food, health, education, to be free from torture, inhuman or degrading treatment – are also interrelated. The improvement of one right facilitates advancement of the others. Likewise, the deprivation of one right adversely affects the others.

Core elements of a right to health

Progressive realization using maximum available resources

No matter what level of resources they have at their disposal, progressive realisation requires that governments take immediate steps within their means towards the fulfilment of these rights. Regardless of resource capacity, the elimination of discrimination and improvements in the legal and juridical systems must be acted upon with immediate effect.

Non-retrogression

States should not allow the existing protection of economic, social, and cultural rights to deteriorate unless there are strong justifications for a retrogressive measure. For example, introducing school fees in secondary education which had formerly been free of charge would constitute a deliberate retrogressive measure. To justify it, a State would have to demonstrate that it adopted the measure only after carefully considering all the options, assessing the impact and fully using its maximum available resources.

Core components of the right to health

The right to health (Article 12) was defined in General Comment 14 of the Committee on Economic, Social and Cultural Rights – a committee of Independent Experts, responsible for overseeing adherence to the Covenant. (4) The right includes the following core components:

Availability

Refers to the need for a sufficient quantity of functioning public health and health care facilities, goods and services, as well as programmes for all. Availability can be measured through the analysis of disaggregated data to different and multiple stratifiers including by age, sex, location and socio-economic status and qualitative surveys to understand coverage gaps and health workforce coverage

Accessibility

Requires that health facilities, goods, and services must be accessible to everyone. Accessibility has four overlapping dimensions:

- non-discrimination
- physical accessibility
- economical accessibility (affordability)
- information accessibility.

Assessing accessibility may require analysis of barriers – physical financial or otherwise – that exist, and how they may affect the most vulnerable, and call for the establishment or application of clear norms and standards in both law and policy to address these barriers, as well as robust monitoring systems of health-related information and whether this information is reaching all populations.

Acceptability

Relates to respect for medical ethics, culturally appropriate, and sensitivity to gender. Acceptability requires that health facilities, goods, services and programmes are people-centred and cater for the specific needs of diverse population groups and in accordance with international standards of medical ethics for confidentiality and informed consent.

Quality

Facilities, goods, and services must be scientifically and medically approved. Quality is a key component of Universal Health Coverage, and includes the experience as well as the perception of health care. Quality health services should be:

- Safe – avoiding injuries to people for whom the care is intended;
- Effective – providing evidence-based healthcare services to those who need them;
- People-centred – providing care that responds to individual preferences, needs and values;
- Timely – reducing waiting times and sometimes harmful delays.
- Equitable – providing care that does not vary in quality on account of gender, ethnicity, geographic location, and socio-economic status;
- Integrated – providing care that makes available the full range of health services throughout the life course;
- Efficient – maximizing the benefit of available resources and avoiding waste

WHO response

WHO has made a commitment to mainstream human rights into healthcare programmes and policies on national and regional levels by looking at underlying determinants of health as part of a comprehensive approach to health and human rights. In addition, WHO has been actively strengthening its role in providing technical, intellectual, and political leadership on the right to health including:

- strengthening the capacity of WHO and its Member States to integrate a human rights-based approach to health;
- advancing the right to health in international law and international development processes; and
- advocating for health-related human rights, including the right to health.

Addressing the needs and rights of individuals at different stages across the life course requires taking a comprehensive approach within the broader context of promoting human rights, gender equality, and equity.

The Purpose of Module 14

The purpose of this module is to provide an overview of the guarantees related to the right to health.

The module

- looks at the development of the concept of the right to health;
- enumerates international, regional and national standards;
- analyzes the state's obligations; and
- considers international and other mechanisms to protect the right.

Health and well-being are deeply personal matters. Nothing is more intimate than the experience of conceiving and bearing a child, and giving birth to a unique human being; none of us can live another's fear or pain; and death itself is something we cannot share, however real the grief we suffer. Facing a particular health related condition, and then being on the receiving end of the decisions or prejudices of others-be they health professionals, religious authorities, family members, neighbours, employers or insurance companies-is something that often gives us a new awareness of how limited is our capacity to control some of the most central aspects of our lives. It gives us an insight into what exclusion feels like.

Current trends suggest that "the enjoyment of the highest attainable standard of health" which WHO describes as "one of the fundamental rights of every human being" is seen almost as a by-product, something that will trickle down to the bottom some time in the future. There is a long way to trickle before this fundamental right reaches those who are destitute (currently one fifth of the human race), those who survive precariously in the informal sector, or those whose access to health care is limited by their age or their disabilities, or by armed conflict.And while seven out of ten of the world's poorest people are female, women's health needs are widely neglected, whatever their background. Yet, if development is not for health, what is it for-and who can expect to enjoy it?

Development of the Concept of the Right to Health

Health was also understood as the "absence of disease." The first laws containing health-related provisions go back to the era of industrialization.ýÿ The Moral Apprentices Act (1802) and Public Health Act (1848) were adopted in the United Kingdom as a means of containing social pressure arising from poor labor conditions. The 1843 Mexican Constitution included references to the state's responsibility for preserving public health. The evolution towards defining health as a social issue led to the founding of the World Health Organization (WHO) in 1946. With the emergence of health as a public issue, the conception of health changed. WHO developed and promulgated the understanding of health as "a state of complete physical, mental and social well-being and not merely the absence of disease or infirmity." It defined an integrated approach linking together all the factors related to human well-being, including physical and social surroundings conducive to good health. Universal recognition of the right to health was further confirmed in the 1978 Declaration of Alma-Ata on Primary Health Care, in which states pledged to progressively develop comprehensive health care systems to ensure effective and equitable distribution of resources for maintaining health.They reiterated their responsibility to provide for the health of their populations, " which can be fulfilled only by the provision of adequate health and social measures. [5] The Declaration develops the bases for implementing primary health care systems, which have implications for the observance of the right. While this instrument is not binding, it does represent a further commitment on the part of states in respect of the right to health, and establishes the framework for an integrated policy aimed at securing its enjoyment.

In the context of the Alma-Ata Conference, WHO designed the plan, Health for All by the Year 2000, which consists of a series of goals and programs to achieve minimum levels of health for all. Nonetheless, in a context in which health problems associated with poverty and inequity continue to pose the main obstacles to attaining minimal levels of well-being for most of the world's population, the failure to achieve these goals points to the need to rework strategies. Promoting health, one of the fundamental aspects of primary health care, has been addressed independently by four successive conferences, the first in Ottawa, Canada, in 1986 and the most recent in Jakarta, Indonesia, in 1997. The Declaration of Jakarta includes an updated conceptualization of health and identifies the requirements for its attainment as we head into the next century. These include "peace, housing, education, social security, social relations, food, income, women's empowerment, a stable ecosystem, the sustainable use of resources, social justice, respect for human rights, and equity. Above all else, poverty is the greatest threat to health."

Other relevant international initiatives in recent years related to health are the Program of Action of the International Conference on Population and Development (Cairo, 1994), which encompassed three goals related to reducing infant and maternal mortality, and guaranteeing universal access to reproductive health and family planning services; and the Platform of Action of the Fourth World Conference on Women (Beijing, 1995), which adopted five strategic objectives aimed at improving women's health worldwide.

Health as a Human Right

International standards

Article 25 of the UDHR emphasizes recognition of the right of all persons to an adequate standard of living, including guarantees for health and well-being. It acknowledges the relationship between health and well-being and its link with other rights, such as the right to food and the right to housing, as well as medical and social services. It adopts a broad view of the right to health as a human right, even though health is but one component of an adequate standard of living. Articles 23 and 24 of the CRC recognize the right to health for all children and identify several steps for its realization. Similarly, CEDAW establishes the obligation to adopt adequate measures to guarantee women access to health and medical care, with no discrimination whatsoever, including access to family planning services. It also establishes the commitment to guarantee adequate maternal and child health care.

Chapter - 5

Implications for Decision-Making in Newborn Medical Care

The 1989 United Nations Convention on the Rights of the Child (UN Convention) provides children with the right of the highest attainable standard of health (article 24). All countries in the world except the United States have now ratified this convention, which has implications for national health policy and priorities regarding health care for every child. The convention places an obligation on all public and private health institutions to ensure that the best interest of the child is assessed and taken as a primary consideration in all actions affecting children. The important point emphasized by the United Nations Committee on the Rights of the Child is that, based on the UN Convention, each child has a right to be assessed individually before a decision is made regarding proper treatment. As a consequence, the UN Convention may change practice in handling of newborns in a wider perspective.

In neonatology, decisions to initiate or forego intensive care for certain infants such as the extremely immature or those with certain syndromes have been heavily debated. However, in recent years, there has been some change in attitudes compatible with the UN Convention. For instance, The International Liaison Committee on Resuscitation (ILCOR) and the American Heart Association's guidelines on newborn resuscitation of 2000 contained a list of diagnoses not compatible with resuscitation in the delivery room: (1) confirmed gestation <23 weeks; (2) birth weight <400 g; (3) anencephaly; and (4) confirmed trisomy 13 or 18. The rationale was that resuscitation of these newly born infants is unlikely to result in survival or survival without severe disability. The ILCOR guidelines published in 2005 reiterated this list; however, the parent's view are now given more weight: "In conditions associated with uncertain prognosis, when there is borderline survival and a relatively high rate of morbidity, and where the burden to the child is high, the parent's view on starting resuscitation should be supported." This less paternalistic view also remains in the 2010 ILCOR guidelines; any specific reference to diagnosis not compatible with resuscitation has been removed completely. The guidelines instead state that resuscitation is not indicated when gestation, birth weight, or congenital anomalies are associated with almost certain early death and an unacceptably high morbidity. The 2015 guidelines have kept this wording.

The introduction of a fixed lower gestational age limit for treatment of newborn infants, as was practiced in the Netherlands and other countries, may violate the UN Convention. Furthermore, the evidence base providing support for such an absolute rule is, in fact, limited. First, it is known that the uncertainty of determining gestational age between 20 and 30 weeks' gestation is <"1 to 2 weeks. In addition, other factors (eg, female gender, singleton birth, higher birth weight, exposure to antenatal steroids) are each associated with an increased survival approximately corresponding to a 1-week increase in gestational age. Thus, Tyson et al estimated that for an infant born between 24 and 25 completed weeks of gestation, the risk of death or profound impairment may vary 2.5-fold.

A 750-g, appropriate for gestational age female singleton who received antenatal steroids has a risk of death of 33% versus 87% for a 525-g, small for gestational age male twin who did not receive antenatal steroids. Thus, the definition of viability is not absolute, and absolute gestational age limits are therefore not acceptable. The 2015 ILCOR/American Heart Association guidelines emphasize that in addition to gestational age, including additional variables such as gender, use of maternal steroids, and multiplicity improves prognostic accuracy. Every newborn, regardless of gestational age, therefore has the right to be assessed beforehand in case a decision is made not to provide intensive care treatment.

In fact, it is peculiar why there has been such a strong focus on immature infants when discussing nontreatment when many other groups of children may have similar outcomes. Selected groups of children with congenital cardiac defects, for instance, develop developmental delay as often as immature infants. Follow-up of children with congenital diaphragmatic hernia at 5 years of age show that 7% had severe neurologic delays.However, nobody would argue that surgical repair of these conditions should never be performed. Another potential issue in conflict with the UN Convention was the previous tacit consensus that trisomy 13 and 18 are lethal, which led to their classification as conditions for which resuscitation was not indicated. However, there has clearly been a change in clinical practice, with more frequent initiation of intensive care therapy for this group that has led in some cases to sustained survival. Parent groups have fought for the right of their children with trisomy 13 or 18 to receive treatment or at least be assessed at birth. Thus, for these infants, decisions of nontreatment should not be made against the parent's will. An individualized comprehensive assessment can be conducted after birth stabilization, and the options and likely consequences of continued supportive medical care and/or surgical intervention can be discussed.

When viewing the best interests of the child as a primary consideration with regard to health care, this approach requires a willingness to give priority to the individual child's interests, especially when the medical decision has an undeniable impact on the child concerned. The UN Convention obviously has practical implications for treatment strategies and should be considered carefully by health workers, administrators, and politicians and be included in the ongoing debate regarding treatment or nontreatment of children. It has been more than a quarter of a century since the introduction of the United Nations Convention on the Rights of the Child ("Convention") – an international treaty recognizing the human rights of children. It asserts that all children – without discrimination in any form – benefit from special protection measures and assistance; have access to services such as education and health care; can develop their personalities, abilities and talents to the fullest potential; grow up in an environment of happiness, love and understanding; and are informed about and participate in, achieving their rights in an accessible and active manner (UNICEF).

The international community, in its near universal ratification of the Convention, has shown a clear commitment to upholding and protecting the rights of the child, however, when it comes to addressing NCDs, children are too frequently left off (or insufficiently acknowledged) in the actual policies which affect their well-being. NCD Child aims to link the intents of the Convention directly to its mission of advocating the prevention, management, and treatment of NCDs in young people. All the commitments have a direct or secondary relationship to addressing NCDs in children, made more evident when taking a life-course approach to child wellness. It starts with ensuring a healthy pregnancy for women, offering immunizations (like Hepatitis B) and metabolic screening at birth, fostering healthy habits throughout adolescence, and guaranteeing consistent, quality access to health care throughout childhood.

The Convention also includes additional articles related to both NCDs and the empowerment of young people in decision making (Article 12). Violence, disabilities, education, play, and drug abuse — all issues which can shape a child's early years and into adulthood, are raised in the Convention. NCD Child is committed to elevating the rights of children living with or affected by NCDs through direct advocacy to governments, civil society, and other key stakeholders. Making a commitment to respect the rights of children has profound implications for the status of children in our society. Nowhere is this more evident than in the field of health care where the decisions and actions of professionals impact on children's lives in profound, intimate, and powerful ways. The UN Convention on the Rights of the Child which was ratified by the UK Government in 1991 places a clear obligation on health authorities and practitioners to evolve policy and practice in accordance with the human rights of children.

Many of the principles embodied in the Convention are not new. (Many of the rights embodied in the Convention on the Rights of the Child derive from earlier human rights treaties—for example, the UN International Covenants on Civil and Political Rights and on Economic, Social, and Cultural Rights.) They are already implemented as a matter of good practice by some health bodies. What is new is the recognition that children are subjects of rights, that those rights impose obligations on adults to ensure their implementation, and that it is necessary to address the inter-relation between the rights embodied in the Convention in order to promote respect for children. Its principles and standards provide a holistic framework with which to analyse and develop the care and treatment of children in the health services. Examination of two important principles in the Convention highlights the implications of taking a rights based approach to children.

Article 12

Article 12 of the Convention states that all children capable of expressing a view have the right to do so freely in all matters of concern to them and that their view shall be given due weight in accordance with their age and maturity. It has been identified by the Committee on the Rights of the Child, the international body responsible for monitoring governments' implementation of the Convention, as a central underlying principle which must be considered in respect of all other rights. Currently, too many children feel excluded from the process by which information is shared and decisions made in all spheres of their lives. Respecting children's right to be heard does not mean that their views must always prevail. However, it does mean that those views should inform decision making processes on matters which concern them. This has significant implications for practice. It involves giving children the necessary information with which to participate fully in decision making. Research by Priscilla Alderson highlights the extent to which even very young children wish to be given and are capable of absorbing complex and painful information. But she also emphasises the need for such information to be given clearly, sensitively, and at an appropriate pace for the individual child.

Research involving interviews with children in child protection procedures shows that children perceive themselves as capable of dealing with distressing and difficult information often denied them by adults. Common sets of scenarios were presented to groups of children and to groups of professionals working in the child protection field. Consistently, the adults identified a need to withhold information from children in order to protect them. Equally consistently, the children took the view not only that they could cope with the information, but would resent being denied access to it. Indeed, they argued persuasively that exclusion would create more distress and anxiety.

The central message is that the child is a subject of rights, not merely a beneficiary of adult good will and as such must be included as an actor in the decision making process. However, the right to participate embodied in Article 12, extends beyond obligations to involve children in individual decisions that affect them. It also applies to matters which affect them as a body: the type of services available, the way those services are provided, where they are provided, what times, and by whom (see, for example, the interpretation of Article 12 by the Committee on the Rights of the Child). These are matters on which traditionally children have had no say whatever. Promoting children's active participation is important as a matter of principle—children like adults have a right to services which take account of their concerns, experiences, and views. But it is also valuable as a means of improving quality, raising standards, and ensuring the development of relevant and appropriate services.

Article 3

An equally central principle is Article 3 of the Convention which states that in all actions affecting the child, the best interests of the child must be a primary consideration. While the Children Act embodies this principle—indeed it goes further, demanding that the child's interests are the paramount consideration—there is no comparable principle as yet incorporated into health legislation. Nevertheless, ratification of the Convention imposes a clear obligation under international law that governments and public authorities comply with its provisions. Giving primary consideration to the best interests of the child does have significant implications. It applies to decisions that affect the individual children—the nature of treatment, the decision to treat, and how that treatment is applied—but it also requires giving consideration to children's best interests within the services as a whole.

Best interests of children as a body

Children do not have access to the powerful lobbies which influence public policy. They cannot vote, they can rarely advocate on their own behalf. It is too easy therefore for children's rights, needs, and interests to be swamped by more vociferous and influential voices. There is ample evidence of the sidelining of children. Despite the fact that we have one of the highest child road accidents rates in Europe, that children suffer disproportionately from the impact of environmental pollution, that rights to play and move freely are restricted by traffic volumes, the interests of the road transport lobby prevail. We appear to value our freedom to drive a car more highly than the health and safety of our children. We know, for example, that the proportion of expenditure on child and adolescent mental health services by health authorities represents on average around 5% of the total NHS mental health budget, although children under 18 represent 25% of the population. It may be, given the heavy call on these services by older people, that this represents an appropriate apportionment, but no attempt to date has been undertaken to analyse whether it does reflect a realistic balance of comparative need. Certainly, we know that child and adolescent mental health services are seriously underfunded in many parts of the country.

Best interests of children as individuals

In respect of actions affecting individual children, the Convention also requires that their best interests are a primary consideration. But how do we determine the best interests of the child? Traditionally, the best interests of the child have been defined in terms of what adults think best, and are too often used, in effect, to "trump" all other rights. In the name of the best interests of children, we have justified decisions, actions, and treatments of children which in retrospect we now consider unacceptable. Mothers were denied access to children in hospital, tonsillectomies were performed almost routinely, and disabled children were removed from their families and placed in long term institutional care. At different periods in history, and within different cultures, the perception of a child's best interests varies widely. So a commitment to its application does not provide us with simple answers to problems. Rather it should be a principle brought to bear in helping to ensure that the rights of children are properly respected. It should be applied as an underlying principle to help in the process of implementing the right of a child, or indeed, to help resolve a situation where there is a conflict between rights. The Convention on the Rights of the Child introduces two clear challenges to health professionals.

Advocating for children within the health service—The Convention imposes obligations to ensure that its principles and standards are respected and promoted within the health service itself. This will necessitate analysis of the Convention as a holistic framework addressing rights to protection, to provision of high quality services, to active participation by children in matters that affect them. It will necessitate better collaboration with partners in education, housing, and social services to address the social factors impacting on child health. It means looking at the organisation of services, the allocation of budgets, the processes by which decisions are made to assess whether the interests of children have been given proper consideration. It means exploring ways in which children themselves can be enabled to influence decision making. It also means addressing professional practice to ensure that it does not itself violate any of these rights. For example, are there adequate policies on restraint and control of young patients, consistent with the right to respect for physical integrity? Are there adequate complaints mechanisms for children who have concerns over their treatment? Are children in psychiatric units treated without their consent and without the protections afforded by the Mental Health Act 1980? Are small children given appropriate access to pain relief?

Advocating for children outside the health service—A significant proportion of the resources of the health service are directed to repairing the damage to children caused by social and economic factors which can only be prevented by decisions and actions well beyond the scope of health professionals. Paediatricians and other health professionals have an enormous body of knowledge pertaining to the impact of public policy on children's lives. It is they who treat the devastating physical consequences of poverty and disadvantage—whether it be the consequences of inadequate diet, poor housing and homelessness, access to drugs and alcohol, early pregnancy, depressed and inadequate parenting. It is they who have evidence of inequality of access to services—the difficulties facing homeless families, or those who do not have English as a first language, refugees and asylum seekers, children in prisons in getting the treatment they require. It is they who treat the children whose health is harmed by the priority given to the transport lobby. Paediatricians, then, have a clear responsibility to advocate on behalf of children for the necessary social, economic, and political changes to guarantee them access to the best possible health.

There are competing calls on public priorities. Children are not the only group in society with unmet needs and rights. However, they are deserving of high priority for principled and instrumental reasons. Without the vote and access to the arenas where decisions are made, children's rights have and will consistently be disregarded, unless adults are prepared to advocate on their behalf and create avenues through which children can be heard in their own right. Investment in children now is probably the most effective strategy for ensuring a stable, humane, democratic, and economically sound society of the future. The challenge rests with those who are committed to respecting children's rights and have the information and power to make a difference.

Impact of the Convention of the Child Rights

A milestone in the international human rights legislation, the 'Convention on the Rights of the Child' has been instrumental in putting all the issues pertaining to children issues on the global as well as national agenda. In addition to this, it has extensively mobilized actions for the realization of the rights and development of children worldwide.

It was not an overnight initiative that resulted in the adoption of the Child Rights. It took several years of movements and activism on shaping favourable, positive and constructive attitudes toward children, and also inciting actions to improve their well-being. The enormous efforts involved toward the implementation of the Convention, the significant amount of resources committed to this cause, and the overall effectiveness of the systems put in place for the execution process have a bearing on the success of child well-being outcomes.

Over the last 20 or so years, implementation of the Convention and its effect on child well-being varied from country to country and from one region of the world to the other. Based on analysis, there has been outstanding progress at a global level in addressing the issues related to children. These include progress in access to services, reaching their fullest potential through education, enactment of laws that upholds the principle of the best interests of child, and child survival.

Though a noteworthy progress has been achieved, yet in developing countries, particularly India, there is still a long way to go in realising the rights of children. Though all the relevant rules and policies are in place, there is a lack in enforcement initiatives. As barriers, there are several factors that forbid effective implementation of the laws. Due to relatively low success in achieving concrete child development outcomes in India, the condition of underprivileged kids and underprivileged youth is harsh and needs urgent attention. There is a need to intensify efforts for children welfare at all levels to implement the rules and provisions of the Convention and contribute to create a world suitable for children.

Child Rights and the world

People from across the world striving for social justice have often directed their efforts toward the most vulnerable in society—the children. From Princess Diana's charitable work on behalf of children to the efforts of activists like Grace Abbott and the youngest Nobel laureate in history—Ms. Malala Yousafzai, these famous children's right activists have put commendable efforts in helping improve the lives of the youngest citizens. 2014 Nobel Peace Prize awardees—Ms. Malala Yousafzai and Mr. Kailash Satyarthi have reminded us all of the need to keep on advancing in providing opportunities that has an important effect on all children. The opportunities are meant to be meaningful enough to allow them to learn and gain the mindsets and skills that would empower them to be free, develop themselves, their communities and the world.

Mr. Kailash Satyarthi's struggle to liberate children from child labour had cost him many life threats, including bullet wounds by those who exploit young boys and girls for economic gain. Wearing flak jackets, and armed with strong determination, he and his team raided many illegal factories and mines to rescue the children who are sold into servitude. It has been 30 years now since he started his movement. A movement that has one clear purpose—no child shall be a slave. On the other hand, when one thinks of Ms. Malala Yousafzai, the first thing that pops in one's mind is education. The second is—education for girls. In 2009, when she was just 11, she wrote to BBC about the norm of banning female education under the Taliban regime in the Swat Valley (her hometown). Her article gained tremendous momentum worldwide. She started her fight for the education of girls at that small age and began to speak publicly and to the press, which caused her and her family receive constant death threats.

"I strongly feel that this is a big honour to hundreds of millions of the children who have been deprived of their childhood and freedom and education." – Mr. Kailash Satyarthi. "I speak not for myself but for those without voice... those who have fought for their rights... their right to live in peace, their right to be treated with dignity, their right to equality of opportunity, their right to be educated." – Ms. Malala Yousafzai. The father of modern education—John Amos Comenius proposed – "all persons should be educated, so we could have peace in the world". Visionaries of the world understood that peace meant guaranteeing every person certain rights that are conditional for humanity—education being one of the most important. The addition of the Right to Education (RTE) in the Universal Declaration of Human Rights in 1948 was the beginning of a remarkable expansion of educational opportunities around the world. The parliament of India enacted the Right of Children to Free and Compulsory Education Act or Right to Education Act (RTE) on August 2009. The same got enforced on April 1st 2010.

As per the act, education is a fundamental right of every child who is between 6 and 14 years old. The act also states that until the completion of elementary education, no child shall be held back, expelled or required to pass a board examination. There is also a provision for special training of school drop-outs to bring them up to par with students of the same age. As a charity for child rights, Smile Foundation has been providing education to marginalized children in poor rural and urban communities in 25 states of the country. Its flagship programme - Mission Education exemplifies the global struggle for universal education. The programme has succeeded in bringing more than 200,000 children to school since its start in the year 2002.

Underprivileged kids lag at all stages of education. When earning a livelihood and taking care of the members of the family becomes a primary matter of concern in one's life, education stands a little or, very often, no chance of pursuance. For the millions of underprivileged people in India, education is a high-priced luxury, and this negative outlook continues on with every new generation. Poverty damages childhood with significant effects on a child's physical and mental health, as well as educational achievement. It limits the expectations of the child's ability to perform well in school, constantly reminding him/her of the miniscule chance he/she has to overcome adversity and poverty. With its development interventions that are focused on social welfare of children, Smile Foundation has raised those expectations among the hardest-to-reach children. Recent mark-sheets of the students in all ME centres has shown Smile Foundation primary school students outperforming their peers, with a very high passing rate. Last year, 51% of the total beneficiaries in Mission Education centres across India were girls. Also, 87% of the total eligible students are successfully mainstreamed in private and government schools.

Article 6 of the Convention on the Rights of the Child (CRC) states that children have the right to live and governments should ensure that children survive and develop healthily. The Convention places a high value on the children's right to survival and states that children have the right to good quality health care, to safe drinking water, nutritious food, a clean and safe environment, and information to help them stay healthy. (Article 24 of CRC) This 20th anniversary of CRC calls for ensuring every child has access to the basic right of survival. Society must save the large number of lives snuffed out within the first few days of life. Eliminating malnourishment should be our top priority as it directly contributes to child mortality, school drop-out rates, gender equality and poverty reduction. Almost 55 million children under five in India are underweight for their age. Children who are chronically undernourished before their second birthday are likely to have diminished cognitive and physical development for the rest of their lives. As adults, they are less productive and earn less than their healthy peers and the cycle of undernutrition and poverty repeats itself, generation after generation.

How is children's health a human rights issue?

Under international human rights law, children are entitled "to the enjoyment of the highest attainable standard of health and to facilities for the treatment of illness and rehabilitation of health." This right is articulated in Article 24 of the 1989 UN Convention on the Rights of the Child (CRC), which is the most widely ratified international human rights instrument1 and consolidates all previous treaties on the rights of children.2 The right to health for children has long been understood as an "inclusive" right, which extends beyond protection from immediately identifiable infringements such as limitations on access to health care or services, and includes the wide range of rights and freedoms that are determinate to children's health, such the rights to non-discrimination, access to health-related education and information, and freedom from harmful traditional practices.3 The realization of a child's right to health also requires access to underlying conditions for health, such as "safe water and adequate sanitation, adequate nutritious food and housing, [and] healthy occupational and environmental conditions."4 The CRC and its Optional Protocols articulate the rights of children (from the perspective of the child "rights-holder") as well as the responsibilities of State Parties ("duty-bearer"). The CRC is legally binding on all signatories, and also establishes a framework for protection of health rights that are not explicitly provided for in the Convention, for example, the rights of children affected by HIV.5 The CRC defines a child as "every human being below the age of eighteen years."6 Such a definition includes adolescence, commonly understood to be between the ages of 10 and 19 years.7 Consequently, the CRC imposes on State Parties a legally binding obligation to give effect to the child-specific health rights of all children, including adolescents, up to 18 years of age

What are the issues and how are they human rights issues?

The fundamental right to health of children, as with adults, stems from the basic human needs that must be met in order for every individual to achieve the highest attainable standard of health, regardless of sex, race, ethnicity, ability, religion, political belief, or economic or social conditions. However, children's health rights differ from those of adults in "important normative ways."9 Children of all ages are uniquely vulnerable to violations of their heath rights due to "the biological and socially constructed characteristics of childhood."10 This includes their developing physical and mental capacity, their dependence on adults to meet their health needs, and their changing social roles and influences, especially during the onset of puberty. As a result, children have a reduced ability to protect themselves and are more vulnerable to negative consequences of violations of their right to health: The physical and psychological effects that children suffer... will generally be greater than those experienced by adults due to their lower level of physical and mental development. This is true both in relation to (a) the immediate impact that violations of the right to health may have on a child's physical and psychological state, and (b) the long-term detrimental effects on the child's development and future capacity for autonomy resulting from such a violation.11

Because children rely on adults for their growth and development, they have historically been treated as passive beings requiring "positive intervention on their behalf to ensure the realization of their rights."12 As such children are "an anomaly in the liberal legal order" which otherwise views rights-holders as autonomous individuals capable of exercising free choice.13 A central concern of children's health right advocates is therefore to promote children's agency and capacity for autonomy.14 A key component is including children, particularly during adolescence, in decision-making processes about their health, not only with respect to their individual health but also at the systematic level of health policy and service delivery.15

International and regional human rights instruments protecting the health rights of children have articulated respect for what are known as the "four

Ps": "participation by children in decisions affecting them; protection of children against discrimination and all forms of neglect and exploitation; prevention of harm to them; and provision of assistance to children for their basic needs."16 The participation of children must be meaningful and should proceed "in a manner consistent with their evolving capacities."17 This requires careful balancing of child protection considerations with efforts to promote the agency and decision-making potential of all children.

Right to Life, Survival and Development

In 2011, there were an estimated 7.6 million deaths of children under 5,18 with more than 70 percent due to preventable causes such as diarrhoea, pneumonia, and malnutrition.19 Another 200 million children under 5 do not achieve their full developmental potential due to poverty, inequality, and inadequate opportunities for learning.20 Adolescents, in particular, experience a high burden of neuropsychiatric disorders (including depression and substance abuse), violence and accidents, maternal conditions, and infectious disease.21 Reducing the mortality and morbidity of children and adolescents is a key priority of the international community.22 Article 6 of the CRC imposes on States a positive obligation to "improve perinatal care for mothers and babies, reduce infant and child mortality, and create conditions that promote the wellbeing of all young children during this critical phase of their lives."23 This obligation is further elaborated in Article 24, which secures the right to the highest attainable standard of health.

The health of children also reflects more broadly on the social and economic conditions in a community.24 In 2011, a child born in the developing world was eight times more likely to die in childhood than her counterpart in the developed world.25 Similarly, children living in countries with greater socioeconomic inequality have poorer health outcomes, with mortality associated with income inequality.26 Both the CRC Committee and the CESCR regularly express concern over failed or insufficient efforts by State parties to reduce child mortality, and have also drawn attention to disparity among certain groups of children such as indigenous children,27 or children living in rural or remote areas28 who are more vulnerable to violations of their right to life, survival and development.

Right to Non-Discrimination

Freedom from discrimination in access to health care, nutrition, adequate standards of living, and education, ensures that all children are equally positioned to attain their maximum level of health and development. However, given their relative dependence on others to realize their human rights, children are at heightened risk of discrimination. Children can face discrimination based on their age and status in society, but also as members of particular groups. Children belonging to minority groups, indigenous communities, and girls generally are more likely to suffer discrimination in accessing their right to health. Article 2 of the CRC enshrines this right to non-discrimination of children, and the CRC Committee has articulated its concern over such violations of the right as:

- Social exclusion and discrimination of children from ethnic minority backgrounds or indigenous children, resulting in disparities of health outcomes.29
- A lack of culturally appropriate services, including the availability of social and health services adapted to culture, history and languages of minority and indigenous children.30
- Discrimination against girls that restricts their capacity to contribute positively to society, such as selective abortion, genital mutilation, neglect and infanticide, including through inadequate feeding in infancy.31

To fulfil their obligation to non-discrimination of children, States must work "actively to identify individual children and groups of children the recognition and realization of whose rights may demand special measures," which may require changes in legislation, administration and resource allocation, as well as educational measures to change attitudes.

Right to Express Views and Have Them Taken into Account

Children are regularly denied the opportunity to be heard and to express their views freely on matters that affect their health and well-being. Yet the right of children to be heard and to participate is one of the fundamental values of the CRC, as it reiterates the understanding that the child is a fully fledged person having the right to express his or her own views in all matters affecting him and her, and having those views heard and given due weight.33 It is also a right that is often infringed not only by legislation and policy that imposes age limits on the right to be heard, but also by socio-attitudinal contexts that prevent children from expressing their views in a variety of forums. Under the CRC, States are required to take all appropriate measures to ensure that the child's "freedom to express views and the right to be consulted in matters that affect him or her is implemented from the earliest stage in ways appropriate to the child's capacities, best interests, and rights to protection from harmful experiences."34

The notion of "evolving capacities" is critical to the realization of this right, particularly with regard to health care, and indicates that there is no single point in development at which all children can or cannot form and articulate their views about their well-being or best interests. This recognition demands that parents, and where necessary, communities, provide "appropriate direction and guidance" in a way that does not undermine the ability of the child to exercise his or her rights.35However, the CRC Committee also goes further and calls on States to introduce legislation or regulations to ensure that children have access to confidential medical counselling and advice without parental consent, irrespective of the child's age, where this is needed for the child's safety or well-being. Right to Information; Right to Sexual and Reproductive Health and Education, including HIV.

Children often lack adequate access to information and services necessary to ensure sexual health, including information related to HIV prevention and care. Critical to youth attaining the highest standard of health and developing in a well-balanced manner is having access to adequate information upon which to understand and make appropriate decisions concerning their well-being. Though children are guaranteed the right to such information under international human rights law,38 often neither health information nor health services are made available, particularly with regard to sexual health. Access to sexual and reproductive services is particularly necessary for the well-being of adolescents, as adolescence is the period when many children begin to explore their sexuality.39 And with 3.4 million children under the age of 15 living with HIV, and teenage pregnancies claiming the lives of young mothers and their children at a substantially higher rate than older mothers, the responsibility of states to provide comprehensive education and information about sexual and reproductive health as well as opportunities to develop the skills necessary for HIV prevention is urgent and critical.40

Where children are denied appropriate health services, including child-sensitive and confidential counselling services, and access to contraceptives, States have failed to uphold their obligation to develop preventive health care. States are responsible for ensuring that sex-education programs exist both inside and outside of school settings, and that efforts are made to raise awareness about the prevention of early pregnancy and the control of sexually transmitted diseases including HIV. The International Guidelines on HIV/AIDS and Human Rights emphasize that "the provision of these services [counseling, testing, and prevention measures] to children/adolescents should reflect the appropriate balance between the rights of the child/adolescent to be involved in decision-making according to his or her evolving capabilities and the rights and duties of parents/guardians for the health and well-being of the child."41 As such, states must also make efforts to empower parents with information about sexual health and HIV transmission, and effective measures should be taken to counter stigma and discrimination faced by children and families infected and affected by HIV. Whether the child's right to health as stipulated in article 24 of the CRC is fully implemented by States Parties can only be judged in the context of how the needs of sick children and their families are met. The most important points are:

- A health care system accessible to all children from age 0 – 18, regardless of status, cultural background, illness or disability, that ensures the highest attainable standard of health care, provided by specifically trained paediatric staff within the necessary infrastructure and environment.

- Parents are considered by the caring team as partners who are as much as possible involved in the treatment of their child. The responsibility of parents for the care of their sick child is acknowledged by States Parties by regulations that allow paid leaves and compensate parents for all costs directly related to a child's illness, disability or stay in hospital.
- Children are treated in children's hospitals or wards by specially trained paediatric staff in an environment adapted to the needs of children of different ages and stages of development.
- Children are not admitted to adult wards with non-paediatric staff and in an environment unsuitable for children. If for rare examinations, surgery or treatments not available in a nearby children's hospital, children are exceptionally admitted to adult wards, they are transferred back to the children's ward as quickly as possible. Doctors or specialists from the adult ward visit child patients in the children's ward and not vice versa.
- Hospitals where children are treated provide trained staff and organizational frameworks to mitigate children's fear, pain and distress. Restraint should be avoided in case of invasive procedures, procedures requiring immobility or minor, but painful procedures (life threatening situations excepted). Restraint is an unacceptable technique in direct contradiction to the child's right to protection from all forms of physical or mental violence.
- Children's hospitals are fully reimbursed for non-medical care of children by professional staff (such as Hospital Play Specialists, Teachers, Psychologists, Social Workers, etc.). The right to therapeutic and recreational play and education during a hospital stay is a basic requirement for the wellbeing of children.
- Due to the enormous success of scientific research in the field of paediatric medicine many once fatal children's diseases can now be cured, great progress has also been achieved in the rehabilitation of disabilities. Many of these children nowadays enjoy a life as healthy adults and are fully valid members of society. They earn their own living and pay taxes. States Parties therefore need to understand that the cost of a holistic health care system for children is not lost money, but an investment in a society's future. The present trends in the health care market as described below do not solve problems but create new ones.

Beginning in the late 19th century and throughout the 20th century huge progress has been achieved in the medical treatment of child specific illnesses and disabilities. At the same time hospitals exclusively for the treatment of children were founded, staffed by doctors and nurses with special paediatric training. On the other hand, until the 1960s parents had no or only limited access to their hospitalized child, which resulted in long-lasting traumatic experiences for many children. Alarming scientific studies by psychologists and paediatricians became known in the 1950s. In order to improve this situation parent's associations were founded in many European countries to promote the unrestricted presence and the participation of parents in the treatment of their children. The first such association, the National Association for the Welfare of Children in Hospital (NAWCH), was founded in 1961 in the UK, other European countries followed in the 1970s.

In 1988 a first international conference of associations from 12 European countries met in Leiden (The Netherlands). Based on experiential learning the Charter for the Rights of Sick Children was drawn up and adopted. The Charter consists of 10 points representing the most basic principles to be considered with regard to the treatment of all sick children before, during and after a hospital stay. In 1993 the umbrella organization EACH European Association for Children in Hospital was founded in order to strengthen the exchange of information and experiences and to promote the implementation of the Charter in all European countries. In 2002 the member associations of EACH adopted the Annotations to the Charter (Enclosure 1) to illustrate the scope of applications for the Charter and to explain to a wider audience the meaning of "family centred care". The Annotations take into consideration the standards to be met with by the national health care systems to comply with the requirements of the child's right to health.

Today National Associations and 8 individual persons from 19 European countries are members of EACH as well as 1 association from Japan (see on the last page list of members endorsing the present submission). II. Health related articles of the CRC and the EACH Charter for the Rights of Sick Children The CRC promotes the child's right to health and the measures to be taken in this regard, and it requires from States Parties "to ensure that the institutions, services and facilities responsible for the care or protection of children shall conform with the standards established by competent authorities". However, as described in the above history of EACH and in view of current political developments all over Europe, such "institutions, services and facilities" need to be looked at from the perspective of the sick child and his family. A few decades ago hospital staff, the scientific audience and health care ministries were convinced and took it for granted that hospitalized children in their countries benefitted from the best possible care and that everything was done for their wellbeing. It did not cross anybody's mind to ask the children concerned and their families.

To provide a holistic view on the implementation of the CRC and the EACH Charter, the concept of family centred care and the differing needs of children depending on age, individual development and illness or disability requires a broader perspective. The EACH Charter was drafted to address the problems that sick children or children with disabilities and their families encounter. CRC articles relating to health and experiences of EACH members For the implementation of the right to health, resp. the rights of sick children not only art. 24, but also the following articles of the CRC need to be considered and should make part of the CRC General Comments on art. 24:

CRC Definition of the age of a child

The CRC defines children as from the age of 0 to 18 years. In quite a number of European countries the upper age limit for children admitted to children's hospitals and wards is 16 years in some countries as low as 12 years. In recent years the age limit has been increased to 18 years – but it is not yet a general standard. For children and adolescents needing psychiatric care many children's hospitals do not provide appropriate infrastructure, and they are inadequately treated in institutions for adults. Even in well-resourced countries, such as Switzerland or France, psychiatric services with staff specifically trained for the care of children of different ages are not sufficiently established and funded. This applies especially to adolescents who need their own space away from smaller children but also away from adults (an increasing problem e.g. with regard to the rising numbers with anorexia, depression or suicide attempts among adolescents).

In our opinion this is the most important article for implementing art. 24. To our regret we are observing in all European countries a rising tendency to continuously reform health care systems with the aim to cut costs in general (and regardless of the ultimate long-term outcome for the public health). Much too often the result are ill-conceived regulations and laws that severely reduce the rights of children to specific paediatric care. The step-by-step privatisation of health care and raising the profitability of hospitals by focussing on high-tech medicine completely neglects the social responsibility of States Parties with regard to the care of sick children in hospitals or in their community. As a result all over Europe specialized independent children's hospitals are closing down or are downgraded to children's departments within an adult hospital. Likewise in many European countries the specific education of paediatric staff has been abolished in favour of a so-called generalist education.

In countries, such as Germany, many children's hospitals were closed following the introduction of the DRG-reimbursement system and more than 50% of the children are now treated in adult hospitals not specialized for the treatment of children. The care children need in addition to the strictly medical treatment is not reimbursed by the DRG-system and many children's hospitals had to close down due to insufficient income. In France where a similar system exists (Tarification à l'activité or T2A) most hospitals even the big university hospitals have a budget in deficit. It is important to note that those payment systems (DRG-T2A) consider only the technical aspects of medical care and leave by side the time spent in the relationship work as well as the time for the necessary information to children and parents, which are both so important in children care.

Freedom from Abuse, Torture and Ill-Treatment

All children have a right to health and to be free from violence, abuse and neglect, yet each year, millions of children are victims of violence, abuse, and neglect, with far-reaching harm to their physical and mental health and development. Children in every country in the world are threatened by violence, where it is often socially approved, and frequently legal and State sanctioned.50 In 2006, the UN conducted the first global study on all forms of violence against children in various settings: family, school, alternative care institutions, detention centers and communities. It found that States often fail to take sufficient measures to protect children from domestic violence, corporal punishment, and/or other forms of abuse and neglect, and that such maltreatment is often justified by adults as "tradition" or "disguised as 'discipline.'"51

Though accurate statistics are hard to ascertain, the UN study estimated that there were 53,000 childhood homicides in 2006.52 Child deaths from maltreatment only represent a small fraction of the problem of child abuse and neglect, with some international studies having shown that, in some parts of the world, between a quarter and a half of all children report severe and frequent physical abuse.53 In 2002, 150 million young girls suffered forced sexual intercourse or other forms of sexual violence.54 And among their peers, children with disabilities are particularly vulnerable to abuse and neglect.

Preventing such abuse and violence against all children is a positive obligation of States. Article 19 of the CRC instructs, "States Parties shall take all appropriate legislative, administrative, social and educational measures to protect the child from all forms of physical or mental violence, injury or abuse, neglect or negligent treatment, maltreatment or exploitation, including sexual abuse, while in the care of parent(s), legal guardian(s) or any other person who has the care of the child." Children have a right to increased protection from maltreatment given the vulnerabilities inherent in their age and dependence on adults for care and security. As such, in cases of abuse, the child explicitly "has the right to the protection of the law against such interference or attacks." The CRC Committee considers the absence of legislation protecting children from domestic violence to be a violation of the obligation of States under Article 19. State Parties are often called to implement legislation that criminalizes domestic violence,55 and absolutely prohibits corporal punishment in all settings. In General Comment 8, the CRC Committee emphasizes that "eliminating violent and humiliating punishment of children, through law reform and other necessary measures, is an immediate and unqualified obligation of States parties. What are human rights-based approaches for upholding the health rights of children?

A basic principle of child rights, as guaranteed by the CRC is to secure the best interest of the child. According to Article 3 of the CRC, the best interest of the child is to be a 'primary consideration' in all actions regarding children. The principle thus underlines all human rights-based approaches for the promotion and protection of children's health rights. The best interests of the child are to guide the implementation of the CRC by State Parties, including all "legislative, administrative and other measures" necessary to realize the human rights of children and adolescents.72 The following list includes objectives and initiatives that support a child-centered, human rights-based approach that serves to prevent and/or defend against some of the violations detailed in the section above.73

Ensuring Early Childhood Survival, Development and Well-being

Given that most children74 under 5 die from one or more of five common (and treatable) conditions – diarrheal dehydration, measles, respiratory infections, malaria, or malnutrition, continuing and comprehensive efforts must be made by States to prevent such deaths. Communication of health information to families and care takers is an underlying premise of effective health interventions, particularly to secure the well being of young children. "Communication is vital: conveying to parents the key information about how to manage diarrhoea at home – or how to recognize pneumonia or malaria and seek timely care from someone with medical training – will save many children's lives."75For example, some of the most effective initiatives to reduce malnutrition were those that enabled "families to understand the causes of malnutrition and to take informed action to address them," including the promotion of breast feeding, and addressing key micronutrient deficiencies.76

Eliminating Barriers to Education and Maximum Development

Education is also critical to the development of communities, and thus eliminating the cultural, social and economic barriers to education for girls and other vulnerable children (including poor children, children living in remote locations, children with disabilities, and children belonging to minority groups) must be a priority of any child-centered education program. However, simply eliminating barriers is insufficient; States must use strategic planning to ensure realistic progress. For example, eliminating school fees as required by the CRC has made significant impact in access to primary education for children in Eastern/Southern Africa,77 where enrollment increased significantly; however, ensuring sustainable and quality education demands acquiring the funds to provide adequate accommodations, supplies, and teachers to these newly enrolled students. A programming approach78 that is guided by the CRC should create conditions that allow families with children and children themselves to participate more fully in community life and in the development of policies that affect them. Consultation with children should make explicit efforts to include vulnerable children and their families, including children of minority groups, poor children, disabled children, and girls, generally. The goal is not just to increase participation of children in decision making and health promotion but to ensure their meaningful participation. "If programmes are to meet the health needs of children it is vital that they are given some ownership of the programmes by having a voice in planning, implementing and monitoring programme activities."79

Countries around the world have undertaken reforms to bring their national legislation into closer conformity with the principles and provisions of the CRC. Such efforts that better safeguard the health rights of children include: laws to protect children from discrimination; laws to protect against domestic violence and prohibit corporal punishment; laws prohibiting forced marriage and raising the legal marriage age; and labor laws prohibiting the involvement of children in hazardous employment and other worst forms of child labor.81 However, changing the law alone is insufficient to guarantee protection if efforts are not made to address the underlying social contexts that require such legislation. Thus, programs committed to achieving substantial changes in the legislative protection of the health and human rights of children must also ensure that children, parents, communities, and enforcement officials are trained and made aware of new regulations and the human rights that warrant such protection.

CHAPTER - 6

RIGHT TO DEVELOPMENT: RELAX AND PLAY

Right To Play is a global organization that attempts to teach children in need with educational games. It was founded in 2000 by Olympic gold medalist Johann Olav Koss. Right To Play's programs are facilitated by more than 14,900 local volunteer coaches and more than 620 international staff. Working in both the humanitarian and development context, Right To Play builds local capacity by training community leaders as coaches to deliver its programs in 18 countries affected by war, poverty, and disease in Africa, Asia, the Middle East, and North America. Right To Play is headquartered in Toronto, Canada and has national offices in Canada, Germany, Norway, the Netherlands, Switzerland, the United Kingdom and the United States. The national offices raise funds, build awareness for Right To Play programs and advocate for play based learning.

Unicef ensures more of the world's children are fed, vaccinated, educated and protected than any other organisation. We have done more to influence laws, policies and customs to help protect children than anyone else in history. We get things done. And we're not going to stop until the world is a safe place for all our children. We receive no funding from the UN budget. Most of our money comes from people, companies and other organisations. In 1989, governments across the world adopted the United Nations Convention on the Rights of the Child (UNCRC), recognising that all children have the right to be treated with dignity and fairness, to be protected, to develop to their full potential and to participate. The Convention sets out the civil, political, economic, social and cultural rights that everyone under 18 is entitled to. It says what countries must do to ensure that all children can enjoy their rights, regardless of who they are, or where they are from. The

UN General Assembly adopted the Convention in 1989 and it was ratified by the UK in 1991. It is the most widely adopted international human rights treaty. The Convention underpins all the work that Unicef does.

Improving Children's Health and Well-being

Playing out's impact includes giving children space and freedom to get much needed exercise outdoors, play freely, gain independence and skills, and make friends close to home

Children's low activity levels – a national picture

Government and health professional guidelines state that children aged 5-18 need an hour each day of what they call 'moderate to vigorous physical activity' to be healthy and well. Evidence shows a staggering 80% of UK children are not getting this, and it's feeding into all kinds of growing health problems in children including clinical obesity and diabetes, as well as storing up future health problems for them as adults. With the cost of obesity alone already costing the NHS £6.1 billion a year and over £27 billion to the economy, as well as the personal cost of any health problems, the decline in children's activity levels is widely being described as a public health crisis, with effective solutions thin on the ground.

What needs to change

In 2016 the World Health Organisation published a report on Ending Childhood Obesity. It stresses how childhood experience "can have an important influence on life-long physical activity habits". In short, what we experience as a child will impact – positively or negatively – on how active we are for the rest of our lives. So it's is a crucial time. The report recommends the creation of: "

Playing out: a simple solution to being more active

If you give children space and freedom outdoors, evidence, experience and common sense all show that they will quite naturally play and be more active. One mum has described it as children "getting exercise without noticing". As actual time spent in formal parks and play spaces is quite low for various reasons, playing out in the street gives children a chance to do this close to home, and playing out sessions can help this to happen. More and more we are seeing that residential streets are spaces – could be spaces – where good habits can form.

What the research says

Research by the University of Bristol has shown that at playing out sessions, children are three to five times more active than they would be on a 'normal' day after school. A more interview-based evaluation of streets in

Hackney, London, also highlighted the significant amount of physical activity at street play sessions, finding it equivalent to 14 additional weekly PE lessons each school term. Professor Angie Page's report from the University of Bristol – "Why temporary street closures for play make sense for public health" – suggests that our low-cost, grassroots model is a scaleable intervention that could make "a meaningful contribution to children's physical activity levels".

Playing Freely

Playing out sessions give children the time, space and opportunity to play freely outdoors when their ability to do so independently has been declining for decades. Research shows that play is not an optional extra, it's fundamental to children's physical, social, mental and emotional development, as well as to their immediate happiness and wellbeing. A child's right to play is enshrined in Article 31 of the UN Convention on the Rights of the Child.

Building physical and practical skills

Through playing out, children can also build physical and practical skills like learning to ride a bike and scoot safely, ready for other local journeys. In our 2017 Survey of streets that have held playing out sessions, the majority of people reported that children had learned or improved these skills including riding a bike (80%), scooting (85%), roller skating (63%) and skipping (66%), as well as other activities like skate boarding, balancing and learning various street games like Hopscotch and Hide and Seek. Jo in Bristol says: "My boy has been practising cycling during our playing out sessions and it's totally paid off. He's now independently cycling."

Growing confidence and independence

Playing out freely with others helps to grow important life skills including the ability to assess risks, have good judgement and problem solve. Also to know whom to trust in emergencies and how to react to new and challenging situations. During playing out sessions children can practise these skills in a safe space with parents and carers nearby.

Making friends and developing social skills

Playing out in the street can mean children make new friends of different ages and backgrounds and often from different schools. They also get to know some of the adults in their street. These things increase their sense of belonging and trust, and help to strengthen the whole street community. In our survey of streets that have played out, the majority of people reported that children had learned or improved social skills, including interacting with other children (88%), interacting with adults (83%) and learning about road safety (56%). All human rights treaties are international agreements that apply equally to children and adults. What is different about the Convention is that it lays out specific rights that only apply to children. It also explains what governments must do at national and local level to make sure that children's rights are promoted, respected, protected and realised. Governments have the lead responsibility for the realisation of children's rights and all adults – including teachers, social workers, doctors and parents – have a responsibility to respect these rights and help children experience their rights. It is very important for children and young people to learn about and understand their rights, as well as know who is responsible for making rights a reality. Governments, schools, the media and all adults should help them with this. The Convention also confirms that children are active participants in the lives of their families, communities and society, so governments and adults must create opportunities for children to play a role in the realisation of their rights.

The Fundraising Years – Supporting International Humanitarian Partners

Between 1994 and 2000, Right to Play, formerly Olympic Aid, continued to raise funds for children in disadvantaged situations, building on the momentum of subsequent Olympic Games. In 1996, Olympic Aid formed a partnership with UNICEF and raised $13 million USD prior to and during the Games in Atlanta. The funds assisted UNICEF in vaccinating approximately 12.2 million children and more than 800,000 women. This vaccination effort was extraordinary as it resulted in temporary Olympic Truces in Afghanistan and the Kurdish region in northern Iraq. All fighting stopped in the regions so the UNICEF staff could safely immunize the children and women of these areas.

Transition to Direct Implementation – Working With International Partners

With its incorporation in late 2000, Olympic Aid (which became Right To Play) made the transition from "fundraising vehicle" to implementing Non-Governmental Organization (NGO). In March 2001, the first sport and play programs began in refugee communities in Angola and Côte d'Ivoire. During the 2002 Olympic Winter Games in Salt Lake City, Olympic Aid hosted a Roundtable Forum entitled "Healthier, Safer, Stronger: Using Sport for Development to build a brighter future for children worldwide". United Nations Secretary-General Kofi Annan gave the keynote address while global leaders in health, sport and development participated in a moderated discussion of the role of sport in relation to four development issues: vaccination, tobacco-free sport, HIV and AIDS prevention and the rehabilitation of refugees. With participants including Archbishop Desmond Tutu and Dr. Jacques Rogge, President of the International Olympic Committee, the Olympic Aid Roundtable placed Sport for Development firmly on the UN agenda.

Controversy

In October 2008, the International Olympic Committee (IOC) and the Vancouver Organizing Committee for the 2010 Olympic and Paralympic Winter Games (VANOC) announced that Right To Play would be banned from an official role at the 2010 Winter Olympics in Vancouver. The two committees cited sponsorship conflicts as the reason behind the ban, identifying Right To Play sponsors such as Canon, Scotiabank, and Mitsubishi as competitors to Olympic sponsors Kodak, Royal Bank of Canada, and General Motors. Right To Play had been present in an official role at every Summer and Winter Olympics since 2004, and since 1994 as Olympic Aid.

Child Rights Partners brings together Unicef UK and local government to ensure all children have the same opportunity to flourish. Launched in November 2013, the partnership is grounded in the UN Convention on the Rights of the Child and puts children's human rights at the heart of public services. Over a period of three years, we are working with local authorities across the UK to transform services for the most vulnerable, including children experiencing poverty, children living in care and young people affected by drug and alcohol misuse. Through training, testing and evaluation, we want to profoundly change the way local authorities work with and for children, ensuring children experience services that are adaptable, connected and empowering.

Together with our partners, we will demonstrate how putting children's rights into action in public organisations can make a real difference to children's lives. When services take a rights-based approach, children know and understand their rights, are treated with dignity and feel nurtured. They have a say in decisions that affect them, experience services that are built with and for them, know what services are available, and feel safe and prioritised. There are four articles in the convention that are seen as special. They're known as the "General Principles" and they help to interpret all the other articles and play a fundamental role in realising all the rights in the Convention for all children. They are:

1. Non-discrimination (article 2)
2. Best interest of the child (article 3)
3. Right to life survival and development (article 6)
4. Right to be heard (article 12)

The Convention also contains a number of agreements to add further unique rights for children which are optional for countries – they are called "Optional Protocols". They include:

1. The Optional Protocol on the involvement of children in armed conflict

This requires governments to increase the minimum age that children can join the armed forces from 15 years and to ensure that members of their armed forces under the age of 18 do not take a direct part in armed conflict.

2. The Optional Protocol to the Convention on the sale of children, child prostitution and child pornography

This provides detailed requirements for governments to end the sexual exploitation and abuse of children. It also protects children from being sold for non-sexual purposes, such as other forms of forced labour, illegal adoption and organ donation.

3. The Optional Protocol on a communications procedure

This allows children to submit a complaint to the United Nations when their rights have been violated and their own country's legal system were not able to offer a solution.

Childhood today: new threats, new opportunities

Despite this progress, the Convention is still not fully implemented or widely known and understood. Millions of children continue to suffer violations of their rights when they are denied adequate health care, nutrition, education and protection from violence. Childhoods continue to be cut short when children are forced to leave school, do hazardous work, get married, fight in wars or are locked up in adult prisons. And global changes, like the rise of digital technology, environmental change, prolonged conflict and mass migration are completely changing childhood. Today's children face new threats to their rights, but they also have new opportunities to realize their rights.

What needs to happen

The hope, vision and commitment of world leaders in 1989 led to the Convention. It is up to today's generation to demand that world leaders from government, business and communities end child rights violations now, once and for all. They must commit to action to make sure every child, has every right.

Play saves lives

It keeps children in school and out of work. It teaches them how to prevent life-threatening diseases like HIV and malaria and keep them safe from exploitation and abuse. It gives girls the power to say no to unwanted sex, and make healthy decisions about their bodies and their futures

Play is powerful

We are transforming the lives of 1.9 million children each week. Using all forms of play - games, sport, poetry, performance, dance, art and music -

we create lasting impact and empower children with the knowledge and skills to drive change in their lives, their families and their communities. Article 31 of the Convention on the Rights of the Child (CRC) recognizes the right of every child to rest, leisure, play, recreational activities and free and full participation in cultural and artistic life. However, the Committee on the Rights of the Child is concerned by the poor recognition given by Governments to these rights.

Rising urban populations, violence in all its forms, the commercialization of play provision, child labour and increasing educational demands are all affecting children's opportunity to enjoy their article 31 rights. In general, where investment is made, it is in the provision of structured and organized activities, but equally important is the need to create time and space for children to engage in spontaneous play, recreation and creativity, and to promote societal attitudes that support and encourage such activity.The Committee on the Rights of the Child is the international body responsible for monitoring governments' implementation of the CRC. To address these concerns, the Committee has produced a 'General Comment' that explains in detail measures governments are urged to take to ensure implementation of the rights in article 31 for all children. The General Comment was adopted by the Committee at its sixty-second session (14 January – 1 February 2013).

The General Comment has three core objectives:

To enhance understanding of the importance of article 31 for children's well being and development. To ensure respect for and strengthen the application of the rights under article 31, as well as other rights in the Convention. To highlight the implications for the determination of obligations of governments, the roles and responsibilities of the private sector, and guidelines for all individuals working with children. The Committee recommends that it is widely disseminated in accessible forms and made available to all interested members of society, including children. This summary provides a short overview of the full text of the General Comment.

Significance of article 31 in children's lives

Play, recreation, rest, leisure, arts and culture are all interlinked and together serve to describe conditions necessary to protect the unique and evolving nature of childhood. Article 31 needs to be understood as a whole. Play and recreation are essential to children's health and well being. They promote the development of creativity, imagination, self-confidence, self-efficacy and physical, social, cognitive and emotional strength and skills. They contribute to all aspects of learning. They are also a form of participation in everyday life, and are of intrinsic value to the child, purely in terms of the enjoyment and pleasure they afford.

Involvement in cultural and artistic life is important for children's sense of belonging to their family, community and society and to their own sense of identity. Children reproduce, transform, create, and transmit culture in many ways. With their peers, they also create a 'culture of childhood'. Children are at the forefront of using digital platforms, such as social media and virtual worlds, to establish new cultural environments and artistic forms. Children's participation in cultural activities also provides opportunities to learn from other cultural and artistic traditions, contributing towards mutual understanding and appreciation of diversity. Rest and leisure are vital to children's development. Lack of sufficient rest will have a physical and psychological impact on children's health, well being, and development. Children also need leisure time to fill as actively or as inactively as they choose. The Committee has interpreted the different terms used in article 31 as follows: 'Rest': Sufficient respite from work, education or any other exertion to ensure optimum health and well being, as well as the opportunity for adequate sleep. 'Leisure': Free time, without obligations, in which play or recreation can take place.

'Play': Children's play is any behaviour, activity or process initiated, controlled and structured by children themselves. Play is non-compulsory, driven by intrinsic motivation and undertaken for its own sake, rather than as a means to an end. It may take infinite forms but the key characteristics of play are fun, uncertainty, challenge, flexibility and non-productivity. While play is often considered non-essential, the Committee reaffirms that it is a fundamental and vital dimension of the pleasure of childhood and is an essential component of children's development. 'Recreation': A broad umbrella term for voluntary activities or experiences chosen by the child for immediate satisfaction or perceived personal or social value. While many such activities may be organized and managed by adults, recreation should be a voluntary activity.

'Appropriate to the age of the child': The age of the child must be taken into account in respect of: time afforded; nature of spaces; degree of adult oversight; safety; risk-taking and challenge; and socializing. 'Cultural life and the arts': The means through which children and their communities express their identity and the meaning they give to their existence, and build their worldview. Culture emerges from within communities, and can be expressed and enjoyed in multiple environments and forms. 'To participate freely': Governments must respect, abstain from interference in, and prevent others from interference in, children's exercising of article 31 rights. 'To participate fully in cultural and artistic life': In order to take part in cultural and artistic life, children must have opportunities to access arts and culture, to participate in creative activities, and to contribute to expressions of culture and the arts. 'Encourage the provision of appropriate opportunities': Governments must provide all the necessary preconditions to facilitate and promote opportunities for the realization of all article 31 rights. 'Equal opportunities': Every child must be afforded equal opportunities to enjoy his or her rights under article 31. It is important to recognize that all rights in the Convention are indivisible and interdependent. Article 31 is central to the realization of many rights. Equally, other rights must be respected in order to guarantee the realization of article 31.

Creating the context for the realization of article 31

Children have a spontaneous urge to play and participate in recreational activities, and will seek out opportunities to do so even in the most unfavourable environments. However, certain conditions need to be assured if they are to realize their article 31 rights fully: Freedom from stress, social exclusion, prejudice or discrimination. An environment secure from social harm and violence, and sufficiently free from pollution, traffic and other hazards that impede free and safe movement. Availability of rest and leisure time, as well as space that is free from adult control and management. Space to play outdoors in diverse and challenging physical environments, with access to supportive adults, when necessary.

Opportunities to experience interact with and play in natural environments and the animal world. Opportunities to invest in their own space and time so as to create and transform their world, using their imagination and languages. Opportunities to explore and understand the cultural and artistic heritage of their community, participate in, create and shape it. Opportunities to participate with other children in games, sports and other recreational activities, supported, where necessary, by trained facilitators or coaches. Recognition by parents, teachers and society as a whole of the value and legitimacy of the rights provided for in article 31. Challenges to be addressed in the realization of article 31 Children throughout the world face significant barriers in realizing their article 31 rights. The challenges differ across regions, but include:

- Lack of recognition of the importance of play and recreation.
- Unsafe and hazardous environments.
- Resistance to children's use of public spaces.
- Balancing risk and safety.
- Lack of access to nature.
- Pressure for educational achievement.
- Overly structured and programmed schedules.
- Neglect of article 31 in development programmes.
- Lack of investment in cultural and artistic opportunities for children.
- Growing role of electronic media.
- Marketing and commercialization of play.

Article 31

"That every child has the right to rest and leisure, to engage in play and recreational activities appropriate to the age of the child and to participate freely in cultural life and the arts. That member governments shall respect and promote the right of the child to participate fully in cultural and artistic life and shall encourage the provision of appropriate and equal opportunities for cultural, artistic, recreational and leisure activity."

Indivisibility of Convention Articles

The rights of the Convention are indivisible and interdependent. The articles of the Convention represent all aspects of the life of a developing child. While a focus on a particular issue is sometimes necessary and desirable, it is important to begin work on any one article from a knowledge of the whole Convention. They are interrelated and mutually supportive.

Of particular importance are the General Principles:

- Article 2: Ensuring all children's rights without discrimination.
- Article 3: Ensuring that best interests of children is a prime consideration.
- Article 6: Ensuring the survival and development of the child.
- Article 12: Ensuring that children (as individuals and as a group) have the right to express their views on matters of concern to them.

Implementation of Article 31

Issues that could be raised by article 31 advocates

Article 31 has become known as 'the forgotten article of the Convention'. Very few of the national reports to the UN Committee (required by signatories of the Convention) have included article 31 in their reports and those which have done so have largely focused on children's physical activity and not embraced all components of the article. Article 31 advocates can do a number of things to raise awareness its importance.

Here are some suggestions

- It is important for article 31 to be included in the national UNCRC implementation plans that are mandatory when a nation ratifies the UN Convention. IPA Branches, member groups and all relevant groups should promote the inclusion of article 31 in national plans or through their official report or through their NGO coalition. Locate your national NGO coalition, or coalitions, which produces a regular report to the UN Committee at about the same time as their national government one (approximately every five years).While the UN Committee encourages such coalitions, not all countries yet have them.

Reports from single or groups of NGOs are therefore also received. IPA representation on NGO coalitions, or at least a close contact with them, would be an advantage for greater recognition and implementation of article 31.

- The range of government ministries or departments, which should be included in article 31 implementation, is a particular challenge. It makes sense for article 31 supporters to help identify key players and organize discussion groups about its implementation priorities. Given the article 31 components of rest and leisure, play and recreation, culture and the arts, there would be a wide range of government departments involved. Those with a responsibility in this field would include, for example, education, recreation, health, social services, labour, social and physical planning, culture, and sports, as well as those concerned with transport, housing and sanitation.
- A goal of IPA Branches and groups would be to support the development of a national policy or framework for article 31. Identify the nation's relevant government departments – as above – and other key national non-government organizations, such as IPA, and encourage comprehensive discussions about article 31. Implementation of the Convention through policy is essential. It can be developed to interpret or build on legislation, or to set out the direction of government or non-governmental organizations in the absence of legislation. Since policy also guides the delivery of programs and services, implementation of the Convention becomes possible through day-to-day practice. (For example: Wales Play Policy, 2002.)
- Orientation and training on article 31 should be accessible for all professionals working with or for children. Is the status of national training, particularly with regard to play, known to IPA Branches, member groups and all relevant groups involved in Article 31? What steps could be taken to improve this? Do you have information that would be useful to other countries?

Children's rights to rest, leisure, recreation and play appropriate to their age, are recognised under Article 31 in the UNCRC (1989). The same Article also recognises their right to be active participants in the cultural and artistic life of their community. Article 31 provides strong support for using play-based approaches to learning in education and care settings.

Children's right to play and leisure time is sometimes threatened by:

- less time for children to play because of a focus on a 'push down' curriculum
- less time to play because of a focus on getting ready for 'tests'
- a focus on commercial toys and products that may not provide open-ended play opportunities

- less time to play and explore outdoors because of educators or parents being worried about safety.

Adults who are committed to children's right to play think seriously about these issues. They ask questions such as: 'Is this a space for children as citizens where they have some control and can take risks, think, wonder, be amazed, have fun and learn with other children and with adults?' A place, as Dahlberg calls it, of 'collective adventure' (as cited in Moss & Petrie, 2002, p. 111). The term 'collective adventure' could be interpreted in a less serious way than was intended. A space or environment for collective adventures is a place where children and adults learn and have fun together; where the time allocation for play is not always ruled by fixed routines or adult agendas and where there is a balance between child-initiated and adult-led learning that has both parties learning in new ways and learning new things together. We should not trivialize the use of play and play materials by early intervention specialists. It is endemic to their work with young children and families (Nwokah, Hui-Chin & Gulker, 2013, p. 211).

The UNCRC's protection and promotion of children's right to play has influenced current policies and practices in early intervention and inclusion for children with disabilities and developmental delay. Previously, the focus for early intervention practices was often on therapeutic interventions to meet goals for children set by professionals. Meeting these goals often required removing a child with special needs from a group and their peers while the child practised a specific skill to achieve a goal. A United Kingdom study involving parents of children with Down syndrome identified that non play-based interventions not only didn't achieve good outcomes for their children, but they also left them with a strong sense of guilt and failure (Rix, Paige-Smith & Jones, 2008). The parents were clear about why highly adult-directed and structured activities failed to meet their children's right to learn through play-based experiences:

- children didn't feel they were in control of the activity
- the activities didn't provide the children with choices
- children did not always enjoy the activities
- the activities often ignored the children's abilities, strengths and interests
- the rigid way the activities were to be implemented generated conflict between the parent and their child.

The highly structured activities described by the parents focused on what the children couldn't do, for example, not being able to use a feeding tool such as a spoon independently. The early intervention goals for the children could have been better promoted through using play-based approaches that recognised the children's interests and strengths. Learning skills like eating or dressing independently can be gained through participating in routine activities at home and through play-based learning in the home corner, or in dress-up play with friends. Families and childhood professionals show respect for children's right to play by their interest, support and involvement. They understand the need to balance child-led and initiated play with adult-guided play and support. Being aware of not taking over children's play and allowing them space, time and resources to engage in play of their choosing is important for meeting the intent of the UNCRC's Article 31 on children's right to play (Lester & Russell, 2010).

Government obligations

1 The obligation to respect article 31 rights

Governments should adopt specific measures aimed at achieving respect for the right of every child, individually or in association with others, to realize his or her rights under article 31, including: Support for caregivers, including guidance, facilitation and support about article 31 which could be in the form of practical guidance. Awareness-raising to challenge widespread cultural attitudes which attach low value to the rights provided for in article 31, including public information on the significance of article 31 and measures to challenge pervasive negative attitudes, especially towards adolescents.

2 The obligation to protect article 31 rights

Governments need to take action to prevent other people or organizations interfering in or restricting the rights provided for in article 31. This will include: Legislation to guarantee access for every child, without discrimination on any ground, to article 31 opportunities. Regulation of non-state actors, to ensure that all members of civil society, including the corporate sector, comply with the provisions of article 31, including in relation to: employment; safety and accessibility of facilities, toys and games; obligations to include provision in urban and rural development proposals; protection from cultural, artistic or recreational material which might be injurious to children's well-being; and prohibiting the production of realistic war games and toys for children. Introduction of child protection measures and professional codes for all adults working with children in the field of play, recreation, sports, culture and the arts.

Measures to promote on-line access and accessibility, as well as safety for children including: reducing impunity of abusive adults; limiting access to harmful material and gaming networks; improving information for parents, teachers and policy makers to raise awareness of risks; and developing strategies for promoting safer and attractive options for children. Development of measures in post conflict situations to restore and protect article 31 rights such as using play and creative expression to promote healing, creating or restoring safe spaces for play and recreation, and removal of landmines and cluster bombs.

Review of policies relating to commercialization of toys and games to children, including through children's television programmes and directly related advertisements, in particular those promoting violence, girls or boys in a sexual way, and gender or disability stereotypes. Introduction of effective and independent complaints mechanisms for children who feel their article 31 rights have been violated.

3 The obligation to fulfil article 31 rights

Governments must introduce a wide range of measures to ensure the fulfilment of all article 31 rights, in full consultation with children.

This includes, in particular:

Legislation and planning for ensuring that every child has sufficient time and space in their life for their article 31 rights, together with a timetable for implementation. Disaggregated data collection and research to find out how far children are able to engage in play, recreation and cultural and artistic life, and to use the results to inform planning and measure progress. Development of cross-departmental collaboration in national and municipal government to ensure a broad and comprehensive approach to implementing article 31. Review of budgets to ensure that allocation for children is inclusive and consistent with their representation as a proportion of the population as a whole, and distributed across the provision for children of all ages, with consideration given to the cost of measures required to ensure access for the most marginalized children. Investment in universal design to promote inclusion and protect children with disabilities from discrimination.

Municipal planning that places a priority on the creation of environments which promote the wellbeing of the child, including: inclusive parks, playgrounds and sports and community centres; zones with priority for pedestrians, players and bikers over motorized traffic; access to landscaped green areas, open spaces and nature, with affordable transport; road safety measures; clubs and facilities for children of all ages; and dedicated and affordable cultural activities for children of all ages.

School environments that provide a major role in article 31 rights, including: physical environments for play, sports, games and drama; active promotion of equal opportunities to play for boys and girls; safe playgrounds and equipment, accessible for all children; adequate time during the school day for play and rest; a curriculum which includes cultural and artistic activities; and a pedagogy which offers active, playful and participatory activities and learning. Training and capacity building on the rights of children including those embodied in article 31 for all professionals working with or for children, or whose work impacts on children. The basic principle underlying the United Nations Convention on the Rights of the Child, often referred to as the UNCRC is that children (defined as being 18 years or under) are born with the same fundamental set of rights as all humans, with a number of additional rights due to their vulnerability. The UNCRC contains a total of 54 articles which were formally adopted by the UN General Assembly in 1989. The United Kingdom government signed the Convention in April 1990, ratified it in December 1991 and it came into force for the UK on 15 January 1992. As a signatory to the convention at national level, all branches of government across the UK (including the NI Assembly, government departments and local councils) are obligated to full implementation of the UNCRC.

The International Play Association (IPA) is an international, non-governmental organization founded in Copenhagen, Denmark in 1961, with an original emphasis on adventure playgrounds. The organization gradually changed its focus to play and children's right to play. Its purpose is to protect, preserve and promote children's right to play as a fundamental human right, according to the Article 31 of the United Nations Convention on the Rights of the Child.

IPA has members in close to 50 countries.

At the IPA Malta Consultation, November 1977, the Declaration of the Child's Right to Play was produced. It was revised by the IPA International Council in Vienna, September 1982, and Barcelona, September 1989. IPA published a report in 2005 stating that children in the United Kingdom were suffering from "play malnourishment". cJanet Dalglish MBE, one of the founders of IPA, received London Play's first Lifetime in Play in London Award in 2006.

How does Right To Play implement their programs?

Play builds life skills like confidence and courage. It helps break down barriers that hold girls back and empower them to learn and lead. We train teachers to use play-based learning to create safe and supportive environments in our five core pillars:

- Education
- Gender Equality
- Health
- Child Protection
- Peace

What does a monthly donations entail?

When you become a monthly donor you'll be donating a set sum every month which goes to support Right To Play programs. Your support will contribute each week towards giving children in our programs protection, education and empowerment through play.

Regular monthly gifts mean a consistent, predictable income so we can plan and budget better, making us more efficient. There are benefits for you too. A regular gift is a hassle-free way to donate, while knowing that you are helping to improve the lives of children rise above adversities, in the long term.

How are my donations spent?

From protecting and educating children, to empowering boys and girls to rise above adversity, you can be sure your donations will go where the need is greatest and will make a lasting difference. 85% of all our fundraising goes towards our work to improve children's lives.

Children's rights are the human rights of children with particular attention to the rights of special protection and care afforded to minors. The 1989 Convention on the Rights of the Child (CRC) defines a child as "any human being below the age of eighteen years, unless under the law applicable to the child, majority is attained earlier." Children's rights includes their right to association with both parents, human identity as well as the basic needs for physical protection, food, universal state-paid education, health care, and criminal laws appropriate for the age and development of the child, equal protection of the child's civil rights, and freedom from discrimination on the basis of the child's race, gender, sexual orientation, genderidentity, nationalorigin, religion, disability, color, ethnicity, or other characteristics. Interpretations of children's rights range from allowing children the capacity for autonomous action to the enforcement of children being physically, mentally and emotionally free from abuse, though what constitutes "abuse" is a matter of debate. Other definitions include the rights to care and nurturing. There are no definitions of other terms used to describe young people such as "adolescents", "teenagers", or "youth" in international law, but the children's rights movement is considered distinct from the youth rights movement. The field of children's rights spans the fields of law, politics, religion, and morality.

Play is work for preschoolers

Children are playful by nature. Their earliest experiences exploring with their senses lead them to play, first by themselves and eventually with others. The National Association for the Education of Young Children (NAEYC) has included play as a criterion in its accreditation process for programs for young children. "They call it their work," says Peter Pizzolongo, associate director for professional development at NAEYC. "When they're learning and playing with joy, then it's a positive experience. They develop a positive approach to learning."

The teacher's role as children grow

As children develop, their play becomes more sophisticated. Up until the age of 2, a child plays by himself and has little interaction with others.

Soon after, he starts watching other children play but may not join in. This is particularly relevant to kids in multi-age settings where younger children can watch and learn from older preschoolers playing nearby. Around 2½ to 3 years, a preschooler starts to play sitting next to another child, often someone with similar interests. This naturally shifts, through the use of language, to the beginnings of cooperative play. An adult can facilitate this process by setting up a space for two or more small bodies and helping children find the words to express their questions or needs. Between 4 and 5 years, preschoolers discover they share similar interests and seek out kids like them. They discuss, negotiate and strategize to create elaborate play scenes; take turns; and work together toward mutual goals.

Types of play

Children's play can be divided into categories, but the types of play often overlap.

- Dramatic — Fantasy-directed play with dressing up in costumes, assuming roles as characters, using toys to represent characters in stories, creating imaginary settings, and pretending to take on the roles of adults.
- Manipulative — Holding and handling small toys often used to build objects but also found in puzzles, characters, beads, etc.
- Physical — Using the whole body in activities with bikes, balls, jump ropes, hoops, play structures, etc.
- Creative — Using art materials such as paint, clay, markers, pencils, glue, etc. The play takes place in the process of using the materials, not in the end product.

Benefits of play

Through play, children develop skills they'll use in their school years.

Physical

Both gross and fine motor development occur through play. When kids play outdoors, if they feel comfortable and supported, they'll push themselves to new challenges and build motor skills. Developing fine motor skills, such as handling small objects, is a way for children to practice using their hands and fingers, which in turn builds the strength and coordination critical for writing skills. "When you're a preschooler or toddler, your attention comes out in a different way," explains Pizzolongo. "Your attention works best if your body is involved, as many parts of it as possible. So children learning to play where they're physically engaged with materials and interacting with each other would work best."

Language

Children build language skills through cooperative play. Their success depends on their ability and patience in explaining themselves. Teachers repeat the words children say to help others understand. They also teach words about the objects the kids are interested in handling. Students may talk to themselves while playing side by side with other children and then begin to repeat what they hear or start talking to each other. This develops into back-and-forth communication about play, becoming increasingly sophisticated by age 4. Children will now set rules, have specific roles, express their interests or objections, and chatter about funny situations that occur in the course of play.

Self-concept

Play builds a strong sense of self-confidence. Trying to do a certain trick on a play structure or build with blocks is hard work for a preschooler. Teachers acknowledge these experiences by articulating what they observe and letting the preschooler absorb these accomplishments again. There are also therapeutic benefits to play that help all children. For example, understanding that a parent is going to work and will come back at pick-up time can be reinforced through a play scenario.

Social development

Listening, negotiating, and compromising are challenging for 4- and 5-year-olds. Though children at this age are still egocentric, or unable to think beyond their own needs, working with others helps them develop an awareness of differences in people around them. These experiences in preschool provide a foundation for learning how to solve problems and communicate with peers. Play also helps build positive leadership qualities for children who are naturally inclined to direct but must learn how to control their impulses.

Loss of play later

For many school-age kids, their time outside of school will include solitary time spent plugged into video games and computers, so it is especially critical for preschoolers to have the opportunity to develop naturally in their play.\ Here is why we believe that playing out is a good thing for children:

1. Children need to play.

It is vital for their physical and emotional development and for their social learning. It is also a human right under the UN Convention on the Rights of the Child.

2. The street is a blank canvas.

It allows for truly child-led free play, providing important benefits over structured, organised activities in designated spaces.

3. Children like to play near home and have traditionally done so.

A 2007 poll found that 71% of adults played out on their street every day compared to only 21% of children today (Playday).

4. Children need ample space to play energetically.

Many homes do not have gardens and in cities these tend to be small. Many children can't get to parks and other open spaces easily whereas the street is instantly accessible.

5. Playing in the street increases community cohesion.

It brings neighbours of all ages together by providing a sense of common space and shared ownership. It can engender a sense of collective responsibility and thereby increase the safety of the neighbourhood.

6. Street play creates new opportunities for socialising and friendships.

These are often across age groups, or with children that go to other schools. Playing out also increases contact between children and adults, helping to build up familiarity and trust.

7. Children learn valuable skills when they play out.

They learn important social skills and they gain understanding about the world around them. They do this through dealing independently with situations as they arise.

8 Playing in the street allows for 'semi-supervised' play.

Parents can get on with housework or looking after other children in the house while allowing children to play outside. Children are far more likely to play outside every day if allowed to play near their home, rather than relying on parents to take them somewhere else, like the park.

9. The street is the "starting point for all journeys" (Tim Gill, 2007)

The ability to play independently in the street is a first step towards greater independent mobility around the neighbourhood – to visit friends, go to the park or walk to school.

10. Streets constitute the vast majority of public space in the city.

To see them only as places to drive and park cars is to massively undervalue them. Streets can and should be places where people can sit, talk, read, play and walk – and even sing and dance if they want to! The only way this will happen is if we start to use them differently.

Justifications

As minors by law, children do not have autonomy or the right to make decisions on their own for themselves in any known jurisdiction of the world. Instead their adult caregivers, including parents, social workers, teachers, youth workers, and others, are vested with that authority, depending on the circumstances. Some believe that this state of affairs gives children insufficient control over their own lives and causes them to be vulnerable. Louis Althusser has gone so far as to describe this legal machinery, as it applies to children, as "repressive state apparatuses". Structures such as government policy have been held by some commentators to mask the ways adults abuse and exploit children, resulting in child poverty, lack of educational opportunities, and child labour. On this view, children are to be regarded as a minority group towards whom society needs to reconsider the way it behaves. Researchers have identified children as needing to be recognized as participants in society whose rights and responsibilities need to be recognized at all ages.

Historic definitions of children's rights

Sir William Blackstone (1765-9) recognized three parental duties to the child: maintenance, protection, and education. In modern language, the child has a right to receive these from the parent. The League of Nations adopted the Geneva Declaration of the Rights of the Child (1924), which enunciated the child's right to receive the requirements for normal development, the right of the hungry child to be fed, the right of the sick child to receive health care, the right of the backward child to be reclaimed, the right of orphans to shelter, and the right to protection from exploitation. The United Nations Universal Declaration of Human Rights (1948) in Article 25(2) recognized the need of motherhood and childhood to "special protection and assistance" and the right of all children to "social protection." The United Nations General Assembly adopted the United Nations Declaration of the Rights of the

Taking action close to home

By organising a playing out session or helping on the day as a steward, residents are taking action to create safe, outdoor free play opportunities for children close to home, and to make their streets a better to place to live for people of all ages.

Active citizens and having a voice

Alongside the health and community impact of playing out sessions, getting more involved in the life of their street also often inspires people to get involved in other things locally. We know of people who have gone on to attend their neighbourhood forums, working on infrastructure changes to make areas more bike and pedestrian friendly. Some have used playing out sessions to collect toys and clothes for donating. Others have gone on to encourage and support playing out sessions beyond their own streets, working as 'activators' in the local areas where they live and beyond.

In our 2017 survey of playing out streets, over a third of survey respondents said that being involved in playing out has led to involvement in other community groups and activities. One said, 'I feel more empowered to make positive change in my community and in the street where I live'. Public health research now shows that this sense of agency and power to change things has a positive impact on people's health.

A positive example for children and young people

Seeing the adults around them meeting, taking action and changing their street from a 'no-go' area to a public space that's open for play and for the whole street community to enjoy is good for children. It demonstrates many positive social values in action: citizenship, a shared sense of public space and pride of place, and community activism. Child (1959), which enunciated ten principles for the protection of children's rights, including the universality of rights, the right to special protection, and the right to protection from discrimination, among other rights. Consensus on defining children's rights has become clearer in the last fifty years.

A 1973 publication by Hillary Clinton (then an attorney) stated that children's rights were a "slogan in need of a definition". According to some researchers, the notion of children's rights is still not well defined, with at least one proposing that there is no singularly accepted definition or theory of the rights held by children. Children's rights law is defined as the point where the law intersects with a child's life. That includes juvenile delinquency, due process for children involved in the criminal justice system, appropriate representation, and effective rehabilitative services; care and protection for children in state care; ensuring education for all children regardless of their race, gender, sexual orientation, gender identity, national origin, religion, disability, color, ethnicity, or other characteristics, and; health care and advocacy.

Classification

Children have two types of human rights under international human rights law. They have the same fundamental general human rights as adults, although some human rights, such as the right to marry, are dormant until they are of age, Secondly, they have special human rights that are necessary to protect them during their minority. General rights operative in childhood include the right to security of the person, to freedom from inhuman, cruel, or degrading treatment, and the right to special protection during childhood. Particular human rights of children include, among other rights, the right to life, the right to a name, the right to express his views in matters concerning the child, the right to freedom of thought, conscience and religion, the right to health care, the right to protection from economic and sexual exploitation, and the right to education. Children's rights are defined in numerous ways, including a wide spectrum of civil, political, economic, social and cultural rights. Rights tend to be of two general types: those advocating for children as autonomous persons under the law and those placing a claim on society for protection from harms perpetrated on children because of their dependency. These have been labeled as the right of empowerment and as the right to protection. United Nations educational guides for children classify the rights outlined in the Convention on the Rights of the Child as the "3 Ps": Provision, Protection, and Participation. They may be elaborated as follows:

- Provision: Children have the right to an adequate standard of living, health care, education and services, and to play and recreation. These include a balanced diet, a warm bed to sleep in, and access to schooling.
- Protection: Children have the right to protection from abuse, neglect, exploitation and discrimination. This includes the right to safe places for children to play; constructive child rearing behavior, and acknowledgment of the evolving capacities of children.
- Participation: Children have the right to participate in communities and have programs and services for themselves. This includes children's involvement in libraries and community programs, youth voice activities, and involving children as decision-makers.

In a similar fashion, the Child Rights International Network (CRIN) categorizes rights into two groups:

- Economic, social and cultural rights, related to the conditions necessary to meet basic human needs such as food, shelter, education, health care, and gainful employment. Included are rights to education, adequate housing, food, water, the highest attainable standard of health, the right to work and rights at work, as well as the cultural rights of minorities and indigenous peoples.
- Environmental, cultural and developmental rights, which are sometimes called "third generation rights," and including the right to live in safe and healthy environments and that groups of people have the right to cultural, political, and economic development.

Amnesty International openly advocates four particular children's rights, including the end to juvenile incarceration without parole, an end to the recruitment of military use of children, ending the death penalty for people under 21, and raising awareness of human rights in the classroom. Human Rights Watch, an international advocacy organization, includes child labor, juvenile justice, orphans and abandoned children, refugees, street children and corporal punishment. Scholarly study generally focuses children's rights by identifying individual rights. The following rights "allow children to grow up healthy and free

Freedom of speech

- Freedom of thought
- Freedom from fear
- Freedom of choice and the right to make decisions
- Ownership over one's body

Physical rights

A report by the Committee on Social Affairs, Health, and Sustainable Development of the Parliamentary Assembly of the Council of Europe identified several areas the Committee was concerned about, including procedures such as "female genital mutilation, the circumcision of young boys for religious reasons, early childhood medical interventions in the case of intersex children and the submission to or coercion of children into piercings, tattoos or plastic surgery". The Assembly adopted a non-binding resolution in 2013 that calls on its 47 member-states to take numerous actions to promote the physical integrity of children.

Article 19 of the Convention on the Rights of the Child enjoins parties to "take all appropriate legislative, administrative, social and educational measures to protect the child from all forms of physical or mental violence, injury or abuse, neglect or negligent treatment, maltreatment or exploitation". The Committee on the Rights of the Child interprets article 19 as prohibiting corporal punishment, commenting on the "obligation of all States Party to move quickly to prohibit and eliminate all corporal punishment." The United Nations Human Rights Committee has also interpreted Article 7 of the International Covenant on Civil and Political Rights prohibiting "cruel, inhuman or degrading treatment or punishment" to extend to children, including corporal punishment of children. The Committee on Bioethics of the American Academy of Pediatrics (AAP) (1997), citing the Convention on the Rights of the Child (1989), asserts that "every child should have the opportunity to grow and develop free from preventable illness or injury."

Parental powers

Parent are given sufficient powers to fulfill their duties to the child.

Parents affect the lives of children in a unique way, and as such their role in children's rights has to be distinguished in a particular way. Particular issues in the child-parent relationship include child neglect, child abuse, freedom of choice, corporal punishment and child custody. There have been theories offered that provide parents with rights-based practices that resolve the tension between "commonsense parenting" and children's rights. The issue is particularly relevant in legal proceedings that affect the potential emancipation of minors, and in cases where children sue their parents.

Limitations of parental powers

Parents do not have absolute power over their children. Parents are subject to criminal laws against abandonment, abuse, and neglect of children. International human rights law provides that manifestation of one's religion may be limited in the interests of public safety, for the protection of public order, health or morals, or for the protection of the rights and freedoms of others.Movement The 1796 publication of Thomas Spence's Rights of Infants is among the earliest English-language assertions of the rights of children. Throughout the 20th century, children's rights activists organized for homeless children's rights and public education. The 1927 publication of The Child's Right to Respect by Janusz Korczak strengthened the literature surrounding the field, and today dozens of international organizations are working around the world to promote children's rights.

In the UK the formation of a community of educationalists, teachers, youth justice workers, politicians and cultural contributors called the New Ideals in Education Conferences (1914–37) stood for the value of 'liberating the child' and helped to define the 'good' primary school in England until the 80s. Their conferences inspired the UNESCO organisation, the New Education Fellowship. A.S. Neill's 1915 book A Dominie's Log (1915), a diary of a headteacher changing his school to one based on the liberation and happiness of the child, can be seen as a cultural product that celebrates the heroes of this movement

Opposition

The opposition to children's rights long predates any current trend in society, with recorded statements against the rights of children dating to the 13th century and earlier.Opponents to children's rights believe that young people need to be protected from the adultcentric world, including the decisions and responsibilities of that world. In a dominantly adult society, childhood is idealized as a time of innocence, a time free of responsibility and conflict, and a time dominated by play. The majority of opposition stems from concerns related to national sovereignty, states' rights, the parent-child relationship. Financial constraints and the "undercurrent of traditional values in opposition to children's rights" are cited, as well. The concept of children's rights has received little attention in the United States.

International human rights law

The Universal Declaration of Human Rights is seen as a basis for all international legal standards for children's rights today. There are several conventions and laws that address children's rights around the world. A number of current and historical documents affect those rights, including the Declaration of the Rights of the Child, drafted by Eglantyne Jebbin 1923, endorsed by the League of Nations in 1924 and reaffirmed in 1934. A slightly expanded version was adopted by the United Nations in 1946, followed by a much expanded version adopted by the General Assembly in 1959. It later served as the basis for the Convention on the Rights of the Child.

International Covenant on Civil and Political Rights

The United Nations adopted the International Covenant on Civil and Political Rights (ICCPR) in 1966. The ICCPR is a multilateral international covenant that has been ratified or acceded to by nearly all nations on Earth. Nations which have become state-parties to the Covenant are required to honor and enforce the rights enunciated by the Covenant. The treaty came into effect on 23 March 1976. The rights codified by the ICCPR are universal, so they apply to everyone without exception and this includes children. Although children have all rights, some rights such as the right to marry and the right to vote come into effect only after the child reaches maturity.

Some general rights applicable to children include:

- the right to life
- the right to security of person
- the right to freedom from torture
- the right to freedom from cruel, inhuman or degrading treatment or punishment
- the right to be separated from adults when charged with a crime, the right to speedy adjudication, and the right to be accorded treatment appropriate to their age

Article 24 codifies the right of the child to special protection due to his minority, the right to a name, and the right to a nationality.

Convention on the Rights of the Child

The United Nations' 1989 Convention on the Rights of the Child, or CRC, is the first legally binding international instrument to incorporate the full range of human rights—civil, cultural, economic, political and social rights. Its implementation is monitored by the Committee on the Rights of the Child. National governments that ratify it commit themselves to protecting and ensuring children's rights, and agree to hold themselves accountable for this commitment before the international community. The CRC is the most widely ratified human rights treaty with 196 ratifications; the United States is the only country not to have ratified it. The CRC is based on four core principles: the principle of non-discrimination; the best interests of the child; the right to life, survival and development; and considering the views of the child in decisions that affect them, according to their age and maturity. The CRC, along with international criminal accountability mechanisms such as the International Criminal Court, the Yugoslavia and Rwanda Tribunals, and the Special Court for Sierra Leone, is said to have significantly increased the profile of children's rights worldwide.

Vienna Declaration and Programme of Action

The Vienna Declaration and Programme of Action urges, at Section II para 47, all nations to undertake measures to the maximum extent of their available resources, with the support of international cooperation, to achieve the goals in the World Summit Plan of Action. And calls on States to integrate the Convention on the Rights of the Child into their national action plans. By means of these national action plans and through international efforts, particular priority should be placed on reducing infant and maternal mortality rates, reducing malnutrition and illiteracy rates and providing access to safe drinking water and basic education. Whenever so called for, national plans of action should be devised to combat devastating emergencies resulting from natural disasters and armed conflicts and the equally grave problem of children in extreme poverty. Further, para 48 urges all states, with the support of international cooperation, to address the acute problem of children under especially difficult circumstances. Exploitation and abuse of children should be actively combated, including by addressing their root causes. Effective measures are required against female infanticide, harmful child labour, sale of children and organs, child prostitution, child pornography, and other forms of sexual abuse. This influenced the adoptions of Optional Protocol on the Involvement of Children in Armed Conflict and Optional Protocol on the Sale of Children, Child Prostitution and Child Pornography.

Enforcement

A variety of enforcement organizations and mechanisms exist to ensure children's rights. They include the Child Rights Caucus for the United Nations General Assembly Special Session on Children. It was set up to promote full implementation and compliance with the Convention on the Rights of the Child, and to ensure that child rights were given priority during the UN General Assembly Special Session on Children and its Preparatory process. The United Nations Human Rights Council was created "with the hope that it could be more objective, credible and efficient in denouncing human rights violations worldwide than the highly politicized Commission on Human Rights." The NGO Group for the Convention on the Rights of the Child is a coalition of international non-governmental organisations originally formed in 1983 to facilitate the implementation of the United Nations Convention on the Rights of the Child.

National law

Many countries around the world have children's rights ombudspeople or children's commissioners whose official, governmental duty is to represent the interests of the public by investigating and addressing complaints reported by individual citizens regarding children's rights. Children's ombudspeople can also work for a corporation, a newspaper, an NGO, or even for the general public.

United States law

The United States has signed but not ratified the CRC. As a result, children's rights have not been systematically implemented in the U.S. Children are generally afforded the basic rights embodied by the Constitution, as enshrined by the Fourteenth Amendment to the United States Constitution. The Equal Protection Clause of that amendment is to apply to children, born within a marriage or not, but excludes children not yet born. This was reinforced by the landmark US Supreme Courtdecision of In re Gault (1967).

In this trial 15-year-old Gerald Gault of Arizona was taken into custody by local police after being accused of making an obscene telephone call. He was detained and committed to the Arizona State Industrial School until he reached the age of 21 for making an obscene phone call to an adult neighbor. In an 8–1 decision, the Court ruled that in hearings which could result in commitment to an institution, people under the age of 18 have the right to notice and counsel, to question witnesses, and to protection against self-incrimination. The Court found that the procedures used in Gault's hearing met none of these requirements. The United States Supreme Court has ruled in the case of Roper v. Simmons that persons may not be executed for crimes committed when below the age of eighteen. It ruled that such executions are cruel and unusual punishment, so they are a violation of the Eighth Amendment to the United States Constitution.

There are other concerns in the United States regarding children's rights. The American Academy of Adoption Attorneys is concerned with children's rights to a safe, supportive and stable family structure. Their position on children's rights in adoption cases states that, "children have a constitutionally based liberty interest in the protection of their established families, rights which are at least equal to, and we believe outweigh, the rights of others who would claim a 'possessory' interest in these children." Other issues raised in American children's rights advocacy include children's rights to inheritance in same-sex marriages and particular rights for youth.

German law

A report filed by the President of the INGO Conference of the Council of Europe, Annelise Oeschger finds that children and their parents are subject to United Nations, European Union and UNICEF human rights violations. Of particular concern is the German (and Austrian) agency, Jugendamt that often unfairly allows for unchecked government control of the parent-child relationship, which have resulted in harm including torture, degrading, cruel treatment and has led to children's death. The problem is complicated by the nearly "unlimited power" of the Jugendamt officers, with no processes to review or resolve inappropriate or harmful treatment. By German law, Jugendamt officers are protected against prosecution. Jugendamt (JA) officers span of control is seen in cases that go to family court where experts testimony may be overturned by lesser educated or experienced JA officers; In more than 90% of the cases the JA officer's recommendation is accepted by family court. Officers have also disregarded family court decisions, such as when to return children to their parents, without repercussions. Germany has not recognized related child-welfare decisions made by the European Parliamentary Court that have sought to protect or resolve children and parental rights violations.

The IPA Declaration of the Child's Right to Play was originally produced in November 1977 at the IPA Malta Consultation held in preparation for the International Year of the Child (1979). It was revised by the IPA International Council in Vienna, September 1982, and Barcelona, September 1989. The IPA Declaration should be read in conjunction with Article 31 of the U.N. Convention on the Rights of the Child (adopted by the General Assembly of the United Nations, November 20, 1989), which states that the child has a right to leisure, play, and participation in cultural and artistic activities.

WHAT IS PLAY?

- CHILDREN are the foundation of the world's future.
- CHILDREN have played at all times throughout history and in all cultures.
- PLAY, along with the basic needs of nutrition, health, shelter and education, is vital to develop the potential of all children.
- PLAY is communication and expression, combining thought and action; it gives satisfaction and a feeling of achievement.
- PLAY is instinctive, voluntary, and spontaneous.
- PLAY helps children develop physically, mentally, emotionally and socially.
- PLAY is a means of learning to live, not a mere passing of time.

ALARMING TRENDS AFFECTING CHILDHOOD

IPA is deeply concerned by a number of alarming trends and their negative impact on children's development:

- Society's indifference to the importance of play
- Over-emphasis on theoretical and academic studies in schools.
- Increasing numbers of children living with inadequate provisions for survival and development.
- Inadequate environmental planning, which results in a lack of basic amenities, inappropriate housing forms, and poor traffic management.
- Increasing commercial exploitation of children, and the deterioration of cultural traditions.
- Lack of access for third world women to basic training in childcare and development.
- Inadequate preparation of children to cope with life in a rapidly changing society.
- Increasing segregation of children in the community.
- The increasing numbers of working children, and their unacceptable working conditions.
- Constant exposure of children to war, violence, exploitation and destruction.
- Over-emphasis on unhealthy competition and "winning at all costs" in children's sports.

PROPOSALS FOR ACTION

The following proposals are listed under the names of government departments having a measure of responsibility for children.

HEALTH

- Play is essential for the physical and mental health of the child.
- Establish programs for professionals and parents about the benefits of play from birth onwards.
- Ensure basic conditions (nutrition, sanitation, clean water and air) which promote the healthy survival and development of all children.
- Incorporate play into community programs designed to maintain children's physical and mental health.
- Include play as an integral part of all children's environments, including hospitals and other institutional settings.

EDUCATION

- Play is part of education.
- Provide opportunities for initiative, interaction, creativity and socialization through play in formal education systems.
- Include studies of the importance of play and the means of play provision in the training of all professionals and volunteers working with and for children.
- Strengthen play provision in primary schools to enhance learning and to maintain attendance and motivation.
- Reduce the incompatibilities between daily life, work and education by involving schools and colleges, and by using public buildings for community play programs.
- Ensure that working children have access to play and learning opportunities outside of the system of formal education.

WELFARE

- Play is an essential part of family and community life.
- Ensure that play is accepted as an integral part of social development and social care.
- Promote measures that strengthen positive relationships between parents and children.
- Ensure that play is part of community-based services designed to integrate children with physical, mental or emotional disabilities into the community.
- Provide safe play environments that protect children against abduction, sexual abuse and physical violence.

LEISURE

- Children need opportunities to play at leisure.
- Provide time, space, materials, natural settings, and programs with leaders where children may develop a sense of belonging, self-esteem, and enjoyment through play.
- Enable interaction between children and people of all backgrounds and ages in leisure settings.
- Encourage the conservation and use of traditional indigenous games.
- Stop the commercial exploitation of children's play, and the production and sale of war toys and games of violence and destruction.
- Promote the use of co-operative games and fair play for children in sports.

- Provide all children, particularly those with special needs, with access to a diversity of play environments, toys and play materials through community programs such as pre-school play groups, toy libraries and play buses.

PLANNING

The needs of the child must have priority in the planning of human settlements.

- Ensure that children and young people can participate in making decisions that affect their surroundings and their access to them.
- When planning new, or reorganizing existing developments, recognize the child's small size and limited range of activity.
- Disseminate existing knowledge about play facilities and play programs to planning professionals and politicians.
- Oppose the building of high-rise housing and provide opportunities to mitigate its detrimental effects on children and families.
- Enable children to move easily about the community by providing safe pedestrian access through urban neighborhoods, better traffic management, and improved public transportation.
- Increase awareness of the high vulnerability of children living in slum settlements, tenements, and derelict neighborhoods.
- Reserve adequate and appropriate space for play and recreation through statutory provision.

AFFIRMATION

IPA is determined to sustain the momentum created by the International Year of the Child in 1979 to arouse world opinion for the improvement of the life of children, and:

- AFFIRMS its belief in the United Nations' Declaration of the Rights of the Child, which in Article 7 states "The child shall have full opportunity to play and recreation, which should be directed to the same purposes as education; society and the public authorities shall endeavor to promote the enjoyment of this right;" and endorses its belief in Article 31 of the Convention on the Rights of the Child.
- RECOGNIZES that the population of children in developing countries is three quarters of the world's total child population, and that efforts directed at the promotion of education and literacy, and the stopping of environmental deprivation would improve the capacities of the poorest.
- AFFIRMS its commitment to working with other national and international organizations to ensure basic conditions of survival for all children in order that they may fully develop as human beings.

- ACKNOWLEDGES that each country is responsible for preparing its own courses of public and political action in the light of its culture, climate and social, political and economic structure;
- RECOGNIZES that the full participation of the community is essential in planning and developing programs and services to meet the needs, wishes, and aspirations of children;
- ASSURES its co-operation with UN agencies and other international and national organizations involved with children;
- APPEALS to all countries and organizations to take action to counteract the alarming trends which jeopardize children's healthy development and to give high priority to long term programs designed to ensure for all time:

THE CHILD'S RIGHT TO PLAY

ORGANIZATION

- IPA is an interdisciplinary non-governmental organization, providing an international forum and advocacy for the promotion of play opportunities.
- IPA membership is open to any individual, group or organization which endorses the IPA Declaration of the Child's Right to Play.
- IPA organizes regional and national conferences, workshops, symposia and study tours and holds a triennial World Congress. IPA also publishes a magazine, PlayRights, and produces publications and audio-visual material on aspects of play.
- IPA offers advice to national governments and UN agencies on issues and problems related to the implementation of the Child's Right to Play.

Erosion of children's freedom

Article 31 of the UN Convention on the Rights of the Child states that children have a right to play. However, in the UK and many other countries, time, space and opportunities for outside free play and playing out have actually been declining for many decades, eroded largely by increases in traffic and attitudinal changes. Funding cuts and reduced recognition of the importance of play within central government have compounded this.

Health and wellbeing impact

The huge impact of this erosion on children's health and wellbeing is only now beginning to be seen, with only one in five children getting the recommended daily physical activity they need to be well – that's 80% of children not getting this – and 20% of children now leaving primary school obese. Children are also increasingly lacking opportunities to socialise outside of school in real life (not on-line), develop independence, problem solve and grow in resilience, as well as the enjoyment of free play with others.

Inequalities Issue

This loss of children's right to simply play out wherever they live – in streets, estates and open spaces, for free, on their doorstep, whether they are rich or poor – also impacts more on children living in social housing whose parents have little say over their own outside space (see this 2019 Guardian article 'Too Poor to Play' where poorer children have been deliberately excluded from the formal play space) and on low income families with less ability to 'compensate' for this loss with paid-for activities or driving to other spaces. We wrote a letter to The Guardian to make this point in response to the article.

Changing things.

The answer – alongside creating a more child-friendly public realm – is to enshrine in law and policy and defend in practice all children's right to play out where they live. Fortunately, there's a growing international movement working towards this. In the UK, this includes many community-based organisations, local play associations and adventure playgrounds and a growing Playing Out network of parents and residents changing things for play where they live.

Playing Out rights based projects

We at Playing Out CIC are also working on specific rights based projects, like the Bristol Child Friendly City initiative and the Safer Streets in Hartcliffe project led by children, where children's voices and participation are key (as in this short film by children from the Hartcliffe Estate in south Bristol calling for more freedom and change). We've also been looking at parent led action to enable playing out on social housing tower block estates where barriers are more complex. And we're increasingly speaking out and calling on local and national government to defend children's right to play out.

Together, we can help change things for all children.

The Impact of Playing Out

This is just what we've managed to record. We're also hearing that much more informal playing out is happening in streets and spaces across the UK because parents, residents and professionals are starting to think differently. Here's the deeper impact taking place each time residents open their front doors to meet, play and use the immediate space in a shared way:

Improving children's health and wellbeing

80% of UK children don't get the basic minimum recommended level of physical activity to be well. Playing out gives children space and freedom to get much needed exercise outdoors, play freely, gain independence and skills, and make new friends close to home. Read more information and evidence here...

Building stronger communities and a sense of belonging

Children and parents are often isolated in their homes. The process of opening a street for play increases connections, friendship and trust between neighbours of all ages and backgrounds, and develops a stronger sense of 'our street'. Read more information and evidence here... Organising playing out, volunteering as a steward and changing the use of the street is a form of community action. It demonstrates citizenship in action to children growing up on the street. Often residents feel inspired to do more within their neighbourhood. Read more information and evidence here...

Changing culture around children's freedom

All this activity, along with smaller important actions like spreading the word and showing support, as well as increasing work around children's rights, is part of a wider, growing national and international movement for children's freedom. Together we are all beginning to change things. Can you join us?

Outdoors without grown ups

For most people, it's not an activity organised by adults, or playing on a bit of park equipment, but something that happened when parents weren't around, and very often something outside: games of Hide and Seek and Cops and Robbers; making up adventures; or even just mucking about in a gang, interacting with each other and the world immediately around. The opportunities for this kind of free, unstructured, imaginative play outside with others are greatly reduced these days, due to increases in traffic, indoor entertainment, parental concerns, changing work patterns and children's involvement in organised clubs and activities. Yet it's now recognised that this kind of play is so important to the cognitive, physical, social and emotional well-being of children, and to their ability to grow into resilient, happy, well adjusted adults.

Benefits of free play

Free play enables children to:

- Use their creativity and find out what they really like
- Discover and act on their own interests, ideas and passions

- Take physical risks in a gradual way, building up what they are capable of doing
- Go at their own pace, make their own decisions, be as involved as they want to be, or drop out when things are not right
- Work collaboratively with other children of different ages and learn how to share, negotiate, resolve conflicts, develop rules and stick up for themselves
- Experience anger, fear, aggression and upset in a safe environment with friends through play fighting, invented games or just interacting with others, and learn how to regulate these important feelings for later life

In our society where children have far fewer chances to play freely like this outdoors, playing out sessions can be a good way of beginning to break the cycle and make it a normal activity again. They provide space and permission for children to play freely together, making good use of public space right outside their homes. Adults may be present, but they simply step back. What children then do in the space is up to them... The right to play: still overlooked one year after landmark UN statement? It's already one year since the United Nations (UN) published its landmark statement on children's right to play. In publishing its 'General Comment', the UN Children's Committee sent a powerful message to the governments of the world that, in their policies and programmes, they must not overlook the importance of play. They emphasised that play is essential to children's health and well-being, to all aspects of learning, to the development of creativity and imagination – and crucially to the simple enjoyment and pleasure of being a child. The UN's message was neatly summed up for the International Play Association (IPA) by children who said: 'If governments take all of this seriously, our lives will be happier and healthier.'

Since the right to play was included in the UN Convention on the Rights of the Child more than twenty years ago, article 31 (where the right to play sits) has been a constant point to which we can refer whenever we need to back up our arguments supporting children's play. The UN General Comment (GC) on article 31 brings the possibility of a richer understanding of the right to play.

The GC calls for governments to take a wide range of measures that would add to conditions in which children's play can flourish. Taking these measures would respond to the children's call for 'all this to be taken seriously'. These measures include legislation and planning to ensure space and time for play in children's lives, investing in research and promoting the inclusion of all children. Governments are urged to review budgets to ensure allocation is consistent with children's representation as a portion of the population and schools are asked to consider play in their environments, timetables, curricula and pedagogy. The year following the adoption of the GC has been one of many celebrations. The GC increased our understanding of the intertwined nature of play, culture and art – and fittingly the right to play has been celebrated with lightness of heart, playfulness, creativity and laughter. For example, IPA created a wonderful video that explains the fundamental importance of play for children's physical, social, mental and emotional development.

The GC offers a renewed source of inspiration and insight but it is also a formal document laying out what is expected of governments and legislators. All European countries, as signatories to the UN Convention on the Rights of the Child, are expected to step up to the standards the GC sets out. Let's now ensure that the underpinning principles of the UN Convention and the need to respect, protect and fulfil children's right to play is firmly embedded in our national and European priorities going forwards. The anniversary of the GC provides a perfect opportunity for European decision makers, in consultation with children and young people, to raise awareness of the importance of play and to strongly encourage the adoption of national plans for play. The Importance of Play in Promoting Healthy Child Development and Maintaining Strong Parent-Child Bonds

Play is so important to optimal child development that it has been recognized by the United Nations High Commission for Human Rights as a right of every child.1 This birthright is challenged by forces including child labor and exploitation practices, war and neighborhood violence, and the limited resources available to children living in poverty. However, even those children who are fortunate enough to have abundant available resources and who live in relative peace may not be receiving the full benefits of play. Many of these children are being raised in an increasingly hurried and pressured style that may limit the protective benefits they would gain from child-driven play. Because every child deserves the opportunity to develop to their unique potential, child advocates must consider all factors that interfere with optimal development and press for circumstances that allow each child to fully reap the advantages associated with play.

No single set of guidelines could do justice to the many factors that impact on children's play, even if it was to focus only on children living in the United States. These guidelines will focus on how American children with adequate resources may be limited from enjoying the full developmental assets associated with play because of a family's hurried lifestyle as well as an increased focus on the fundamentals of academic preparation in lieu of a broader view of education. Those forces that prevent children in poverty and the working class from benefiting fully from play deserve full, even urgent, attention, and will be addressed in a future document. Those issues that impact on play for children with limited resources will be mentioned briefly here to reinforce that play contributes to optimal child development for all children and that we must advocate for the changes specific to the need of each child's social and environmental context that would enhance the opportunities for play.

These guidelines were written in response to the multiple forces that challenge play. The overriding premise is that play (or some available free time in the case of older children and adolescents) is essential to the cognitive, physical, social, and emotional well-being of children and youth. Although the guidelines were written in defense of play, they should not be interpreted as being against other forces that compete for children's time. Academic enrichment opportunities are vital for some children's ability to progress academically, and participation in organized activities is known to promote healthy youth development.23 It is essential that a wide variety of programming remain available to meet the needs of both children and families. Rather, these guidelines call for an inclusion of play as we seek the balance in children's lives that will create the optimal developmental milieu to prepare our children to be academically, socially, and emotionally equipped to lead us into the future.

Play allows children to use their creativity while developing their imagination, dexterity, and physical, cognitive, and emotional strength. Play is important to healthy brain development.46 It is through play that children at a very early age engage and interact in the world around them. Play allows children to create and explore a world they can master, conquering their fears while practicing adult roles, sometimes in conjunction with other children or adult caregivers.714 As they master their world, play helps children develop new competencies that lead to enhanced confidence and the resiliency they will need to face future challenges. Undirected play allows children to learn how to work in groups, to share, to negotiate, to resolve conflicts, and to learn self-advocacy skills. When play is allowed to be child driven, children practice decision-making skills, move at their own pace, discover their own areas of interest, and ultimately engage fully in the passions they wish to pursue. Ideally, much of play involves adults, but when play is controlled by adults, children acquiesce to adult rules and concerns and lose some of the benefits play offers them, particularly in developing creativity, leadership, and group skills.17 In contrast to passive entertainment, play builds active, healthy bodies. In fact, it has been suggested that encouraging unstructured play may be an exceptional way to increase physical activity levels in children, which is one important strategy in the resolution of the obesity epidemic.1819 Perhaps above all, play is a simple joy that is a cherished part of childhood.

Children's developmental trajectory is critically mediated by appropriate, affective relationships with loving and consistent caregivers as they relate to children through play.4When parents observe their children in play or join with them in child-driven play, they are given a unique opportunity to see the world from their child's vantage point as the child navigates a world perfectly created just to fit his or her needs. (The word "parent" is used in this report to represent the wide range of adult caregivers who raise children.) The interactions that occur through play tell children that parents are fully paying attention to them and help to build enduring relationshipsParents who have the opportunity to glimpse into their children's world learn to communicate more effectively with their children and are given another setting to offer gentle, nurturing guidance. Less verbal children may be able to express their views, experiences, and even frustrations through play, allowing their parents an opportunity to gain a fuller understanding of their perspective. Quite simply, play offers parents a wonderful opportunity to engage fully with their children.

Play is integral to the academic environment. It ensures that the school setting attends to the social and emotional development of children as well as their cognitive development. It has been shown to help children adjust to the school setting and even to enhance children's learning readiness, learning behaviors, and problem-solving skills.2232 Social-emotional learning is best integrated with academic learning; it is concerning if some of the forces that enhance children's ability to learn are elevated at the expense of others. Play and unscheduled time that allow for peer interactions are important components of social-emotional learning

Despite the numerous benefits derived from play for both children and parents, time for free play has been markedly reduced for some children. This trend has even affected kindergarten children, who have had free play reduced in their schedules to make room for more academics. A 1989 survey taken by the National Association of Elementary School Principals found that 96% of surveyed school systems had at least 1 recess period. Another survey a decade later found that only 70% of even kindergarten classrooms had a recess period. Currently, many schoolchildren are given less free time and fewer physical outlets at school; many school districts responded to the No Child Left Behind Act of 200137 by reducing time committed to recess, the creative arts, and even physical education in an effort to focus on reading and mathematics.

This change may have implications on children's ability to store new information, because children's cognitive capacity is enhanced by a clear-cut and significant change in activity.3540 A change in academic instruction or class topic does not offer this clear-cut change in cognitive effort and certainly does not offer a physical release. Even a formal structured physical education class may not offer the same benefit as free-play recess.3541 Reduced time for physical activity may be contributing to the discordant academic abilities between boys and girls, because schools that promote sedentary styles of learning become a more difficult environment for boys to navigate successfully. Some children are given less time for free exploratory play as they are hurried to adapt into adult roles and prepare for their future at earlier ages.4446 Parents are receiving carefully marketed messages that good parents expose their children to every opportunity to excel, buy a plethora of enrichment tools, and ensure their children participate in a wide variety of activities.4547 Children are exposed to enrichment videos and computer programs from early infancy as well as specialized books and toys designed to ensure that they are well-rounded and adequately stimulated for excelled development. Specialized gyms and enrichment programs designed for children exist in many communities, and there is an abundance of after-school enrichment activities.

These tools and programs are heavily marketed, and many parents have grown to believe that they are a requirement of good parenting and a necessity for appropriate development. As a result, much of parent-child time is spent arranging special activities or transporting children between those activities. In addition to time, considerable family financial resources are being invested to ensure that the children have what are marketed as the "very best" opportunities. It is clear that organized activities have a developmental benefit for children, especially in contrast to completely unsupervised time.2 Some research substantiates that for most children, benefits increase with higher levels of participation.2 In addition, it has been suggested that because this lifestyle is associated with middle-class families, it may have a benefit in maintaining social class or in creating upward mobility.50 It is less clear, however, at what point a young person may be "overscheduled" to their developmental detriment or emotional distress. Free child-driven play known to benefit children is decreased, and the downtime that allows parents and children some of the most productive time for interaction is at a premium when schedules become highly packed with adult-supervised or adult-driven activities.

Although most highly scheduled children are thriving,2 some are reacting to the associated pressures with anxiety and other signs of increased stress.454653 In this regard, highly scheduled children have less time for free, child-driven, creative play,45464754 which offers benefits that may be protective against the effects of pressure and stress.4554 There is evidence that childhood and adolescent depression is on the rise through the college years.5560 Although there are certainly many factors involved, and a direct link between the early pressure-filled intense preparation for a high-achieving adulthood and these mental health concerns cannot be made on the basis of current research, it is important that we consider the possibility of this linkage. We can be certain that in some families, the protective influences of both play and high-quality family time are negatively affected by the current trends toward highly scheduling children. As trusted child advocates, pediatric health professionals are ideally suited to help parents consider the appropriate balance between preparing for the future and living fully in the present through play, child-centered organized activities, and rich parent-child interaction. It is likely that the balance that needs to be achieved will be different for every child on the basis of the child's academic needs, temperament, environment, and the family's needs. Because there are so many forces that influence the trend toward focusing on future preparation, it is important that parents have a medical home that can reinforce the importance of some of the basic, tried-and-true aspects of child rearing. There may be as many explanations for the current trends as there are families, but several key factors that have led to decreased free play should be considered.

1. There are more families with a single head of household or 2 working parents and fewer multigenerational households in which grandparents and extended family members can watch the children. Therefore, fewer families have available adult supervision in the home during the workday, which makes it necessary for children to be in child care or other settings in which they can be monitored by adults throughout the day.61 Organized after-school activities and academic enrichment opportunities offer valuable alternatives to children who might otherwise be left with minimal or no adult supervision.
2. Many parents have learned how to become increasingly efficient in balancing work and home schedules. They wish to make the most effective use of limited time with their children and believe that facilitating their children to have every opportunity is the best use of that time. Some may use some of the standards of efficiency and productivity they have mastered at work to judge their own effectiveness as parents; this is sometimes referred to as the professionalization of parenthood.51 This phenomenon may create guilt in parents who find it difficult to balance competing demands after a taxing workday. Parents who understand that high-interaction, at-home activities (eg, reading or playing with children) present opportunities for highly effective parenting may feel less stress than those who feel compelled to arrange out-of-home opportunities.
3. Parents receive messages from a variety of sources stating that good parents actively build every skill and aptitude their child might need from the earliest ages. They are deluged in parenting magazines and in the media with a wide range of enrichment tools and activities that tout their ability to produce super-achieving children. They read about parents who go to extreme efforts, at great personal sacrifice, to make sure their children participate in a variety of athletic and artistic opportunities. They hear other parents in the neighborhood talk about their overburdened schedules and recognize it is the culture and even expectation of parents.
4. The college-admissions process has become much more rigorous in recent years, largely because of a baby boom hitting the college years.

Parents receive the message that if their children are not well prepared, well balanced, and high-achieving, they will not get a desired spot in higher education. Even parents who wish to take a lower-key approach to child rearing fear slowing down when they perceive everyone else is on the fast track.6263 Children are encouraged to build a college resume through both academic excellence and a wide variety of activities and volunteer efforts starting at younger ages. In some cases, parents feel pressured to help their child build a strong resume.

5. In response to the increasingly rigorous college-admissions process, many secondary schools are judged by the rates in which their students are accepted by the most prestigious centers of higher learning. Partly in response to this, many students have been encouraged to carry increasingly rigorous academic schedules, including multiple advanced-placement courses. In addition, many students are taking preparation courses for standardized entrance examinations. These students are left with less free time because of the home preparatory time needed for their classes.
6. The pressure for admission to select schools begins for some families long before college. Selection for private preschool programs can even be competitive, and parents may need to consider how best to "package" their preschoolers.
7. There is a national trend to focus on the academic fundamentals of reading and arithmetic. This trend, spearheaded by the No Child Left Behind Act of 2001, is a reaction to the unacceptable educational performance of America's children in some educational settings. One of the practical effects of the trend is decreased time left during the school day for other academic subjects, as well as recess, creative arts, and physical education.3839 This trend may have implications for the social and emotional development of children and adolescents.33 In addition, many after-school child care programs prioritize an extension of academics and homework completion over organized play, free play, and physical activity.
8. The decrease in free play can also be explained by children being passively entertained through television or computer/video games. In sharp contrast to the health benefits of active, creative play and the known developmental benefits of an appropriate level of organized activities, there is ample evidence that this passive entertainment is not protective and, in fact, has some harmful effects.
9. In many communities, children cannot play safely outside of the home unless they are under close adult supervision and protection. This is particularly true in areas that are unsafe because of increased violence or other environmental dangers.

It would be wrong to assume that the current trends are a problem for all children; some excel with a highly driven schedule. Because we need skilled young people to be well prepared to be tomorrow's leaders, we must recognize the advantages to the increased exposures and enriched academics some of our children are receiving. In fact, many of our children, particularly those in poverty, should receive more enrichment activities. But even children who are benefiting from this enrichment still need some free unscheduled time for creative growth, self-reflection, and decompression and would profit from the unique developmental benefits of child-driven play. However, for some children, this hurried lifestyle is a source of stress and anxiety and may even contribute to depression.4546 Increased pressure to achieve is likely to manifest in school avoidance and somatic symptoms.6972 The challenge for society, schools, and parents is to strike the balance that allows all children to reach their potential without pushing them beyond their personal comfort limits and while allowing them personal free playtime.

It appears that the increased pressures of adolescence have left some young people less equipped to manage the transition toward the college years. Many student health services and counseling centers on college campuses have not been able to keep pace with the increased need for mental health services, and surveys have substantiated this need by reporting an increase in depression and anxiety among college students.5759 A survey by the American College Health Association reported that 61% of college students had feelings of hopelessness during the previous academic year, 45% felt so depressed they had trouble functioning, and 9% suffered suicidal ideation.57 Several studies have linked feelings of anxiety and depression with that of perfectionism and an overly critical self-evaluation.7277Other studies have linked this perfectionism with highly critical parents who instill pressures to excel.7882 Perfectionism is challenging to the individual and has a broader effect cn society because it may stifle creativity and unencumbered thinking.83 There are no longitudinal studies that directly link intense preparation for adulthood during childhood to this rise in mental health needs, and there certainly are other causes, but some experts believe today's pressured lifestyle is an important contributor.

Children may also have received an unintended message from this hurried, intense preparation for adulthood. They may have learned that the end-point goal—the best school or the best job—must be reached at all costs. High schools, colleges, and universities throughout the country are reporting that more students may be cheating to achieve the desired end result of a superior grade.8586 Despite grade inflation over the last decades, many teachers report increased stress in students when they achieve less-than-perfect scores.8789 This competitive era may be producing a minority of young people so intensely worried about the appearance of high achievement that they will forsake core values such as fairness and honesty for the sake of acquiring good grades.

FAMILY CONSIDERATIONS

Some families whose children are highly scheduled may also suffer. Adults who may already be burdened by work responsibilities and maintaining a household find themselves sacrificing their downtime because they need to arrange activities and transport children between appointments.4547 In addition, because of the pressures they feel to meet every one of the needs they perceive (or are told) their child requires to excel, they may feel inadequate and ultimately have less personal satisfaction in parenting.5152 Most importantly, parents lose the opportunity for perhaps the highest-quality time with their children. Some of the best interactions occur during downtime—just talking, preparing meals together, and working on a hobby or art project, playing sports together, or being fully immersed in child-centered play.

As parents prepare their children for the future, they cannot know precisely which skills each will need for the workforce. With added anxiety over their inability to adequately predict the future, they become susceptible to the promises of success and full preparation offered by all of the special enrichment programs and vulnerable to the belief that if their children are at least exposed to everything, they will have the best chance to be prepared. Although no one can be sure what skills will be needed, certain character traits will produce children capable of navigating an increasingly complex world as they grow older.

These traits include confidence, competence or the ability to master the environment, and a deep-seated connectedness to and caring about others that create the love, safety, and security that children need to thrive. In addition, to be resilient—to remain optimistic and be able to rebound from adversity—young people need the essential character traits of honesty, generosity, decency, tenacity, and compassion. Children are most likely to gain all of these essential traits of resiliency within a home in which parents and children have time to be together and to look to each other for positive support and unconditional love.9095Many families are successfully navigating a wide variety of commitments without sacrificing high-quality parent-child time,2 but some families' ability to maintain essential parent-child time may be compromised by this hurried lifestyle. In these families, overscheduling may lead to less emotionally competent, well-buffered children.

WHAT ARE THE SOLUTIONS?

Because there are at least several causes for the decreased amount of child-directed play, there is no single position that child advocates should take. For example, in the case of a child who is economically disadvantaged and does not reside in a safe neighborhood, it may be unwise to simply propose more child-centered play. Although parents can be encouraged to optimize conditions for this kind of play in the home, there must be broad societal responses that address poverty, social inequities, and violence before we can advise parents to allow unsupervised play. In addition, for children in poverty, enhanced child care services, early community-based education (eg, Head Start), increased academic programming, more enrichment activities, and greater opportunities for community-based adult-supervised activities are warranted. Some of the needed solutions for this group of disadvantaged children remain beyond the scope of this article and are raised here to emphasize that the suggestions offered here need to be individualized; one size does not fit all.

For all children, however, advocates need to promote the implementation of those strategies known to promote healthy youth development and resiliency. Some of those strategies are community based, and others are school based, but many reside within the family. They are rooted in the deep connection that develops when parents engage with their children.929395 Play remains an ideal venue for parents to engage fully, and child professionals must reinforce the value of this play. Some play must remain entirely child driven, with parents either not present or as passive observers, because play builds some of the individual assets children need to develop and remain resilient.

Parents need to feel supported to not passively accept the media and advertising messages that suggest there are more valuable means of promoting success and happiness in children than the tried, trusted, and traditional methods of play and family togetherness. Purveyors of these special programs should be encouraged to produce long-term evidence that define how their products/strategies produce more successful children. In parallel, we would encourage independent researchers to evaluate both the benefits and problems associated with these enrichment tools. Researchers should also continue to explore the type and quantity of activities that are likely to be enriching for children with different needs.

Colleges are seeing a generation of students who appear to be manifesting increased signs of depression, anxiety, perfectionism, and stress. They should clarify their messages about the type of students they seek in the face of widespread folklore that they seek only super-achieving students. Colleges certainly seek a physically and emotionally healthy student body with the character traits that support learning. Colleges could reduce the stress levels of young people and their parents if they offered clear, more realistic expectations about the type of students they seek and helped families to understand that there is a match for each reasonably prepared student. In addition, colleges should address the myth that desirable students are those who excel in every area. In the adult world, people rarely excel in more than 1 or 2 areas, while well-balanced individuals enjoy several others. Colleges should recognize the possibility that when children believe that they must excel in all areas to gain admission, they might respond to those perceived and unrealistic expectations with stress and anxiety.6263

ADVICE FOR PEDIATRICIANS*

In the midst of so many conflicting messages about what parents should do to prepare their child for what is perceived to be an increasingly complicated, competitive world, pediatricians have a natural role to serve as caring, objective child professionals with whom parents can discuss their approach to child rearing and reflect on their own desires for their children. Because pediatricians have a unique and important role in promoting the physical, emotional, and social well-being of children and adolescents, it is important that they promote strategies that will support children to be resilient and to reduce excessive stressors in their lives.

- Pediatricians can promote free play as a healthy, essential part of childhood. They should recommend that all children are afforded ample, unscheduled, independent, nonscreen time to be creative, to reflect, and to decompress. They should emphasize that although parents can certainly monitor play for safety, a large proportion of play should be child driven rather than adult directed.
- Pediatricians should emphasize the advantages of active play and discourage parents from the overuse of passive entertainment (eg, television and computer games).
- Pediatricians should emphasize that active child-centered play is a time-tested way of producing healthy, fit young bodies.
- Pediatricians should emphasize the benefits of "true toys" such as blocks and dolls, with which children use their imagination fully, over passive toys that require limited imagination.
- Pediatricians can educate families regarding the protective assets and increased resiliency developed through free play and some unscheduled time.
- Pediatricians can reinforce that parents who share unscheduled spontaneous time with their children and who play with their children are being wonderfully supportive, nurturing, and productive.
- Pediatricians can discuss that, although very well intentioned, arranging the finest opportunities for their children may not be parents' best opportunity for influence and that shuttling their children between numerous activities may not be the best quality time. Children will be poised for success, basking in the knowledge that their parents absolutely and unconditionally love them. This love and attention is best demonstrated when parents serve as role models and family members make time to cherish one another: time to be together, to listen, and to talk, nothing more and nothing less. Pediatricians can

remind parents that the most valuable and useful character traits that will prepare their children for success arise not from extracurricular or academic commitments but from a firm grounding in parental love, role modeling, and guidance.

- Pediatricians should be a stable force, reminding parents that the cornerstones of parenting—listening, caring, and guiding through effective and developmentally appropriate discipline—and sharing pleasurable time together are the true predictors of childhood, and they serve as a springboard toward a happy, successful adulthood.
- Pediatricians should help parents evaluate the claims made by marketers and advertisers about the products or interventions designed to produce super-children.
- Pediatricians should emphasize the proven benefits of reading to their children, even at very early ages.
- Pediatricians can be available to parents as sounding boards to help parents evaluate the specific needs of their child in terms of promoting resiliency, developing confidence and competence, and ultimately enhancing that child's trajectory toward a successful future.
- Pediatricians can support parents to organize playgroups beginning at an early preschool age of approximately 2.5 to 3 years, when many children move from parallel play to cooperative play in the process of socialization.
- Pediatricians can advocate for developing "safe spaces" in underresourced neighborhoods, perhaps by opening school, library, or community facilities to be used by children and their parents after school hours and on weekends.
- Pediatricians can educate themselves about appropriate resources in their own community that foster play and healthy child development and have this information available to share with parents.
- Pediatricians should support children having an academic schedule that is appropriately challenging and extracurricular exposures that offer appropriate balance. What is appropriate has to be determined individually for each child on the basis of their unique needs, skills, and temperament, not on the basis of what may be overly pressurized or competitive community standards or a perceived need to gain college admissions.
- Pediatricians should encourage parents to allow children to explore a variety of interests in a balanced way without feeling pressured to excel in each area. Pediatricians should encourage parents to avoid conveying the unrealistic expectation that each young person needs to excel in multiple areas to be considered successful or prepared to

compete in the world. In parallel, they should promote balance in those youth who are strongly encouraged to become expert in only 1 area (eg, a particular sport or musical instrument) to the detriment of having the opportunity to explore other areas of interest.

- As parents choose child care and early education programs for their children, pediatricians can reinforce the importance of choosing settings that offer more than "academic preparedness." They should be guided to also pay attention to whether the settings attend to the social and emotional developmental needs of the children.
- Pediatricians can join with other child professionals and parents to advocate for educational settings that promote optimal academic, cognitive, physical, social, and emotional development for children and youth.
- Pediatricians should assess their patients for the manifestations of stress, anxiety, and depression in family-centered interviews for children and privately conducted interviews with adolescents.
- Because stress often manifests with physical sensations, pediatricians should be highly sensitized to stress as an underlying cause of somatic illness.
- Pediatricians should refer to appropriate mental health professionals when children or their parents show signs of excessive stress, anxiety, or depression.

Play is a cherished part of childhood that offers children important developmental benefits and parents the opportunity to fully engage with their children. However, multiple forces are interacting to effectively reduce many children's ability to reap the benefits of play. As we strive to create the optimal developmental milieu for children, it remains imperative that play be included along with academic and social-enrichment opportunities and that safe environments be made available to all children. Additional research is needed to explore the appropriate balance of play, academic enrichment, and organized activities for children with different temperaments and social, emotional, intellectual, and environmental needs.

The importance of play and recreation in the life of every child has long been acknowledged by the international community, as evidenced by the proclamation in the 1959 Declaration of the Rights of the Child: "The child shall have full opportunity for play and recreation [...]; society and the public authorities shall endeavour to promote the enjoyment of this right" (art. 7). This proclamation was further strengthened in the Convention on the Rights of the Child (the Convention) of 1989 which explicitly states in article 31 that "States Parties recognize the right of the child to rest and leisure, to engage in play and recreational activities appropriate to the age of the child and and to participate freely in cultural life and the arts."

However, based on its reviews of the implementation of the rights of the child under the Convention, the Committee is concerned by the poor recognition given by States to the rights contained in article 31. Poor recognition of their significance in the lives of children results in lack of investment in appropriate provisions, weak or non-existent protective legislation and the invisibility of children in national and local-level planning. In general, where investment is made, it is in the provision of structured and organized activities, but equally important is the need to create time and space for children to engage in spontaneous play, recreation and creativity, and to promote societal attitudes that support and encourage such activity.

The Committee is particularly concerned about the difficulties faced by particular categories of children in relation to enjoyment and conditions of equality of the rights defined in article 31, especially girls, poor children, children with disabilities, indigenous children, children belonging to minorities, among others.

Furthermore, profound changes in the world are having a major impact on children's opportunities to enjoy the rights provided for in article 31. The urban population, especially in developing countries, is increasing significantly, as is violence worldwide in all its forms – at home, in schools, in mass media, in the streets. The implications, along with the commercialization of play provisions, are influencing the ways children engage in recreation, as well as in cultural and artistic activities. For many children in both rich and poor countries, child labour, domestic work or increasing educational demands serve to reduce the time available for the enjoyment of these rights.

This general comment has been developed to address these concerns, raise the profile, awareness and understanding among States of the centrality of the rights in article 31 in the life and development of every child, and urge them to elaborate measures to ensure their implementation. The rights in article 31 have universal application in the diversity of communities and societies in the world and respect the value of all cultural traditions and forms. Every child should be able to enjoy these rights regardless of where he or she lives, his or her cultural background or his or her parental status. This general comment only touches tangentially on the issue of sport, as it is a major issue in its own right. In respect of cultural life, the general comment focuses primarily on aspects related to creative or artistic activities, rather than the broader definition embraced in article 30 on the right of the child to enjoy his or her own culture.

The present general comment seeks to enhance the understanding of the importance of article 31 for children's well-being and development; to ensure respect for and strengthen the application of the rights under article 31, as well as other rights in the Convention, and to highlight the implications for the determination of:

(a) Consequent obligations of States in the elaboration of all implementation measures, strategies and programmes aimed at the realization and full implementation of the rights defined in article 31;

(b) The role and responsibilities of the private sector, including companies working in the areas of recreation, cultural and artistic activities, as well as civil society organizations providing such services for children;

(c) Guidelines for all individuals working with children, including parents, on all actions undertaken in the area of play and recreation.

Our Charter for Children's Play describes play as: 'what children and young people do when they follow their own ideas and interests, in their own way, and for their own reasons.' Play has also frequently been described as 'what children and young people do when they are not being told what to do by adults'. Having time and space to play gives children the opportunity to meet and socialise with their friends, keeps them physically active, and gives the freedom to choose what they want to do. Research shows that play has many benefits for children, families and the wider community, as well as improving health and quality of life. Recent research suggests that children's access to good play provision can:

- increase their self-awareness, self-esteem, and self-respect
- improve and maintain their physical and mental health
- give them the opportunity to mix with other children
- allow them to increase their confidence through developing new skills
- promote their imagination, independence and creativity
- offer opportunities for children of all abilities and backgrounds to play together
- provide opportunities for developing social skills and learning
- build resilience through risk taking and challenge, problem solving, and dealing with new and novel situations
- provide opportunities to learn about their environment and the wider community.

Evidence is also available that outlines wider benefits of play provision for families and communities, suggesting that:

- parents can feel more secure knowing that their children are happy, safe and enjoying themselves
- families benefit from healthier, happier children
- buildings and facilities used by play services are frequently seen as a focal point for communities
- it offers opportunities for social interaction for the wider community and supports the development of a greater sense of community spirit, promoting social cohesion

- public outside spaces have an important role in the everyday lives of children and young people, especially as a place for meeting friends
- parks and other green spaces are popular with adults taking young children out to play and for older children and young people to spend time together.

Children's right to play is a human right

On 1 February 2013 the United Nations Committee on the Rights of the Child adopted a General Comment that clarifies for governments worldwide the meaning and importance of Article 31 of the Convention on the Right of the Child. A General Comment is an official statement that elaborates on the meaning of an aspect of the United Nations Convention on the Rights of the Child that seems to require further interpretation or emphasis. The aim of the General Comment is to raise the importance of an Article and increase accountability among countries that have signed up to the Convention.\ In the United Nations Convention on the Rights of a Child, it states that 'play' is the right of all children. This reinforces the value placed on 'play' both here in Australia and internationally.

You will often hear educators use the terms 'play-based learning' or discussing the importance of play in early childhood. At The Scots College, our early learning program is inspired by the Reggio Emilia education philosophy which models a partnership with children, teachers and parents. At Scots, the Early Years Centre is a place of adventure, growth and learning. Our aim is to support the boys' natural curiosity, eagerness to learn and their love of communication with others. Our learning environment is designed to provoke curiosity and constantly challenge boys' thinking.

Here are our top 5 reasons why play is important in the early years:

1. Developing secure attachments: Through play children begin to foster secure attachments to their peers, families and educators. Strong relationships are the key to children feeling safe, secure and supported, which impacts their learning, happiness and self-esteem. Parents are a child's first teacher and much of that teaching happens through play.
2. The effect of play on brain development: Play has intellectual and cognitive benefits for the brain and it is believed that play can in fact shape the structural development of the brain.
3. Development of learning skills: Through play children develop important learning and life skills such as exploring, identifying, negotiating, risk-taking and imagining.
4. Speech and language development through play: During play children are watching, listening, exploring and imitating. Even when your child is playing silently, they are learning important information and exposed to new vocabulary that they will carry with them and use later.

5. The ability to regulate their behaviour: As children play they are learning skills such as how to concentrate on a task, how to take turns and how to share. In turn these will aid them in regulating their behaviour and emotions.

Play leads to enhanced school adjustment and, most importantly, a love of learning. When children play and learn new things they discover that learning can be fun and go on to view learning as something enjoyable, rather than a chore.

The right to play is central to childhood

Little did I know seven years ago that play would form such an important part of my life as Commissioner. My journey on play began in my first few months in post. In fact, the first report I published as Commissioner was all about children with disabilities' access to play. It was the culmination of a project which my predecessor had begun, analysing the content of local authorities' play strategies and gathering the views of children and young people with disabilities.

Seven years on, I am still acutely aware of how important play is to children and young people. During my final year in post, I was lucky to be appointed to a working group assisting on the drafting of a general comment for the UN Committee on the Rights of the Child which wanted State Parties across the world to give greater attention to children's rights to play and leisure activities in Article 31 of the UN Convention on the Rights of the Child. Here in Wales and across the world, the publication of the General Comment on Article 31 provides an opportunity for every child in every school, in every community, to exercise the right to play. Whilst the rights embodied in Article 31 may not necessarily be at the forefront of policy makers' minds, they are central to childhood itself. They contribute to the joy, fun and sheer pleasure of growing up. Furthermore, their implementation will contribute to children's development, not only as individuals, but also as competent members of society aware of the perspectives of others, and capable of cooperation and conflict resolution.

Wales and the Welsh Government have taken great strides in promoting and implementing play as the right of every child and young person and are viewed very highly on the international stage. But I can't help but think that whilst we have ground-breaking legislation here in Wales, it's having little or no immediate impact on the ground for children and young people. By way of an example I'm going full circle, back to children and young people with disabilities' access to play. The Children and Families (Wales) Measure 2010 saw Wales become the first country in the world to establish a duty in relation to play. This Measure introduced a Play Sufficiency Duty, which comes in two parts: the first involves local authorities in carrying out Play Sufficiency Assessments. I reviewed them all, focussing in particular on children and young people from disadvantaged communities and households and on children and young people with disabilities. The provision of play and recreation opportunities for children and young people with disabilities, as reported in these Play Sufficiency Assessments, is diverse, with a number of local authorities even having difficulties identifying how many children and young people with disabilities resided within their authority. There is some wonderful work ongoing, with some authorities evidencing a framework of policy and practice firmly directed at delivering on Article 31 for children with disabilities. But, the picture remains inconsistent.

Austerity is also hitting us hard in Wales and is having a direct impact on the implementation of Article 31. One devastating example of the impact was shared with me via film by a group of young people in rural west Wales. It told the story, a true story, of how a new housing development destroyed a play space. The play area was a muddy bank. A piece of land used by children and young people extensively. At no point during the planning process for this new housing development did anybody consult with children and young people. The new housing has no play provision as part of the development and the one area that children used has been flattened by bulldozers and built over. The film is powerful and demonstrates that these children and young people should have had a say in the planning process and they should have been heard.

The UN Convention on the Rights of the Child is embedded in Welsh law. This 'ground-breaking' legislation, was meant to 'make a positive change to the way in which all support and services for children and young people in Wales will be designed and delivered in the future'. This legislative measure provides me with the framework to hold adults to account if children report a limiting of play opportunities. Wales has made a bold and positive commitment. Let's make sure legislation made in Wales and across Europe makes a practical, positive difference to each and every child, whatever their circumstance.

Although play is important for people of all ages (witness the current fitness craze for adults, grown-ups who are 'just playing'), it is especially meaningful and important for young children. Actually play is their work, and they give a tremendous amount of energy and effort to it. If you doubt this, just watch for a few minutes as a 1-year-old struggles to get a ring on a color cone, or stand in the background as a 3-year-old tries to fit a puzzle piece into the proper spot. Or, if you roll a ball back and forth to a 2-year-old, just expect to be the first one to want to quit the game; your partner often wants to go on and on. There are at least three ways in which play is important for young children: skill development, social development, and imagination and creativity. Learning occurs in all areas of development as young children play—and the learning, too, is for keeps.

We can observe skill development as we watch young children play with their toys. When, as very young infants, they reach for and do something with a rattle, they learn to coordinate movements of their hands with what their eyes see. The great pediatrician, Dr. Arnold Gesell, once wrote that 'The mind of man is hand-made.' This statement recognizes the tremendous importance to a young child of having exciting objects to hold and listen to and feel and manipulate. And, as young children struggle to create a desired effect with a toy, they discover that it isn't always easy. They realize that there is perhaps a problem to be solved and that they have to practice to acquire and improve the skills necessary to achieve their goal.

Play with other children is critical for the development of social skills. At first adults are their most important playmates, but soon they become eager to interact with children of similar ages. And it is through such play that they learn how to get along with others: that hitting may get them a desired toy, but lose an equally desired friend; that the other children have wants, just as they do; that sharing and kindnesses bring more rewards than snatching and pushing.

Play is the crucible in which imagination and creativity can be cultivated and expressed. The child who pretends to be a cowboy, a mother, a fairy, a firefighter is demonstrating some knowledge of these roles and is working through his or her own ideas about all that they entail. And the child who 'spanks' a doll while saying, 'I don't want you to do that again,' is releasing some of his or her own aggressive impulses via this make-believe route instead of trying to mount a direct attack on another person. Play provides just such an outlet for young children.

Children's right to learn in their own languages

Education is power and language is the key to accessing that power. A child who thrives at school and develops self-esteem and pride will have better employment opportunities and is more likely to realise his or her potential. Ethnicity, language and culture aredeeply intertwined. They are also intertwined with inequity, discrimination andconflict. Since most countries in the world are multiethnic and multilingual,opinions about provision of education, curriculum content, and the language ofteaching and learning are often fiercely held and hotly debated.

The languages of elite groups or former colonisers often dominatethe languages of others, particularly in official settings like the school. Yetit is now well established that when a child begins learning in his or herfirst language (also known as a home language or mother tongue) that child ismore likely to succeed academically and is better able to learn additionallanguages. A child who begins learning in a second (or foreign) languagewill, at least initially, find learning anything that much harder. The barrierof school language is often enough for children not to enrol in school or, ifthey do, for them to experience difficulties, become discouraged, repeat years,or drop out of school.

What arethe challenges?

With almost7,000 languages worldwide, how realistic is it to expect every child to havethe opportunity to begin school in his or her first language? How difficult(and expensive) is it for a ministry or department of education to developwriting systems and provide curricula, teachers and materials for everylanguage in the country? If families of marginalised groups speaking non-dominantlanguages want their children to learn in a dominant language, shouldpedagogical arguments override their views? Each articlein this issue of 'id21 insightseducation' demonstrates the value for children (particularly those frommarginalised groups) of learning in their first language, while recognising the challenges of turning sound educational principles intopractice.

What are the benefits?

The United Nations Convention on theRights of the Child states that all children have the right to education (Article 28) the right to learn and usethe language of their family (Article30). Tove Skutnabb-Kangas argues that wheneducation is in a language the child doesn't know, whether due to family choiceor lack of an alternative, this is violating the child's rights. She alsocontends that if languages are not protected, they will disappear (estimatedrates vary), along with the knowledge held by their speakers.

Bolivia's successful language model, Intercultural andBilingual Education, described by XavierAlbó, shows that indigenous children are lesslikely to repeat years and more likely to perform well. Evidence fromGuinea-Bissau, Niger and Mozambique, gathered by Carol Benson, shows that mother tongue-based primary schooling isparticularly beneficial for girls and leads to increased parental involvementin their education, reduced exploitation by male teachers and improvededucational access and performance. Now that child labor had been effectively eradicated in parts of the world, the movement turned to other things, but it again stalled when World War II broke out and children and women began to enter the work force once more. With millions of adults at war, the children were needed to help keep the country running. In Europe, children served as couriers, intelligence collectors, and other underground resistance workers in opposition to Hitler's regime.

Natural rights

The concept of children having particular rights is a relatively new one. Traditional attitudes towards children tended to consider them as mere extensions of the household and 'owned' by their parents and/or legal guardian, who exerted absolute parental control. Views began to change during the Enlightenment, when tradition was increasingly challenged and the value of individual autonomy and natural rights began to be asserted. The Foundling Hospital in London was founded in 1741 as a children's home for the "education and maintenance of exposed and deserted young children". Thomas Spence, an English political radical wrote the first modern defence of the natural rights of children in The Rights of Infants, published in 1796.

Social reform

With the onset of the Industrial Revolution, children as young as six began to be employed in the factories and coal mines in often inhumane conditions with long hours and little pay. During the early 19th century this exploitation began to attract growing opposition. The terrible conditions of the poor urban children was exposed to liberal middle-class opinion, notably by the author Charles Dickens in his novel Oliver Twist. Social reformers, such as the Lord Shaftesbury, began to mount a vigorous campaign against this practice. Ameliorating legislation was achieved with a series of Factory Acts passed during the 19th century, where working hours for children were limited and they were no longer permitted to work during the night. Children younger than nine were not allowed to work and those between 9-16 were limited to 16 hours per day. Factories were also required to provide education to the apprentices in reading, writing and arithmetic for the first four years.

An influential social reformer was Mary Carpenter, who campaigned on behalf of neglected children who had turned to juvenile delinquency. In 1851 she proposed the establishment of three types of schools; free day schools for the general population, industrial schools for those in need and reformatory schools for young offenders. She was consulted by the drafters of educational bills, and she was invited to give evidence before House of Commons committees. In 1852 she established a reformatory school at Bristol. In the United States, the Children's Rights Movement began with the orphan train. In the big cities, when a child's parents died or were extremely poor, the child frequently had to go to work to support himself and/or his family. Boys generally became factory or coal workers, and girls became prostitutes or saloon girls, or else went to work in a sweat shop. All of these jobs paid only starvation wages. Her experiences there and later in Russia, led her to believe that the rights of a child needed be especially protected and enforced, and her stipulations consisted of the following criteria:

1. The child must be given the means requisite for its normal development, both materially and spiritually.
2. The child that is hungry must be fed, the child that is sick must be nursed, the child that is backward must be helped, the delinquent

child must be reclaimed, and the orphan and the waif must be sheltered and succored.

3. The child must be the first to receive relief in times of distress.
4. The child must be put in a position to earn a livelihood, and must be protected against every form of exploitation.
5. The child must be brought up in the consciousness that its talents must be devoted to the service of its fellow men.

This manifesto was adopted by the International Save the Children Union and endorsed by the League of Nations General Assembly in 1924 as the World Child Welfare Charter.In 1925, the first International Child Welfare Congress was held in Geneva, where the Declaration was widely discussed and supported by organisations and governments.

Declaration of the Rights of the Child

The SCIU also pressed the newly formed United Nations in 1946 to adopt the World Child Welfare Charter. This was achieved in 1959, when the United Nations General Assemblyadopted an expanded version as the Declaration of the Rights of the Child. Its main provisions are:

- protection rights: the right to be protected against maltreatment and neglect, the right to be protected from all forms of exploitation
- provision rights: the right to food and to health care, the right to education, the right to benefit from social security
- participation rights: the right to act in certain circumstances and the right to be involved in decision-making

From the formation of the United Nations to the present day, the Children's Rights Movement has become global in focus. Children around the world still suffer from forced child labor, genital mutilation, military service, and sex trafficking. Several international organizations have rallied to the assistance of children. These include Save the Children, Free the Children, and the Children's Defense Fund. The Child Rights Information Network, or CRIN, formed in 1983, is a group of 1,600 non-governmental organizations from around the world which advocate for the implementation of the Convention on the Rights of the Child. Organizations report on their countries' progress towards implementation, as do governments that have ratified the Convention. Every 5 years reporting to the United Nations Committee on the Rights of the Child is required for governments.

Children's rights by country

Many countries have created an institute of children's rights commissioner or ombudsman, the first being Norway in 1981. Others include Finland, Sweden, and Ukraine, which was the first country worldwide to install a child in that post in 2005.

Argentina

In 2005, in order to implement the UN Convention on the Rights of the Child, national Law for the Integral Protection of Children and Adolescents was enacted. This not only allows for protective measures for children, but also created the groundwork for a juvenile justice system. This system allows for children to be integrated back into society and established tactics to protect children from abuse and exploitation.

Australia

Australia is a participant to all significant treaties that impact on children's rights. The rights and protection of children are governed by both Federal and state and territory law.

Brazil

Brazil is a founding member of the UN and a signatory of the Universal Declaration of Human Rights, which was adopted by General Assembly resolution in 1948. The Universal Declaration of the Rights of the Child emphasizes that motherhood and childhood are entitled to special care and that children born out of wedlock are allowed the same social protection. In 1990, Brazil approved the UN Convention on the Rights of the Child and fully incorporated it onto Brazil's positive law.

China

China has ratified many international documents with regard to children's rights protection, including the 1989 Convention on Rights of the Child, the Optional Protocol to the Convention on Rights of Child on the Sale of Children, Child Prostitution, and Child Pornography 2000, the Worst Forms of Child Labor Convention 1999, and The Hague Convention on the Protection of Children and Cooperation in Respect of Intercountry Adoption 1993.

France

France is in cooperation with all the major treaties dealing with children rights. It has in place several mechanisms to monitor the implementation of the 1989 Convention on the Rights of the Child, in particular, an ombudsman for children.

Germany

Germany is in agreement with the global conventions that protect the rights of the child. However, Germany prefers to interpret these according to the principles of European agreements, specifically the European Human Rights Convention and also in accordance with German Constitutional guarantees.

Greece

Greece has various laws and a number of measures and services to promote and advance the rights of children. In 2002, the Greek Parliament adopted a new law on human trafficking; in 2003 the juvenile system was reformed; in 2006 an additional law was created to combat intra-family violence which states a prohibition of corporal punishment of children.

United States

There is a long history of children's rights in the U.S. Many children's rights advocates in the U.S. today advocate for a smaller agenda than their international peers. According to the U.S, for the purposes of the present Convention, a child means every human being below the age of eighteen years unless under the law applicable to the child, majority is attained earlier. Groups predominately focus on child abuse and neglect, child fatalities, foster care, youth aging out of foster care, preventing foster care placement, and adoption.A longstanding movement promoting youth rights in the United States has made substantial gains in the past. Refer to the Convention of the Rights of a Child.

United Kingdom

The Children's Rights Movement assert that it is the case that children have rights which adults, states and government have a responsibility to uphold. The UK maintains a position that UNCRC is not legally enforceable and is hence 'aspirational' only - albeit a 2003 ECHR ruling states: "The human rights of children and the standards to which all governments must aspire in realizing these rights for all children are set out in the Convention on the Rights of the Child." (Extract from Sahin v Germany, Grand Chamber judgment of the ECHR, July 8, 2003). 18 years after ratification, the four Children's Commissioners in the devolved administrations have united in calling for adoption of the Convention into domestic legislation, making children's rights legally enforceable..

The United Nations Convention on the Rights of the Child has 54 articles, each outlining a different right. They cover four different groupings of rights; survival, protection, development and participation. The Convention establishes a standard premise for the children's rights movement. It has been ratified by all but two countries; the United States and South Sudan. The US administration under Bush opposed ratifying the Convention, stating that there were "serious political and legal concerns that it conflicts with US policies on the central role of parents, sovereignty, and state and local law." The Convention is supplemented by the Optional Protocol on the Involvement of Children in Armed Conflict (against military use of children) and the Optional Protocol on the Sale of Children, Child Prostitution and Child Pornography (against sale of children, child prostitution and child pornography).

Children in power

Presently, there are at least thirty countries that have some kind of non-adult structure of parliament, whether nationally or in cities, villages or schools. Many children's parliaments, especially in wealthier nations, are oriented more toward children's education in politics than toward the actual exercise of power in adult political systems. On the other hand, some children's parliaments do exercise a degree of political power. One of the first children's parliaments, set up in the 1990s in village schools in Rajasthan, India, involves children aged six to fourteen electing child representatives who have been able to make genuine differences for their communities. Some children's parliaments, such as in the city of Barra Mansa in Brazil, have extensive powers over children's issues and control parts of the government budget.

There are also private institutions which are largely governed by children, for instance democratic schools (including Sudbury schools). The GMC seeks to jointly promote global advocacy campaigns for child rights and accountability of governments vis-à-vis their children. The GMC was created as a result of the success of the Say Yes for Children campaign which led to the [UN Special Session on Children] in 2002 resolving to help mobilize citizens of every nation families, communities, civil society, organizations of every kind and children within an active, influential and united movement.

The objectives of the GMC are to:

- unite and coordinate organisations and people to influence public opinion and organise collective action;
- promote and support child participation;
- encourage political commitments and accountability.

The children's rights movement has existed since the early years of the twentieth century when individuals, public institutions and NGOs began to unite their efforts to improve the fate of children around the world. In recent years the movement has seen a dramatic growth and gained greater coherence with the drafting and entry into force of the Convention on the Rights of the Child (1989) passed on the 30th anniversary of the 'Declaration of the Rights of the Child'. Events following the adoption of the convention enhanced the significance of the movement even more, namely:

- the World Summit for Children in 1990.
- Graça Machel's study on the Impact of Armed Conflict on Children (1996)
- a series of global campaigns against landmines, child labour, sexual exploitation, and the use of child soldiers;
- the GMC Convening Committee for the Say Yes for Children campaign (2000), formally established the Global Movement for Children in 2002 bringing together some of the biggest organisations working with children.

- the UN General Assembly's Special Session on Children (2002).

At the UN General Assembly's Special Session on Children in 2002 the name Global Movement for Children (GMC) was first coined. The purpose of naming the Global Movement for Children was to help make visible to the world's leaders the thousands of organisations and millions of citizens, voters – and children themselves – who are today united in this cause. Nelson Mandela and Graça Machel launched the GMC at the United Nations and since then, it has brought together thousands of organisations in advocating for children rights. Over the years, the GMC has focused on the following issues:

- Girl's education
- Children and AIDS
- Violence against children
- Child survival
- Children on the move and child traffic

UN General Assembly resolution regarding the GMC

In 2002, the General Assembly of the United Nations agreed the following: Article 62: "We hereby recommit ourselves to spare no effort in continuing with the creation of a world fit for children, building on the achievements of the past decade and guided by the principles of first call for children. In solidarity with a broad range of partners, we will lead a Global Movement for Children that creates an unstoppable momentum for change." Article 62, Section D, A World Fit for Children, Report of the United Nations General Assembly Special Session on Children (A/S-27/19/Rev.1)

Convening committee

At present, the GMC is led by a coalition of the largest organisations and networks focused on children composed at a global level by ENDA Tiers Monde, Plan International,REDLAMYC, Save the Children, UNICEF and World Vision, which together make up the Convening Committee. At a regional level, the GMC is led by the Regional Platforms which are in turn integrated by national platforms of organisations working with child rights.

Focus of the convening committee

Child rights-based approach: the CC focuses on the realisation of child rights as defined by the Convention on the Rights of the Child.

- Children's participation: the best advocates for children are children themselves. Those who are marginalised, vulnerable or living in poverty are better able to understand how this affects their daily lives, and should be able to fully participate in planning and implementing solutions. Children have an active role in the GMC, mainly at the local and national levels but also at the international level.

- Gender equity: girls and boys have the same rights and the CC works for the attainment of such principle. This implies an approach that is gender sensitive and that pays particular attention to the rights of girls.
- Multisectoral and holistic approach: the group seeks to build partnerships with those existing national, regional and international coalitions advocating for children's rights.
- Institutional and long term reform: the organisations pay attention to advocacy. They focus on lobbying for institutional change to create the conditions for the full implementation of the Convention of the Rights of the Child.

From arights-based perspective, we know why it must happen. From a pedagogicalperspective, we know what should be done. From a practical perspective, thereare many success stories – from PapuaNew Guinea, Eritrea,Nigeria,Guatemala,Mali,Bolivia– demonstrating how it can work.

More is needed, however:

- Teachers, educators andnon-government organisations (NGOs) can increase awareness of and commitment tothe importance of language diversity and multilingualism in education.
- Donor agencies and NGOs can learnfrom the success stories and adapt them for countries without the same level ofpolitical support.
- Researchers need to find more effectiveways to convince policymakers and budget holders.
- Researchers can also raise the issuesat the annual international Education for All forum and monitor progress.
- National governments and donoragencies need to mobilise sufficient resources.

Approximately 1.38 billion people speak local languages – languages that are less well-known, without writtenforms and not used in formal education. This includes an estimated 221 millionschool-aged children. Mother tongue-based education can ensure a better qualityeducation for these children – a significant contribution towards Education forAll. Under the Bolsheviks, Russia became the first country in human history to provide free abortions to women in state run hospitals.

North America

Canada

Women's rights activism in Canada during the 19th and early 20th centuries focused on increasing women's role in public life, with goals including women's suffrage, increased property rights, increased access to education, and recognition of women as "persons" under the law. The Famous

Five were five Canadian women – Emily Murphy, Irene Marryat Parlby, Nellie Mooney McClung, Louise Crummy McKinney and Henrietta Muir Edwards – who, in 1927, asked the Supreme Court of Canada to answer the question, "Does the word 'Persons' in Section 24 of the British North America Act, 1867, include female persons?" in the case Edwards v. Canada (Attorney General). After Canada's Supreme Court summarized its unanimous decision that women are not such "persons", the judgment was appealed and overturned in 1929 by the British Judicial Committee of the Imperial Privy Council, at that time the court of last resort for Canada within the British Empire and Commonwealth.

United States

The Women's Christian Temperance Union (WCTU) was established in 1873 and championed women's rights, including advocating for prostitutes and for women's suffrage.Under the leadership of Frances Willard, "the WCTU became the largest women's organization of its day and is now the oldest continuing women's organization in the United States."

East Asia

Japan

The extent to which women could participate in Japanese society has varied over time and social classes. In the 8th century, Japan had women emperors, and in the 12th century (Heian period) women in Japan occupied a relatively high status, although still subordinated to men. From the late Edo period, the status of women declined. In the 17th century, the "Onna Daigaku", or "Learning for Women", by Confucianist author Kaibara Ekken, spelled out expectations for Japanese women, lowering significantly their status. During the Meiji period, industrialization and urbanization reduced the authority of fathers and husbands, but at the same time the Meiji Civil Code of 1898 denied women legal rights and subjugated them to the will of household heads.

From the mid 20th century the status of women improved greatly. Although Japan is often considered a very conservative country, it was in fact earlier than many European countries on giving women legal rights in the 20th century, as the 1947 Constitution of Japan provided a legal framework favorable to the advancement of women's equality in Japan. Japan for instance enacted women's suffrage in 1946, earlier than several European countries such as Switzerland (1971 at federal level; 1990 on local issues in the canton of Appenzell Innerrhoden), Portugal (1976 on equal terms with men, with restrictions since 1931), San Marino in 1959, Monaco in 1962, Andorra in 1970, and Liechtenstein in 1984.

Central Asia

Central Asian cultures largely remain patriarchal, however, since the fall of the former Soviet Union, the secular societies of the region have become more progressive to women's roles outside the traditional construct of being wholly subservient to men. In Mongolia, more women than men complete school and are higher earners as result. The UN Development Programme notes "significant progress" in gender equality in Kazakhstan but discrimination persists.Marriage by abduction remains a serious problem in this region; the practice of bride kidnapping is prevalent in Kyrgyzstan Kazakhstan, Turkmenistan, and Karakalpakstan, an autonomous region of Uzbekistan.

Oceania

Australia

The history of women's rights in Australia is a contradictory one: while Australia led the world in women's suffrage rights in the 19th century, it has been very slow in recognizing women's professional rights - it was not until 1966 that its marriage bar was removed. On the other hand, reforms which allowed women both to vote and stand for office in South Australia in the late 19th century were a cornerstone for women's political rights in other parts of the world. In this regard, Australia differs from other cultures, in that women's suffrage in Australia was one of the earliest objectives of the feminist movement there (beginning with South Australia and Western Australia) unlike other cultures, such as Eastern European cultures, where at the turn of the 20th century the feminist movement focused on labour rights, access to professions and education, rather than political rights. To this day, Australia has a quite low percentage of women in business executive roles compared to other countries with equivalent corporate structures.

Core concepts

Natural rights

17th century natural law philosophers in Britain and America, such as Thomas Hobbes, Jean-Jacques Rousseau and John Locke, developed the theory of natural rights in reference to ancient philosophers such as Aristotle and the Christian theologist Aquinas. Like the ancient philosophers, 17th century natural law philosophers defended slavery and an inferior status of women in law. Relying on ancient Greek philosophers, natural law philosophers argued that natural rights were not derived from god, but were "universal, self-evident, and intuitive", a law that could be found in nature. They believed that natural rights were self-evident to "civilised man" who lives "in the highest form of society". Natural rights derived from human nature, a concept first established by the ancient Greek philosopher Zeno of Citium in Concerning Human Nature. Zenon argued that each rational and civilized male Greek citizen had a "divine spark" or "soul" within him that existed independent of the body. Zeno founded the Stoic philosophy and the idea of a human nature was adopted by other Greek philosophers, and later natural lawphilosophers and western humanists. Aristotle developed the widely adopted idea of rationality, arguing that man was a "rational animal" and as such a natural power of reason. Concepts of human nature in ancient Greece depended on gender, ethnic, and other qualifications and 17th century natural law philosophers came to regard women along with children, slaves and non-whites, as neither "rational" nor "civilised".

Natural law philosophers claimed the inferior status of women was "common sense" and a matter of "nature". They believed that women could not be treated as equal due to their "inner nature". The views of 17th century natural law philosophers were opposed in the 18th and 19th century by evangelical natural theology philosophers such as William Wilberforce and Charles Spurgeon, who argued for the abolition of slavery and advocated for women to have rights equal to that of men. Modern natural law theorists, and advocates of natural rights, claim that all people have a human nature, regardless of gender, ethnicity or other qualifications, therefore all people have natural rights.

Equal employment

Employment rights for women include non-discriminatory access of women to jobs and equal pay. The rights of women and men to have equal pay and equal benefits for equal work were openly denied by the British Hong Kong Government up to the early 1970s, 1917–2009), President of the Hong Kong Chinese Civil Servants' Association (1965–68), contributed to the establishment of equal pay for men and women, including the right for married women to be permanent employees. Before this, the job status of a woman changed from permanent employee to temporary employee once she was married, thus losing the pension benefit. Some of them even lost their jobs. Since nurses were mostly women, this improvement of the rights of married women meant much to the nursing profession. In some European countries, married women could not work without the consent of their husbands until a few decades ago, for example in France until 1965 and in Spain until 1975. In addition, marriage bars, a practice adopted from the late 19th century to the 1970s across many countries, including Austria, Australia, Ireland, Canada, and Switzerland, restricted married women from employment in many professions.

A key issue towards insuring gender equality in the workplace is the respecting of maternity rights and reproductive rights of women.Maternity leave (and paternity leave in some countries) and parental leave are temporary periods of absence from employment granted immediately before and after childbirth in order to support the mother's full recovery and grant time to care for the baby. Different countries have different rules regarding maternity leave, paternity leave and parental leave. In the European Union (EU) the policies vary significantly by country, but the EU members must abide by the minimum standards of the Pregnant Workers Directive and Parental Leave Directive.

Right to vote

During the 19th century some women began to ask for, demand, and then agitate and demonstrate for the right to vote – the right to participate in their government and its law making. Other women opposed suffrage, like Helen Kendrick Johnson, who argued in the 1897 pamphlet Woman and the Republic that women could achieve legal and economic equality without having the vote.The ideals of women's suffrage developed alongside that of universal suffrage and today women's suffrage is considered a right (under the Convention on the Elimination of All Forms of Discrimination Against Women). During the 19th century the right to vote was gradually extended in many countries, and women started to campaign for their right to vote. In 1893 New Zealand became the first country to give women the right to vote on a national level. Australia gave women the right to vote in 1902.

Property rights

During the 19th century some women, such as Ernestine Rose, Paulina Wright Davis, Elizabeth Cady Stanton, Harriet Beecher Stowe, in the United States and Britain began to challenge laws that denied them the right to their property once they married. Under the common law doctrine of coverture husbands gained control of their wives' real estate and wages. Beginning in the 1840s, state legislatures in the United States and the British Parliament began passing statutes that protected women's property from their husbands and their husbands' creditors. These laws were known as the Married Women's Property Acts.

Courts in the 19th-century United States also continued to require privy examinations of married women who sold their property. A privy examination was a practice in which a married woman who wished to sell her property had to be separately examined by a judge or justice of the peace outside of the presence of her husband and asked if her husband was pressuring her into signing the document. Property rights for women continued to be restricted in many European countries until legal reforms of the 1960-70s. For example, in West Germany, the law pertaining to rural farm succession favored male heirs until 1963. In the US, Head and master laws, which gave sole control of marital property to the husband, were common until a few decades ago. The Supreme Court, in Kirchberg v. Feenstra (1981), declared such laws unconstitutional.

Freedom of movement

Freedom of movement is an essential right, recognized by international instruments, including Article 15 (4) of CEDAW. Nevertheless, in many regions of the world, women have this right severely restricted, in law or in practice. For instance, in some countries women may not leave the home without a male guardian, or without the consent of the husband – for example the personal law of Yemenstates that a wife must obey her husband and must not get out of the home without his consent.Even in countries which do not have legal restrictions, women's movement may be prevented in practice by social and religious norms such as purdah. Laws restricting women from travelling existed until relatively recently in some Western countries: until 1983, in Australia the passport application of a married woman had to be authorized by her husband. Various practices have been used historically to restrict women's freedom of movement, such as foot binding, the custom of applying painfully tight binding to the feet of young Chinese girls, which was common between the 10th and 20th century.

Women's freedom of movement may be restricted by laws, but it may also be restricted by attitudes towards women in public spaces. In areas where it is not socially accepted for women to leave the home, women who are outside may face abuse such as insults, sexual harassment and violence. Many of the restrictions on women's freedom of movement are framed as measures to "protect" women.For example, in the summer of 2017, an India women named Varnika Kundu shared a story on Facebook about being stalked by two men late at night. Kundu was coming home after a night out with friends when two men began following her. Kundu made it home unharmed, but was understandably shaken after the incident. She posted her story on Facebook, hoping to bring awareness and warn other women, but was instead met with a backlash of trolls telling her she shouldn't have been out that late and that it was her fault for being in that situation. This incident spawned the #AintNoCinderella movement, where women all over the world shared pictures of them being out past midnight with the hashtag in order to combat gender stereotypes and bias.

Informing women about their legal rights

The lack of legal knowledge among many women, especially in developing countries, is a major obstacle in the improvement of women's situation. International bodies, such as the United Nations, have stated that the obligation of states does not only consist in passing relevant laws, but also in informing women about the existence of such laws, in order to enable them to seek justice and realize in practice their rights. Therefore, states must popularize the laws, and explain them clearly to the public, in order to prevent ignorance, or misconceptions originating in popular myths, about the laws. The United Nations Development Programme states that, in order to advance gender justice, "Women must know their rights and be able to access legal systems", and the 1993 UN Declaration on the Elimination of Violence Against Women states at Art. 4 (d) [...] "States should also inform women of their rights in seeking redress through such mechanisms".What are women's rights? Human rights are the basic rights and freedoms that all humans should be guaranteed. These rights apply to everyone equally, but many women are prevented from realising their rights because of tradition, prejudice, social and economic interests.

When many international human rights laws were being drawn up the typical citizen they imagined (and often the person writing the law) was a man. Since then women's movements around the world have campaigned for the violence and discrimination experienced every day by women to be given greater visibility and to be understood as a violation of women's fundamental human rights.

International women's rights instruments

Today there are several international instruments which protect women's rights, including:

- The Convention on the Elimination of All Forms of Discrimination against Women(CEDAW), adopted in 1979 by the UN General Assembly, and often described as an international bill of rights for women. Consisting of a preamble and 30 articles, it defines what constitutes discrimination against women and sets up an agenda for national action to end such discrimination.
- The Beijing Declaration and Platform for Action, a historic agreement between 189 governments, including the UK, to empower women globally. It can be seen as the blueprint for action to advance women's rights and empowerment across the globe and was adopted at the UN Fourth World Conference on Women in 1995. It covers 12 key vital areas on women's rights, including violence against women and access to power and decision-making.
- The United Nations Security Council Resolution 1325 (UNSCR 1325), adopted in 2000. It was the first resolution to recognise the important role of women in peacebuilding and calls on governments to ensure that women are included in all peace negotiations and processes.
- The Sustainable Development Goals (SDGs) succeed the Millennium Development Goals on 1 January 2016. The SDGs are a new, universal set of goals, targets and indicators that UN member states will use to frame their development priorities over the next 15 years. They include a standalone goal on gender equality and targets on violence against women and girls and women's participation and leadership (thanks in part to campaigning by Womankind and our partners).

These policy frameworks may seem detached from the realities of most women's lives, but they are an important tool for activists. From advocating for new laws, to securing justice for survivors of violence, or making sure women are at the table during peace processes, women's rights organisations hold governments to account and deliver real change for women.

Women's rights organisations champion change

Even though it was campaigning by the global women's movement which led to the women's rights agreements above, when it comes to international decision-making the experience and expertise of women's rights organisations are often overlooked. Local and national women's rights organisations are the champions of change. They must be heard at the international level and be involved in setting commitments and targets. Women's rights organisations around the world are also critically underfunded, reliant on piecemeal project funding which often restricts their ability to do policy and advocacy work. Although there have been huge strides forward for women's rights over the last few decades there is still urgent work to be done and an ever-present danger that women's hard-won rights could be rolled back.

Discrimination

Women's rights movements focus on ending discrimination of women. In this regard, the definition of discrimination itself is important. According to the jurisprudence of the ECHR, the right to freedom from discrimination includes not only the obligation of states to treat in the same way persons who are in analogous situations, but also the obligation to treat in a different way persons who are in different situations. In this regard equity, not just "equality" is important. Therefore, states must sometimes differentiate between women and men – through for example offering maternity leave or other legal protections surrounding pregnancy and childbirth (to take into account the biological realities of reproduction), or through acknowledging a specific historical context. For example, acts of violence committed by men against women do not happen in a vacuum, but are part of a social context: in Opuz v Turkey, the ECHR defined violence against women as a form of discrimination against women; this is also the position of the Istanbul Convention which at Article 3 states that "violence against women" is understood as a violation of human rights and a form of discrimination against women [...]".

There are different views on where it is appropriate to differentiate between women and men, and one view is that the act of sexual intercourse is an act where this difference must be acknowledged, both due to the increased physical risks for the woman, and due to the historical context of women being systematically subjected to forced sexual intercourse while in a socially subordinated position (particularly within marriage and during war). States must also differentiate with regard to healthcare by ensuring that women's health - particularly with regard to reproductive health such as pregnancy and childbirth - is not neglected. According to the World Health Organization "Discrimination in health care settings takes many forms and is often manifested when an individual or group is denied access to health care services that are otherwise available to others.

It can also occur through denial of services that are only needed by certain groups, such as women." The refusal of states to acknowledge the specific needs of women, such as the necessity of specific policies like the strong investment of states in reducing maternal mortality can be a form of discrimination. In this regard treating women and men similarly does not work because certain biological aspects such as menstruation, pregnancy, labor, childbirth, breastfeeding, as well as certain medical conditions, only affect women. The Committee on the Elimination of Discrimination against Women stipulates in its General recommendation No. 35 on gender based violence against women, updating general recommendation No. 19 that states should "Examine gender neutral laws and policies to ensure that they do not create or perpetuate existing inequalities and repeal or modify them if they do so". (paragraph 32).Another example of gender neutral policy which harms women is that where medication tested in medical trials only on men is also used on women assuming that there are no biological differences.

Right to health

Health is defined by the World Health Organization as "a state of complete physical, mental and social well-being and not merely the absence of disease or infirmity". Women's health refers to the health of women, which differs from that of men in many unique ways. Women's health is severely impaired in some parts of the world, due to factors such as inequality, confinement of women to the home, indifference of medical workers, lack of autonomy of women, lack of financial resources of women. Discrimination against women occurs also through denial of medical services that are only needed by women. Violations of women's right to health may result in maternal death, accounting for more than 300.000 deaths per year, most of them in developing countries. Certain traditional practices, such as female genital mutilation, also affect women's health. Worldwide, young women and adolescent girls are the population most affected by HIV/AIDS.

Right to education

The right to education is a universal entitlement to education. The Convention against Discrimination in Education prohibits discrimination in education, with discrimination being defined as "any distinction, exclusion, limitation or preference which, being based on race, colour, sex, language, religion, political or other opinion, national or social origin, economic condition or birth, has the purpose or effect of nullifying or impairing equality of treatment in education". The International Covenant on Economic, Social and Cultural Rights states at Article 3 that "The States Parties to the present Covenant undertake to ensure the equal right of men and women to the enjoyment of all economic, social and cultural rights set forth in the present Covenant", with Article 13 recognizing "the right of everyone to education".While women's right to access to academic education is recognized as very important, it is increasingly recognized that academic education must be supplemented with education on human rights, non-discrimination, ethics and gender equality, in order for social advancement to be possible.

This was pointed out by Zeid Ra'ad Al Hussein, the current United Nations High Commissioner for Human Rights, who stressed the importance of human rights education for all children: "What good was it to humanity that Josef Mengele had advanced degrees in medicine and anthropology, given that he was capable of committing the most inhuman crimes? Eight of the 15 people who planned the Holocaust at Wannsee in 1942 held PhDs. They shone academically, and yet they were profoundly toxic to the world. Radovan Karad•iæ was a trained psychiatrist. Pol Pot studied radio electronics in Paris. Does this matter, when neither of them showed the smallest shred of ethics and understanding?" There has been increased attention given in recent decades to the raising of student awareness to the importance of gender equality.

Reproductive rights

Legal rights

Reproductive rights are legal rights and freedoms relating to reprod uction and reproductive health. Reproductive rights were endorsed by the twenty-year Cairo Programme of Action which was adopted in 1994 at the International Conference on Population and Development (ICPD) in Cairo, and by the Beijing Declaration and Beijing Platform for Action in 1995. In the 1870s feminists advanced the concept of voluntary motherhood as a political critique of involuntary motherhoodand expressing a desire for women's emancipation. Advocates for voluntary motherhood disapproved of contraception, arguing that women should only engage in sex for the purpose of procreation and advocated for periodic or permanent abstinence. Reproductive rights represents a broad concept, that may include some or all of the following rights: the right to legal or safe abortion, the right to control one's reproductive functions, the right to access quality reproductive healthcare, and the right to education and access in order to make reproductive choices free from coercion, discrimination, and violence. Reproductive rights may also be understood to include education about contraception and sexually transmitted infections. Reproductive rights are often defined to include freedom from female genital mutilation (FGM), and forced abortion and forced sterilization. The Istanbul Convention recognizes these two rights at Article 38 – Female genital mutilation and Article 39 – Forced abortion and forced sterilisation. Reproductive rights are understood as rights of both men and women, but are most frequently advanced as women's rights. In the 1960s, reproductive rights activists promoted women's right to bodily autonomy, with these social movements leading to the gain of legal access to contraception and abortion during the next decades in many countries.

Birth control

In the early 20th century birth control was advanced as alternative to the then fashionable terms family limitation and voluntary motherhood. The phrase "birth control" entered the English language in 1914 and was popularised by Margaret Sanger,who was mainly active in the US but had gained an international reputation by the 1930s. The British birth control campaigner Marie Stopes made contraception acceptable in Britain during the 1920s by framing it in scientific terms. Stopes assisted emerging birth control movements in a number of British colonies. The birth control movement advocated for contraception so as to permit sexual intercourse as desired without the risk of pregnancy. By emphasizing control, the birth control movement argued that women should have control over their reproduction, an idea that aligned closely to the theme of the feminist movement. Slogans such as "control over our own bodies" criticised male domination and demanded women's liberation, a connotation that is absent from the family planning, population control and eugenics movements. In the 1960s and 1970s the birth control movement advocated for the legalisation of abortion and large-scale education campaigns about contraception by governments. In the 1980s birth control and population control organisations co-operated in demanding rights to contraception and abortion, with an increasing emphasis on "choice".

Birth control has become a major theme in United States politics. Reproductive issues are cited as examples of women's powerlessness to exercise their rights. The societal acceptance of birth control required the separation of sex from procreation, making birth control a highly controversial subject in the 20th century. Birth control in the United States has become an arena for conflict between liberal and conservative values, raising questions about family, personal freedom, state intervention, religion in politics, sexual morality and social welfare. Reproductive rights, that is rights relating to sexual reproduction and reproductive health, were first discussed as a subset of human rights at the United Nation's 1968 International Conference on Human Rights.

Abortion

Women's reproductive rights may be understood as including the right to easy access to a safe and legal abortion. Abortion laws vary from a full prohibition (the Dominican Republic, El Salvador, Malta, Nicaragua, the Vatican) to countries such as Canada, where there are no legal restrictions. In many countries where abortion is permitted by law, women may only have limited access to safe abortion services. In some countries abortion is permitted only to save the pregnant woman's life, or if the pregnancy resulted from rape or incest. There are also countries where the law is liberal, but in practice it is very difficult to have an abortion, due to most doctors being conscientious objectors. The fact that in some countries where abortion is legal it is de facto very difficult to have access to one is controversial; the UN in its 2017 resolution on Intensification of efforts to prevent and eliminate all forms of violence against women and girls: domestic violence urged states to guarantee access to "safe abortion where such services are permitted by national law".

The Committee on the Elimination of Discrimination against Women considers the criminalization of abortion a "violations of women's sexual and reproductive health and rights" and a form of "gender based violence"; paragraph 18 of its General recommendation No. 35 on gender based violence against women, updating general recommendation No. 19 states that: "Violations of women's sexual and reproductive health and rights, such as forced sterilizations, forced abortion, forced pregnancy, criminalisation of abortion, denial or delay of safe abortion and post abortion care, forced continuation of pregnancy, abuse and mistreatment of women and girls seeking sexual and reproductive health information, goods and services, are forms of gender based violence that, depending on the circumstances, may amount to torture or cruel, inhuman or degrading treatment." The same General Recommendation also urges countries at paragraph 31 to [...] In particular, repeal: a) Provisions that allow, tolerate or condone forms of gender based violence against women, including legislation that criminalises abortion".

According to Human Rights Watch, "Abortion is a highly emotional subject and one that excites deeply held opinions. However, equitable access to safe abortion services is first and foremost a human right. Where abortion is safe and legal, no one is forced to have one. Where abortion is illegal and unsafe, women are forced to carry unwanted pregnancies to term or suffer serious health consequences and even death. Approximately 13% of maternal deaths worldwide are attributable to unsafe abortion—between 68,000 and 78,000 deaths annually." According to Human Rights Watch, "the denial of a pregnant woman's right to make an independent decision regarding abortion violates or poses a threat to a wide range of human rights." One can argue that even though women die from unsafe abortion, the legalization of abortion is considered a human right violation since it supports a cause that deprives the unborn of their humanity, which must be respected, and therefore another solution is needed in order to avoid maternal deaths (e.g., psychological and physiological support during and after pregnancy) whilst also avoiding abortion. According to World Health Organization, 56 million abortions on average occurred worldwide each year in 2010-2014. African American women are 5 times likely to have an abortion rather than a white woman. The Catholic Church and many other Christian faiths, particularly those considered the Christian right, and most Orthodox Jews regard abortion not as a right, but as a moral evil and a Mortal sin. Russia was the first country to legalise abortions and offer free medical care in state hospitals to do so. After the October Revolution, the Women's wing of the Bolshevik Party (the Zhenotdel) persuaded the Bolsheviks to legalise abortion (as a 'temporary measure'). The Bolsheviks legalised abortion in November 1920. This was the first time in world history that women had won the right to free abortions in state hospitals.

Abuse during childbirth

The abuse of women during childbirth is a recently identified global problem and a basic violation of a woman's rights. Abuse during childbirth is the neglect, physical abuseand lack of respect during childbirth. This treatment is regarded as a violation of the woman's rights. It also has the effect of preventing women from seeking pre-natal care and using other health care services.

Child marriage

Child marriage is a practice which is widespread across the world, and is often connected to poverty and gender inequality. Child marriage endangers the reproductive health of young girls, leading to an increased risk of complications in pregnancy or childbirth. Such complications are a leading cause of death among girls in developing countries

Forced pregnancy

Forced pregnancy is the practice of forcing a woman or girl to become pregnant, often as part of a forced marriage, including by means of bride kidnapping, through rape (including marital rape, war rape and genocidal rape) or as part of a program of breeding slaves (see Slave breeding in the United States). It is a form of reproductive coercion, was common historically, and still occurs in parts of the world. In the 20th century, state mandated forced marriage with the aim of increasing the population was practiced by some authoritarian governments, notably during the Khmer Rouge regime in Cambodia, which systematically forced people into marriages ordering them to have children, in order to increase the population and continue the revolution. Forced pregnancy is strongly connected to the custom of bride price.

Freedom from violence

Violence against women is, collectively, violent acts that are primarily or exclusively committed against women. The UN Declaration on the Elimination of Violence Against Womenstates, "violence against women is a manifestation of historically unequal power relations between men and women" and "violence against women is one of the crucial social mechanisms by which women are forced into a subordinate position compared with men." The Council of Europe Convention on preventing and combating violence against women and domestic violence, also known as the Istanbul Convention, provides the following definition of violence against women: "violence against women" is understood as a violation of human rights and a form of discrimination against women and shall mean all acts of gender-based violence that result in, or are likely to result in, physical, sexual, psychological or economic harm or suffering to women, including threats of such acts, coercion or arbitrary deprivation of liberty, whether occurring in public or in private life".Violence against women may be perpetrated by individuals, by groups, or by the State. It may occur in private or in public. Violence against women may be sexual violence, physical violence, psychological violence, socioeconomic violence. Some forms of violence against women have long cultural traditions: honor killings, dowry violence, female genital mutilation. Violence against women is considered by the World Health Organization "a major public health problem and a violation of women's human rights."

Family law

Under male dominated family law, women had few, if any, rights, being under the control of the husband or male relatives. Legal concepts that existed throughout the centuries, such as coverture, marital power, Head and Master laws, kept women under the strict control of their husbands. Restrictions from marriage laws also extended to public life, such as marriage bars. Practices such as dowry or bride price were, and still are to this day in some parts of the world, very common. Some countries continue to require to this day a male guardian for women, without whom women cannot exercise civil rights. Other harmful practices include marriage of young girls, often to much older men.

Modern movements

In the subsequent decades women's rights again became an important issue in the English speaking world. By the 1960s the movement was called "feminism" or "women's liberation." Reformers wanted the same pay as men, equal rights in law, and the freedom to plan their families or not have children at all. Their efforts were met with mixed results. The International Council of Women (ICW) was the first women's organization to work across national boundaries for the common cause of advocating human rights for women. In March and April 1888, women leaders came together in

Washington D.C. with 80 speakers and 49 delegates representing 53 women's organizations from 9 countries: Canada, the United States, Ireland, India, England, Finland, Denmark, France and Norway. Women from professional organizations, trade unions, arts groups and benevolent societies participate. National Councils are affiliated to the ICW and thus make themselves heard at international level. In 1904, the ICW met in Berlin, Germany. The ICW worked with the League of Nations during the 1920s and the United Nations post-World War II. Today the ICW holds Consultative Status with the United Nations Economic and Social Council, the highest accreditation an NGO can achieve at the United Nations. Currently, it is composed of 70 countries and has a headquarters in Lasaunne, Switzerland. International meetings are held every three years.

In the UK, a public groundswell of opinion in favour of legal equality had gained pace, partly through the extensive employment of women in what were traditional male roles during both world wars. By the 1960s the legislative process was being readied, tracing through MP Willie Hamilton's select committee report, his equal pay for equal work bill, the creation of a Sex Discrimination Board, Lady Sear's draft sex anti-discrimination bill, a government Green Paper of 1973, until 1975 when the first British Sex Discrimination Act, an Equal Pay Act, and an Equal Opportunities Commission came into force With encouragement from the UK government, the other countries of the EEC soon followed suit with an agreement to ensure that discrimination laws would be phased out across the European Community.

In the US, the National Organization for Women (NOW) was created in 1966 with the purpose of bringing about equality for all women. NOW was one important group that fought for the Equal Rights Amendment (ERA). This amendment stated that "equality of rights under the law shall not be denied or abridged by the United States or any state on account of sex." But there was disagreement on how the proposed amendment would be understood. Supporters believed it would guarantee women equal treatment. But critics feared it might deny women the right be financially supported by their husbands. The amendment died in 1982 because not enough states had ratified it. ERAs have been included in subsequent Congresses, but have still failed to be ratified.

Women for Women International (WfWI) is a nonprofit humanitarian organization that provides practical and moral support to women survivors of war. WfWI helps such women rebuild their lives after war's devastation through a year-long tiered program that begins with direct financial aid and emotional counseling and includes life skills (e.g., literacy, numeracy) training if necessary, rights awareness education, health education, job skills training and small business development. The organization was co-founded in 1993 by Zainab Salbi, an Iraqi American who is herself a survivor of the Iran–Iraq

War and Salbi's then-husband Amjad Atallah. Since June 2012, WfWI has been led by Afshan Khan, a long-time former executive with UNICEF who became WfWI's first new CEO since founder Zainab Salbi stepped down to devote more time to her writing and lecturing.

The National Council of Women of Canada (Conseil national des femmes du Canada), is a Canadian advocacy organization based in Ottawa aimed at improving conditions for women, families, and communities. A federation of nationally organized societies of men and women and local and provincial councils of women, it is the Canadian member of the International Council of Women (ICW). The Council has concerned itself in areas including women's suffrage, immigration, health care, education, mass media, the environment, and many others. Formed on 27 October 1857 in Toronto, Ontario, it is one of the oldest advocacy organizations in the country.

The Association for the Protection and Defense of Women's Rights in Saudi Arabia is a Saudi Non-governmental organization founded to provide activism for women's rights. It was founded by Wajeha al-Huwaider and Fawzia Al-Uyyouni, and grew out of a 2007 movement to gain women the right to drive. The association is not officially licensed by the government of Saudi Arabia, and has been warned not to mount demonstrations. In a 2007 interview, al-Huwaider described the goals: "The association will consist of a number of leagues, with each league pursuing a different issue or right... representation for women in shari'a courts; setting a [minimum] age for girls' marriages; allowing women to take care of their own affairs in government agencies and allowing them to enter government buildings; protecting women from domestic violence, such as physical or verbal violence, or keeping her from studies, work, or marriage, or forcing her to divorce..." In Ukraine, FEMEN was founded in 2008. The organisation is internationally known for its topless protests against sex tourists, international marriage agencies, sexism and other social, national and international social illnesses. FEMEN has sympathisers groups in many European countries through social media.

United Nations and World Conferences

In 1946 the United Nations established a Commission on the Status of Women. Originally as the Section on the Status of Women, Human Rights Division, Department of Social Affairs, and now part of the Economic and Social Council (ECOSOC). Since 1975 the UN has held a series of world conferences on women's issues, starting with the World Conference of the International Women's Year in Mexico City. These conferences created an international forum for women's rights, but also illustrated divisions between women of different cultures and the difficulties of attempting to apply principles universally. Four World Conferences have been held, the first in Mexico City (International Women's Year, 1975), the second in Copenhagen (1980) and the third in Nairobi(1985). At the Fourth World Conference on Women in Beijing (1995), The Platform for Action was signed. This included a commitment to achieve "gender equality and the empowerment of women". The same commitment was reaffirmed by all U.N. member nations at the Millennium Summit in 2000 and was reflected in the Millennium Development Goals to be achieved by 2015.

Field organisations

Regions where women's rights are less developed have produced interesting local organisations, such as:

- IIDA Women's Development Organisation, a Somali non-governmental organisation, created by women in order to work for peacebuilding and women's rights defence in Somalia, a country deprived of state structures and security since 1991,
- the All Pakistan Women's Association, a civil society organisation founded in 1949, which develops a range of programmes in the field of health, nutrition, education, birth controland legal aid.

Human rights

United Nations convention

The Universal Declaration of Human Rights, adopted in 1948, enshrines "the equal rights of men and women", and addressed both the equality and equity issues. In 1979, the United Nations General Assembly adopted the Convention on the Elimination of All Forms of Discrimination against Women (CEDAW) for legal implementation of the Declaration on the Elimination of Discrimination against Women. Described as an international bill of rights for women, it came into force on 3 September 1981. The UN member states that have not ratified the convention are Iran, Palau, Somalia, Sudan, Tonga, and the United States. Niue and the Vatican City, which are non-member states, have also not ratified it. The latest state to become a party to the convention is South Sudan, on 30 April 2015. The Convention defines discrimination against women in the following terms: Any distinction, exclusion or restriction made on the basis of sex which has the effect or purpose of impairing or nullifying the recognition, enjoyment or exercise by women, irrespective of their marital status, on a basis of equality of men and women, of human rights and fundamental freedoms in the political, economic, social, cultural, civil or any other field.

It also establishes an agenda of action for putting an end to sex-based discrimination for which states ratifying the Convention are required to enshrine gender equality into their domestic legislation, repeal all discriminatory provisions in their laws, and enact new provisions to guard against discrimination against women. They must also establish tribunals and public institutions to guarantee women effective protection against discrimination, and take steps to eliminate all forms of discrimination practiced against women by individuals, organizations, and enterprises.

Marriage, divorce, and family law

Article 16 of the Universal Declaration of Human Rights enshrines the right of consenting men and women to marry and found a family.

"(1) Men and women of full age, without any limitation due to race, nationality or religion, have the right to marry and to found a family. They are entitled to equal rights as to marriage, during marriage and at its dissolution.

(2) Marriage shall be entered into only with the free and full consent of the intending spouses.

(3) The family is the natural and fundamental group unit of society and is entitled to protection by society and the State."

Article 16 of CEDAW stipulates that, "1. States Parties shall take all appropriate measures to eliminate discrimination against women in all matters relating to marriage and family relations ". Among the rights included are a woman's right to freely and consensually choose her spouse; to have parental rights to her children irrespective of her marital status; the right of a married woman to choose a profession or an occupation, and to have property rights within marriage. In addition to these, "The betrothal and the marriage of a child shall have no legal effect". Polygamous marriage is a controversial practice, prevalent in some parts of the world. The General recommendations made by the Committee on the Elimination of Discrimination against Women, state at General Recommendation No. 21, Equality in marriage and family relations "14. Polygamous marriage contravenes a woman's right to equality with men, and can have such serious emotional and financial consequences for her and her dependents that such marriages ought to be discouraged and prohibited."

Cohabitation of unmarried couples as well as single mothers are common in some parts the world. The Human Rights Committee has stated: "27. In giving effect to recognition of the family in the context of article 23, it is important to accept the concept of the various forms of family, including unmarried couples and their children and single parents and their children and to ensure the equal treatment of women in these contexts (General Comment 19 paragraph 2 last sentence). Single parent families frequently consist of a single woman caring for one or more children, and States parties should describe what measures of support are in place to enable her to discharge her parental functions on the basis of equality with a man in a similar position."

Vienna Declaration and Programme of Action

The Vienna Declaration and Programme of Action, also known as VDPA, is a human rights declaration adopted by consensus at the World Conference on Human Rights on 25 June 1993 in Vienna, Austria. This declaration recognizes women's rights as being protected human rights. Paragraph 18 reads: "The human rights of women and of the girl-child are an inalienable, integral and indivisible part of universal human rights. The full and equal participation of women in political, civil, economic, social and cultural life, at the national, regional and international levels, and the eradication of all forms of discrimination on grounds of sex are priority objectives of the international community".

United Nations Security Council Resolution 1325

On 31 October 2000, the United Nations Security Council unanimously adopted United Nations Security Council Resolution 1325, the first formal and legal document from the United Nations Security Council that requires all states to respect fully international humanitarian law and international human rights law applicable to the rights and protection of women and girls during and after the armed conflicts.

Maputo Protocol

The Protocol to the African Charter on Human and Peoples' Rights on the Rights of Women in Africa, better known as the Maputo Protocol, was adopted by the African Union on 11 July 2003 at its second summit in Maputo, Mozambique. On 25 November 2005, having been ratified by the required 15 member nations of the African Union, the protocol entered into force. The protocol guarantees comprehensive rights to women including the right to take part in the political process, to social and political equality with men, and to control of their reproductive health, and an end to female genital mutilation.

Violence against women

United Nations Declaration

The Declaration on the Elimination of Violence Against Women was adopted by the United Nations in 1993. It defines violence against women as "any act of gender-based violence that results in, or is likely to result in, physical, sexual or psychological harm or suffering to women, including threats of such acts, coercion or arbitrary deprivation of liberty, whether occurring in public or in private life." This resolution established that women have a right to be free from violence. As a consequence of the resolution, in 1999, the General Assembly declared the day of 25 November to be the International Day for the Elimination of Violence against Women.

Article 2 of The Declaration on the Elimination of Violence Against Women outlines several forms of violence against women: Violence against women shall be understood to encompass, but not be limited to, the following:

(a) Physical, sexual and psychological violence occurring in the family, including battering, sexual abuse of female children in the household, dowry-related violence, marital rape, female genital mutilation and other traditional practices harmful to women, non-spousal violence and violence related to exploitation;

(b) Physical, sexual and psychological violence occurring within the general community, including rape, sexual abuse, sexual harassment and intimidation at work, in educational institutions and elsewhere, trafficking in women and forced prostitution;

(c) Physical, sexual and psychological violence perpetrated or condoned by the State, wherever it occurs.

Istanbul Convention

The Council of Europe Convention on preventing and combating violence against women and domestic violence, also known as the Istanbul Convention, is the first legally binding instrument in Europe in the field of domestic violence and violence against women, and came into force in 2014. Countries which ratify it must ensure that the forms of violence defined in its text are outlawed. In its Preamble, the Convention states that "the realisation of de jure and de facto equality between women and men is a key element in the prevention of violence against women". The Convention also provides a definition of domestic violence as "all acts of physical, sexual, psychological or economic violence that occur within the family or domestic unit or between former or current spouses or partners, whether or not the perpetrator shares or has shared the same residence with the victim".Although it is a Convention of the Council of Europe, it is open to accession by any country.

Rape and sexual violence

Rape, sometimes called sexual assault, is an assault by a person involving sexual intercourse with or sexual penetration of another person without that person's consent. Rape is generally considered a serious sex crime as well as a civil assault. When part of a widespread and systematic practice, rape and sexual slavery are now recognised as a crime against humanity as well as a war crime. Rape is also now recognised as a form of genocide when committed with the intent to destroy, in whole or in part, a targeted group.

As genocide

In 1998, the International Criminal Tribunal for Rwanda established by the United Nations made landmark decisions that rape is a crime of genocideunder international law. The trial of Jean-Paul Akayesu, the mayor of Taba Commune in Rwanda, established precedents that rape is an element of the crime of genocide. The Akayesu judgement includes the first interpretation and application by an international court of the 1948 Convention on the Prevention and Punishment of the Crime of Genocide. The Trial Chamber held that rape, which it defined as "a physical invasion of a sexual nature committed on a person under circumstances which are coercive", and sexual assault constitute acts of genocide insofar as they were committed with the intent to destroy, in whole or in part, a targeted group. It found that sexual assault formed an integral part of the process of destroying the Tutsi ethnic group and that the rape was systematic and had been perpetrated against Tutsi women only, manifesting the specific intent required for those acts to constitute genocide.

Judge Navanethem Pillay said in a statement after the verdict: "From time immemorial, rape has been regarded as one of the spoils of war. Now it will be considered a war crime. We want to send out a strong message that rape is no longer a trophy of war." An estimated 500,000 women were raped during the 1994 Rwandan Genocide.

As a crime against humanity

The Rome Statute Explanatory Memorandum, which defines the jurisdiction of the International Criminal Court, recognises rape, sexual slavery, enforced prostitution, forced pregnancy, enforced sterilization, "or any other form of sexual violence of comparable gravity" as a crime against humanity if the action is part of a widespread or systematic practice. The Vienna Declaration and Programme of Action also condemn systematic rape as well as murder, sexual slavery, and forced pregnancy, as the "violations of the fundamental principles of international human rights and humanitarian law." and require a particularly effective response.

Rape was first recognised as a crime against humanity when the International Criminal Tribunal for the former Yugoslavia issued arrest warrants based on the Geneva Conventionsand Violations of the Laws or Customs of War. Specifically, it was recognised that Muslim women in Foca (southeastern Bosnia and Herzegovina) were subjected to systematic and widespread gang rape, torture, and sexual enslavement by Bosnian Serb soldiers, policemen, and members of paramilitary groups after the takeover of the city in April 1992. The indictment was of major legal significance and was the first time that sexual assaults were investigated for the purpose of prosecution under the rubric of torture and enslavement as a crime against humanity. The indictment was confirmed by a 2001 verdict by the International Criminal Tribunal for the former Yugoslavia that rape and sexual enslavement are crimes against humanity. This ruling challenged the widespread acceptance of rape and sexual enslavement of women as intrinsic part of war. The International Criminal Tribunal for the former Yugoslavia found three Bosnian Serb men guilty of rape of Bosniak (Bosnian Muslim) women and girls (some as young as 12 and 15 years of age), in Foca, eastern Bosnia and Herzegovina. Furthermore, two of the men were found guilty of the crime against humanity of sexual enslavement for holding women and girls captive in a number of de facto detention centres. Many of the women subsequently disappeared.

Forced marriage and slavery

The 1956 Supplementary Convention on the Abolition of Slavery, the Slave Trade, and Institutions and Practices Similar to Slavery defines "institutions and practices similar to slavery" to include:

c) Any institution or practice whereby:

- (i) A woman, without the right to refuse, is promised or given in marriage on payment of a consideration in money or in kind to her parents, guardian, family or any other person or group; or
- (ii) The husband of a woman, his family, or his clan, has the right to transfer her to another person for value received or otherwise; or
- (iii) A woman on the death of her husband is liable to be inherited by another person;

The Istanbul Convention requires countries which ratify it to prohibit forced marriage (Article 37) and to ensure that forced marriages can be easily voided without further victimization (Article 32).Chapter 7: Women's health Women's health refers to the health of women, which differs from that of men in many unique ways. Women's health is an example of population health, where health is defined by the World Health Organization as "a state of complete physical, mental and social well-being and not merely the absence of disease or infirmity". Often treated as simply women's reproductive health, many groups argue for a broader definition pertaining to the overall health of women, better expressed as "The health of women". These differences are further exacerbated in developing countries where women, whose health includes both their risks and experiences, are further disadvantaged.

Although women in industrialised countries have narrowed the gender gap in life expectancy and now live longer than men, in many areas of health they experience earlier and more severe disease with poorer outcomes. Gender remains an important social determinant of health, since women's health is influenced not just by their biology but also by conditions such as poverty, employment, and family responsibilities. Women have long been disadvantaged in many respects such as social and economic power which restricts their access to the necessities of life including health care, and the greater the level of disadvantage, such as in developing countries, the greater adverse impact on health.

Women's reproductive and sexual health has a distinct difference compared to men's health. Even in developed countries pregnancyand childbirth are associated with substantial risks to women with maternal mortality accounting for more than a quarter of a million deaths per year, with large gaps between the developing and developed countries. Comorbidity from other non reproductive disease such as cardiovascular disease contribute to both the mortality and morbidity of pregnancy, including preeclampsia. Sexually transmitted infections have serious consequences for women and infants, with mother-to-child transmission leading to outcomes such as stillbirths and neonatal deaths, and pelvic inflammatory disease leading to infertility. In addition infertility from many other causes, birth control, unplanned pregnancy, unconsensual sexual activity and the struggle for access to abortion create other burdens for women.

While the rates of the leading causes of death, cardiovascular disease, cancer and lung disease, are similar in women and men, women have different experiences. Lung cancer has overtaken all other types of cancer as the leading cause of cancer death in women, followed by breast cancer, colorectal, ovarian, uterine and cervical cancers. While smoking is the major cause of lung cancer, amongst nonsmoking women the risk of developing cancer is three times greater than amongst nonsmoking men. Despite this, breast cancer remains the commonest cancer in women in developed countries, and is one of the more important chronic diseases of women, while cervical cancer remains one of the commonest cancers in developing countries, associated with human papilloma virus (HPV), an important sexually transmitted disease. HPV vaccine together with screening offers the promise of controlling these diseases. Other important health issues for women include cardiovascular disease, depression, dementia, osteoporosis and anemia. A major impediment to advancing women's health has been their underrepresentation in research studies, an inequity being addressed in the United States and other western nations by the establishment of centers of excellence in women's health research and large scale clinical trials such as the Women's Health Initiative.

Definitions and scope

Women's experience of health and disease differ from those of men, due to unique biological, social and behavioural conditions. Biological differences vary all the way from phenotype to the cellular, and manifest unique risks for the development of ill health. The World Health Organization (WHO) defines health as "a state of complete physical, mental and social well-being and not merely the absence of disease or infirmity". Women's health is an example of population health, the health of a specific defined population. Women's health has been described as "a patchwork quilt with gaps". Although many of the issues around women's health relate to their reproductive health, including maternaland child health, genital health and breast health, and endocrine (hormonal) health, including menstruation, birth control and menopause, a broader understanding of women's health to include all aspects of the health of women has been urged, replacing "Women's Health" with "The Health of Women". The WHO considers that an undue emphasis on reproductive health has been a major barrier to ensuring access to good quality health care for all women. Conditions that affect both men and women, such as cardiovascular disease, osteoporosis, also manifest differently in women. Women's health issues also include medical situations in which women face problems not directly related to their biology, such as gender-differentiated access to medical treatment and other socioeconomic factors. Women's health is of particular concern due to widespread discrimination against women in the world, leaving them disadvantaged.

A number of health and medical research advocates, such as the Society for Women's Health Research in the United States, support this broader definition, rather than merely issues specific to human female anatomy to include areas where biological sex differences between women and men exist. Women also need health care more and access the health care system more than do men. While part of this is due to their reproductive and sexual health needs, they also have more chronic non-reproductive health issues such as cardiovascular disease, cancer, mental illness, diabetes and osteoporosis. Another important perspective is realising that events across the entire life cycle (or life-course), from in utero to aging effect the growth, development and health of women. The life-course perspective is one of the key strategies of the World Health Organization.

Global perspective

Gender differences in susceptibility and symptoms of disease and response to treatment in many areas of health are particularly true when viewed from a global perspective.Much of the available information comes from developed countries, yet there are marked differences between developed and developing countries in terms of women's roles and health. The global viewpoint is defined as the "area for study, research and practice that places a priority on improving health and achieving health equity for all people worldwide". In 2015 the World Health Organization identified the top ten issues in women's health as being cancer, reproductive health, maternal health, human immunodeficiency virus (HIV), sexually transmitted infections, violence, mental health, non communicable diseases, youth and aging.

Life expectancy

Women's life expectancy is greater than that of men, and they have lower death rates throughout life, regardless of race and geographic region.

Historically though, women had higher rates of mortality, primarily from maternal deaths (death in childbirth). In industrialised countries, particularly the most advanced, the gender gap narrowed and was reversed following the industrial revolution. Despite these differences, in many areas of health, women experience earlier and more severe disease, and experience poorer outcomes. Despite these differences, the leading causes of death in the United States are remarkably similar for men and women, headed by heart disease, which accounts for a quarter of all deaths, followed by cancer, lung disease and stroke. While women have a lower incidence of death from unintentional injury (see below) and suicide, they have a higher incidence of dementia (Gronowski and Schindler, Table I).

The major differences in life expectancy for women between developed and developing countries lie in the childbearing years. If a woman survives this period, the differences between the two regions become less marked, since in later life non-communicable diseases (NCDs) become the major causes of death in women throughout the world, with cardiovascular deaths accounting for 45% of deaths in older women, followed by cancer (15%) and lung disease (10%). These create additional burdens on the resources of developing countries. Changing lifestyles, including diet, physical activity and cultural factors that favour larger body size in women, are contributing to an increasing problem with obesity and diabetes amongst women in these countries and increasing the risks of cardiovascular disease and other NCDs. Women who are socially marginalized are more likely to die at younger ages than women who are not. Women who have substance abuse disorders, who are homeless, who are sex workers, and/or who are imprisoned have significantly shorter lives than other women. At any given age, women in these overlapping, stigmatized groups are approximately 10 to 13 times more likely to die than typical women of the same age.

Social and cultural factors

Women's health is positioned within a wider body of knowledge cited by, amongst others, the World Health Organization, which places importance on gender as a social determinant of health. While women's health is affected by their biology, it is also affected by their social conditions, such as poverty, employment, and family responsibilities, and these aspects should not be overshadowed. Women have traditionally been disadvantaged in terms of economic and social status and power, which in turn reduces their access to the necessities of life including health care. Despite recent improvements in western nations, women remain disadvantaged with respect to men. The gender gap in health is even more acute in developing countries where women are relatively more disadvantaged. In addition to gender inequity, there remain specific disease processes uniquely associated with being a woman which create specific challenges in both prevention and health care.

Even after succeeding in accessing health care, women have been discriminated against, a process that Iris Young has called "internal exclusion", as opposed to "external exclusion", the barriers to access. This invisibility effectively masks the grievances of groups already disadvantaged by power inequity, further entrenching injustice. Behavioral differences also play a role, in which women display lower risk taking including consume less tobacco, alcohol, and drugs, reducing their risk of mortality from associated diseases, including lung cancer, tuberculosis and cirrhosis. Other risk factors that are lower for women include motor vehicle accidents. Occupational differences have exposed women to less industrial injuries, although this is likely to change, as is risk of injury or death in war. Overall such injuries contributed to 3.5% of deaths in women compared to 6.2% in the United States in 2009. Suicide rates are also less in women.

The social view of health combined with the acknowledgement that gender is a social determinant of health inform women's health service delivery in countries around the world. Women's health services such as Leichhardt Women's Community Health Centre which was established in 1974 and was the first women's health centre established in Australia is an example of women's health approach to service delivery. Women's health is an issue which has been taken up by many feminists, especially where reproductive health is concerned and the international women's movement was responsible for much of the adoption of agendas to improve women's health.

Biological factors

Women and men differ in their chromosomal makeup, protein gene products, genomic imprinting, gene expression, signaling pathways, and hormonal environment. All of these necessitate caution in extrapolating information derived from biomarkers from one sex to the other. Women are particularly vulnerable at the two extremes of life. Young women and adolescents are at risk from STIs, pregnancy and unsafe abortion, while older women often have few resources and are disadvantaged with respect to men, and also are at risk of dementia and abuse, and generally poor health.

Reproductive and sexual health

Women experience many unique health issues related to reproduction and sexuality and these are responsible for a third of all health problems experienced by women during their reproductive years (aged 15–44), of which unsafe sex is a major risk factor, especially in developing countries. Reproductive health includes a wide range of issues including the health and function of structures and systems involved in reproduction, pregnancy, childbirth and child rearing, including antenatal and perinatal care. Global women's health has a much larger focus on reproductive health than that of developed countries alone, but also infectious diseases such as malaria in pregnancy and non-communicable diseases (NCD). Many of the issues that face women and girls in resource poor regions are relatively unknown in developed countries, such as female genital cutting, and further lack access to the appropriate diagnostic and clinical resources.

Maternal health

Pregnancy presents substantial health risks, even in developed countries, and despite advances in obstetrical science and practice.Maternal mortality remains a major problem in global health and is considered a sentinel event in judging the quality of health care systems. Adolescent pregnancy represents a particular problem, whether intended or unintended, and whether within marriage or a union or not. Pregnancy results in major changes in a girl's life, physically, emotionally, socially and economically and jeopardises her transition into adulthood. Adolescent pregnancy, more often than not, stems from a girl's lack of choices. or abuse. Child marriage (see below) is a major contributor worldwide, since 90% of births to girls aged 15–19 occur within marriage.

Maternal death

In 2013 about 289,000 women (800 per day) in the world died due to pregnancy-related causes, with large differences between developed and developing countries. Maternal mortality in western nations had been steadily falling, and forms the subject of annual reports and reviews.Yet, between 1987 and 2011, maternal mortality in the United States rose from 7.2 to 17.8 deaths per 100,000 live births, this is reflected in the Maternal Mortality Ratio (MMR). By contrast rates as high as 1,000 per birth are reported in the rest of the world, with the highest rates in Sub-Saharan Africa and South Asia, which account for 86% of such deaths. These deaths are rarely investigated, yet the World Health Organization considers that 99% of these deaths, the majority of which occur within 24 hours of childbirth, are preventable if the appropriate infrastructure, training, and facilities were in place.

In these resource-poor countries, maternal health is further eroded by poverty and adverse economic factors which impact the roads, health care facilities, equipment and supplies in addition to limited skilled personnel. Other problems include cultural attitudes towards sexuality, contraception, child marriage, home birth and the ability to recognise medical emergencies. The direct causes of these maternal deaths are hemorrhage, eclampsia, obstructed labor, sepsis and unskilled abortion. In addition malaria and AIDS complicate pregnancy. In the period 2003–2009 hemorrhage was the leading cause of death, accounting for 27% of deaths in developing countries and 16% in developed countries.

Non-reproductive health remains an important predictor of maternal health. In the United States, the leading causes of maternal death are cardiovascular disease (15% of deaths), endocrine, respiratory and gastrointestinal disorders, infection, hemorrhage and hypertensive disorders of pregnancy (Gronowski and Schindler, Table II).

In 2000, the United Nations created Millennium Development Goal (MDG) 5 to improve maternal health. Target 5A sought to reduce maternal mortality by three quarters from 1990 to 2015, using two indicators, 5.1 the MMR and 5.2 the proportion of deliveries attended by skilled health personnel (physician, nurse or midwife). Early reports indicated MDG 5 had made the least progress of all MDGs. By the target date of 2015 the MMR had only declined by 45%, from 380 to 210, most of which occurred after 2000. However this improvement occurred across all regions, but the highest MMRs were still in Africa and Asia, although South Asia witnessed the largest fall, from 530 to 190 (64%).

The smallest decline was seen in the developed countries, from 26 to 16 (37%). In terms of assisted births, this proportion had risen globally from 59 to 71%. Although the numbers were similar for both developed and developing regions, there were wide variations in the latter from 52% in South Asia to 100% in East Asia. The risks of dying in pregnancy in developing countries remains fourteen times higher than in developed countries, but in Sub-Saharan Africa, where the MMR is highest, the risk is 175 times higher. In setting the MDG targets, skilled assisted birth was considered a key strategy, but also an indicator of access to care and closely reflect mortality rates. There are also marked differences within regions with a 31% lower rate in rural areas of developing countries (56 vs. 87%), yet there is no difference in East Asia but a 52% difference in Central Africa (32 vs. 84%). With the completion of the MDG campaign in 2015, new targets are being set for 2030 under the Sustainable Development Goalscampaign. Maternal health is placed under Goal 3, Health, with the target being to reduce the global maternal mortality ratio to less than 70. Amongst tools being developed to meet these targets is the WHO Safe Childbirth Checklist.

Improvements in maternal health, in addition to professional assistance at delivery, will require routine antenatal care, basic emergency obstetric care, including the availability of antibiotics, oxytocics, anticonvulsants, the ability to manually remove a retained placenta, perform instrumented deliveries, and postpartum care. Research has shown the most effective programmes are those focussing on patient and community education, prenatal care, emergency obstetrics (including access to cesarean sections) and transportation.As with women's health in general, solutions to maternal health require a broad view encompassing many of the other MDG goals, such as poverty and status, and given that most deaths occur in the immediate intrapartum period, it has been recommended that intrapartum care (delivery) be a core strategy. New guidelines on antenatal care were issued by WHO in November 2016.

Complications of pregnancy

In addition to death occurring in pregnancy and childbirth, pregnancy can result in many non-fatal health problems including obstetrical fistulae, ectopic pregnancy, preterm labor, gestational diabetes, hyperemesis gravidarum, hypertensive states including preeclampsia, and anemia. Globally, complications of pregnancy vastly outway maternal deaths, with an estimated 9.5 million cases of pregnancy-related illness and 1.4 million near-misses (survival from severe life-threatening complications). Complications of pregnancy may be physical, mental, economic and social. It is estimated that 10–20 million women will develop physical or mental disability every year, resulting from complications of pregnancy or inadequate care. Consequently, international agencies have developed standards for obstetric care.

Obstetrical fistula

Of near miss events, obstetrical fistulae (OF), including vesicovaginal and rectovaginal fistulae, remain one of the most serious and tragic. Although corrective surgery is possible it is often not available and OF is considered completely preventable. If repaired, subsequent pregnancies will require cesarean section. While unusual in developed countries, it is estimated that up to 100,000 cases occur every year in the world, and that about 2 million women are currently living with this condition, with the highest incidence occurring in Africa and parts of Asia. OF results from prolonged obstructed labor without intervention, when continued pressure from the fetus in the birth canalrestricts blood supply to the surrounding tissues, with eventual fetal death, necrosis and expulsion.

The damaged pelvic organs then develop a connection (fistula) allowing urine or feces, or both, to be discharged through the vagina with associated urinary and fecal incontinence, vaginal stenosis, nerve damage and infertility. Severe social and mental consequences are also likely to follow, with shunning of the women. Apart from lack of access to care, causes include young age, and malnourishment. The UNFPA has made prevention of OF a priority and is the lead agency in the Campaign to End Fistula, which issues annual reports and the United Nations observes May 23 as the International Day to End Obstetric Fistula every year. Prevention includes discouraging teenage pregnancy and child marriage, adequate nutrition, and access to skilled care, including caesarean section.

Sexual health

The ability to determine if and when to become pregnant, is vital to a woman's autonomy and well being, and contraception can protect girls and young women from the risks of early pregnancy and older women from the increased risks of unintended pregnancy. Adequate access to contraception can limit multiple pregnancies, reduce the need for potentially unsafe abortion and reduce maternal and infant mortality and morbidity. Some barrier forms of contraception such as condoms, also reduce the risk of STIs and HIV infection. Access to contraception allows women to make informed choices about their reproductive and sexual health, increases empowerment, and enhances choices in education, careers and participation in public life. At the societal level, access to contraception is a key factor in controlling population growth, with resultant impact on the economy, the environment and regional development. Consequently, the United Nations considers access to contraception a human right that is central to gender equality and women's empowerment that saves lives and reduces poverty, and birth control has been considered amongst the 10 great public health achievements of the 20th century.

To optimise women's control over pregnancy, it is essential that culturally appropriate contraceptive advice and means are widely, easily, and affordably available to anyone that is sexually active, including adolescents. In many parts of the world access to contraception and family planning services is very difficult or non existent and even in developed counties cultural and religious traditions can create barriers to access. Reported usage of adequate contraception by women has risen only slightly between 1990 and 2014, with considerable regional variability. Although global usage is around 55%, it may be as low as 25% in Africa. Worldwide 222 million women have no or limited access to contraception. Some caution is needed in interpreting available data, since contraceptive prevalence is often defined as "the percentage of women currently using any method of contraception among all women of reproductive age (i.e., those aged 15 to 49 years, unless otherwise stated) who are married or in a union. The "in-union" group includes women living with their partner in the same household and who are not married according to the marriage laws or customs of a country." This definition is more suited to the more restrictive concept of family planning, but omits the contraceptive needs of all other women and girls who are or are likely to be sexually active, are at risk of pregnancy and are not married or "in-union".

Three related targets of MDG5 were adolescent birth rate, contraceptive prevalence and unmet need for family planning (where prevalence+unmet need = total need), which were monitored by the Population Division of the UN Department of Economic and Social Affairs. Contraceptive use was part of Goal 5B (universal access to reproductive health), as Indicator 5.3. The evaluation of MDG5 in 2015 showed that amongst couples usage had increased worldwide from 55% to 64%. with one of the largest increases in Subsaharan Africa (13 to 28%). The corollary, unmet need, declined slightly worldwide

(15 to 12%). In 2015 these targets became part of SDG5 (gender equality and empowerment) under Target 5.6: Ensure universal access to sexual and reproductive health and reproductive rights, where Indicator 5.6.1 is the proportion of women aged 15–49 years who make their own informed decisions regarding sexual relations, contraceptive use and reproductive health care (p. 31).

There remain significant barriers to accessing contraception for many women in both developing and developed regions. These include legislative, administrative, cultural, religious and economic barriers in addition to those dealing with access to and quality of health services. Much of the attention has been focussd on preventing adolescent pregnancy. The Overseas Development Institute (ODI) has identified a number of key barriers, on both the supply and demand side, including internalising socio-cultural values, pressure from family members, and cognitive barriers (lack of knowledge), which need addressing. Even in developed regions many women, particularly those who are disadvantaged, may face substantial difficulties in access that may be financial and geographic but may also face religious and political discrimination. Women have also mounted campaigns against potentially dangerous forms of contraception such as defective intrauterine devices (IUD)s, particularly the Dalkon Shield.

Abortion

Abortion is the intentional termination of pregnancy, as compared to spontaneous termination (miscarriage). Abortion is closely allied to contraception in terms of women's control and regulation of their reproduction, and is often subject to similar cultural, religious, legislative and economic constraints. Where access to contraception is limited, women turn to abortion. Consequently, abortion rates may be used to estimate unmet needs for contraception. However the available procedures have carried great risk for women throughout most of history, and still do in the developing world, or where legal restrictions force women to seek clandestine facilities. Access to safe legal abortion places undue burdens on lower socioeconomic groups and in jurisdictions that create significant barriers. These issues have frequently been the subject of political and feminist campaigns where differing viewpoints pit health against moral values.

Globally, there were 87 million unwanted pregnancies in 2005, of those 46 million resorted to abortion, of which 18 million were considered unsafe, resulting in 68,000 deaths. The majority of these deaths occurred in the developing world. The United Nations considers these avoidable with access to safe abortion and post-abortion care. While abortion rates have fallen in developed countries, but not in developing countries. Between 2010–2014 there were 35 abortions per 1000 women aged 15–44, a total of 56 million abortions per year. The United nations has prepared recommendations for health care workers to provide more accessible and safe abortion and post-abortion care. An inherent part of post-abortion care involves provision of adequate contraception.

Sexually transmitted infections

Important sexual health issues for women include Sexually transmitted infections (STIs) and female genital cutting (FGC). STIs are a global health priority because they have serious consequences for women and infants. Mother-to-child transmission of STIs can lead to stillbirths, neonatal death, low-birth-weight and prematurity, sepsis, pneumonia, neonatal conjunctivitis, and congenital deformities. Syphilis in pregnancy results in over 300,000 fetal and neonatal deaths per year, and 215,000 infants with an increased risk of death from prematurity, low-birth-weight or congenital disease.

Diseases such as chlamydia and gonorrhoea are also important causes of pelvic inflammatory disease (PID) and subsequent infertility in women. Another important consequence of some STIs such as genital herpes and syphilis increase the risk of acquiring HIV by three-fold, and can also influence its transmission progression. Worldwide, women and girls are at greater risk of HIV/AIDS. STIs are in turn associated with unsafe sexual activity that is often unconsensual.

Female genital mutilation

Female genital mutilation (also referred to as female genital cutting) is defined by the World Health Organization (WHO) as "all procedures that involve partial or total removal of the external female genitalia, or other injury to the female genital organs for non-medical reasons". It has sometimes been referred to as female circumcision, although this term is misleading because it implies it is analogous to the circumcision of the foreskin from the male penis. Consequently, the term mutilation was adopted to emphasise the gravity of the act and its place as a violation of human rights. Subsequently, the term cutting was advanced to avoid offending cultural sensibility that would interfere with dialogue for change. To recognise these points of view some agencies use the composite female genital mutilation/cutting (FMG/C).

It has affected more than 200 million women and girls who are alive today. The practice is concentrated in some 30 countries in Africa, the Middle East and Asia. FGC affects many religious faiths, nationalities, and socioeconomic classes and is highly controversial. The main arguments advanced to justify FGC are hygiene, fertility, the preservation of chastity, an important rite of passage, marriageability and enhanced sexual pleasure of male partners. The amount of tissue removed varies considerably, leading the WHO and other bodies to classify FGC into four types. These range from the partial or total removal of the clitoris with or without the prepuce (clitoridectomy) in Type I, to the additional removal of the labia minora, with or without excision of the labia majora (Type II) to narrowing of the vaginal orifice (introitus) with the creation of a covering seal by suturing the remaining labial tissue over the urethra and introitus, with or without excision of the clitoris (infibulation). In this type a small opening is created to allow urine and menstrual blood to be discharged. Type 4 involves all other procedures, usually relatively minor alterations such as piercing.

While defended by those cultures in which it constitutes a tradition, FGC is opposed by many medical and cultural organizations on the grounds that it is unnecessary and harmful. Short term health effects may include hemorrhage, infection, sepsis, and even result in death, while long term effects include dyspareunia, dysmenorrhea, vaginitis and cystitis. In addition FGC leads to complications with pregnancy, labor and delivery. Reversal (defibulation) by skilled personnel may be required to open the scarred tissue. Amongst those opposing the practice are local grassroots groups, and national and international organisations including WHO, UNICEF, UNFPA and Amnesty International. Legislative efforts to ban FGC have rarely been successful and the preferred approach is education and empowerment and the provision of information about the adverse health effects as well the human rights aspects.

Progress has been made but girls 14 and younger represent 44 million of those who have been cut, and in some regions 50% of all girls aged 11 and younger have been cut.Ending FGC has been considered one of the necessary goals in achieving the targets of the Millennium Development Goals, while the United Nations has declared ending FGC a target of the Sustainable Development Goals, and for February 6 to known as the International Day of Zero Tolerance for Female Genital Mutilation, concentrating on 17 African countries and the 5 million girls between the ages of 15 and 19 that would otherwise be cut by 2030.

Infertility

In the United States, infertility affects 1.5 million couples. Many couples seek assisted reproductive technology (ART) for infertility. In the United States in 2010, 147,260 in vitro fertilization (IVF) procedures were carried out, with 47,090 live births resulting. In 2013 these numbers had increased to 160,521 and 53,252. However, about a half of IVF pregnancies result in multiple-birth deliveries, which in turn are associated with an increase in both morbidity and mortality of the mother and the infant. Causes for this include increased maternal blood pressure, premature birth and low birth weight. In addition, more women are waiting longer to conceive and seeking ART.

Child marriage

Child marriage (including union or cohabitation) is defined as marriage under the age of eighteen and is an ancient custom. In 2010 it was estimated that 67 million women, then, in their twenties had been married before they turned eighteen, and that 150 million would be in the next decade, equivalent to 15 million per year. This number had increased to 70 million by 2012. In developing countries one third of girls are married under age, and 1:9 before 15. The practice is commonest in South Asia (48% of women), Africa (42%) and Latin America and the Caribbean (29%). The highest prevalence is in Western and Sub-Saharan Africa. The percentage of girls married before the age of eighteen is as high as 75% in countries such as Niger (Nour, Table I). Most child marriage involves girls. For instance in Mali the ratio of girls to boys is 72:1, while in countries such as the United States the ratio is 8:1. Marriage may occur as early as birth, with the girl being sent to her husbands home as early as age seven.

There are a number of cultural factors that reinforce this practice. These include the child's financial future, her dowry, social ties and social status, prevention of premarital sex, extramarital pregnancy and STIs. The arguments against it include interruption of education and loss of employment prospects, and hence economic status, as well as loss of normal childhood and its emotional maturation and social isolation. Child marriage places the girl in a relationship where she is in a major imbalance of power and perpetuates the gender inequality that contributed to the practice in the first place. Also in the case of minors, there are the issues of human rights, non-consensual sexual activity and forced marriage and a 2016 joint report of the WHO and Inter-Parliamentary Union places the two concepts together as Child, Early and Forced Marriage (CEFM), as did the 2014 Girl Summit (see below). In addition the likely pregnancies at a young age are associated with higher medical risks for both mother and child, multiple pregnancies and less access to care with pregnancy being amongst the leading causes of death amongst girls aged 15–19. Girls married under age are also more likely to be the victims of domestic violence.

There has been an international effort to reduce this practice, and in many countries eighteen is the legal age of marriage. Organizations with campaigns to end child marriage include the United Nations and its agencies, such as the Office of the High Commissioner for Human Rights, UNFPA, UNICEF and WHO. Like many global issues affecting women's health, poverty and gender inequality are root causes, and any campaign to change cultural attitudes has to address these. Child marriage is the subject of international conventions and agreements such as The Convention on the Elimination of All Forms of Discrimination against Women (CEDAW, 1979) (article 16) and the Universal Declaration of Human Rights and in 2014 a summit conference (Girl Summit) co-hosted by UNICEF and the UK was held in London (see illustration) to address this issue together with FGM/C. Later that same year the General Assembly of the United Nations passed a resolution, which inter alia. Urges all States to enact, enforce and uphold laws and policies aimed at preventing and ending child, early and forced marriage and protecting those at risk, and ensure that marriage is entered into only with the informed, free and full consent of the intending spouses (5 September 2014)

Amongst non-governmental organizations (NGOs) working to end child marriage are Girls not Brides, Young Women's Christian Association (YWCA), the International Center for Research on Women (ICRW) and Human Rights Watch (HRW). Although not explicitly included in the original Millennium Development Goals, considerable pressure was applied to include ending child marriage in the successor Sustainable Development Goals adopted in September 2015, where ending this practice by 2030 is a target of SDG 5 Gender Equality (see above). While some progress is being made in reducing child marriage, particularly for girls under fifteen, the prospects are daunting. The indicator for this will be the percentage of women aged 20–24 who were married or in a union before the age of eighteen. Efforts to end child marriage include legislation and ensuring enforcement together with empowering women and girls. To raise awareness, the inaugural UN International Day of the Girl Child in 2012 was dedicated to ending child marriage.

Menstrual cycle

Women's menstrual cycles, the approximately monthly cycle of changes in the reproductive system, can pose significant challenges for women in their reproductive years (the early teens to about 50 years of age). These include the physiological changes that can effect physical and mental health, symptoms of ovulation and the regular shedding of the inner lining of the uterus (endometrium) accompanied by vaginal bleeding (menses or menstruation). The onset of menstruation (menarche) may be alarming to unprepared girls and mistaken for illness. Menstruation can place undue burdens on women in terms of their ability to participate in activities, and access to menstrual aids such as tampons and "sanitary pads". This is particularly acute amongst poorer socioeconomic groups where they may represent a financial burden and in developing countries where menstruation can be an impediment to a girl's education.

Equally challenging for women are the physiological and emotional changes associated with the cessation of menses (menopause or climacteric). While typically occurring gradually towards the end of the fifth decade in life marked by irregular bleeding the cessation of ovulation and menstruation is accompanied by marked changes in hormonal activity, both by the ovary itself (oestrogen and progesterone) and the pituitary gland (follicle stimulating hormone or FSH and luteinizing hormone or LH). These hormonal changes may be associated with both systemic sensations such as hot flashes and local changes to the reproductive tract such as reduced vaginal secretions and lubrication. While menopause may bring relief from symptoms of menstruation and fear of pregnancy it may also be accompanied by emotional and psychological changes associated with the symbolism of the loss of fertility and a reminder of aging and possible loss of desirability. While menopause generally occurs naturally as a physiological process it may occur earlier (premature menopause) as a result of disease or from medical or surgical intervention. When menopause occurs prematurely the adverse consequences may be more severe.

Other issues

Other reproductive and sexual health issues include sex education, puberty, sexuality and sexual function. Women also experience a number of issues related to the health of their breasts and genital tract, which fall into the scope of gynaecology.

Non-reproductive health

Women and men have different experiences of the same illnesses, especially cardiovascular disease, cancer, depression and dementia, and are more prone to urinary tract infections than men.

Cardiovascular disease

Cardiovascular disease is the leading cause of death (30%) amongst women in the United States, and the leading cause of chronic disease amongst them, affecting nearly 40% (Gronowski and Schindler, Tables I and IV). The onset occurs at a later age in women than in men. For instance the incidence of stroke in women under the age of 80 is less than that in men, but higher in those aged over 80. Overall the lifetime risk of stroke in women exceeds that in men. The risk of cardiovascular disease amongst those with diabetes and amongst smokers is also higher in women than in men. Many aspects of cardiovascular disease vary between women and men, including risk factors, prevalence, physiology, symptoms, response to intervention and outcome.

Cancer

Women and men have approximately equal risk of dying from cancer, which accounts for about a quarter of all deaths, and is the second leading cause of death. However the relative incidence of different cancers varies between women and men. In the United States the three commonest types of cancer of women in 2012 were lung, breast and colorectalcancers. In addition other important cancers in women, in order of importance, are ovarian, uterine (including endometrial and cervical cancers (Gronowski and Schindler, Table III). Similar figures were reported in 2016. While cancer death rates rose rapidly during the twentieth century, the increase was less and later in women due to differences in smoking rates. More recently cancer death rates have started to decline as the use of tobacco becomes less common. Between 1991 and 2012, the death rate in women declined by 19% (less than in men). In the early twentieth century death from uterine (uterine body and cervix) cancers was the leading cause of cancer death in women, who had a higher cancer mortality than men.

From the 1930s onwards, uterine cancer deaths declined, primarily due to lower death rates from cervical cancer following the availability of the Papanicolaou (Pap) screening test. This resulted in an overall reduction of cancer deaths in women between the 1940s and 1970s, when rising rates of lung cancer led to an overall increase. By the 1950s the decline in uterine cancer left breast cancer as the leading cause of cancer death till it was overtaken by lung cancer in the 1980s. All three cancers (lung, breast, uterus) are now declining in cancer death rates (Siegel et al. Figure 8), but more women die from lung cancer every year than from breast, ovarian, and uterine cancers combined. Overall about 20% of people found to have lung cancer are never smokers, yet amongst nonsmoking women the risk of developing lung cancer is three times greater than amongst men who never smoked. In addition to mortality, cancer is a cause of considerable morbidity in women. Women have a lower lifetime probability of being diagnosed with cancer (38% vs 45% for men), but are more likely to be diagnosed with cancer at an earlier age.

Breast cancer

Breast cancer is the second most common cancer in the world and the most common among women. It is also among the ten most common chronic diseases of women, and a substantial contributor to loss of quality of life (Gronowski and Schindler, Table IV). Globally, it accounts for 25% of all cancers. In 2016, breast cancer is the most common cancer diagnosed among women in both developed and developing countries, accounting for nearly 30% of all cases, and worldwide accounts for one and a half million cases and over half a million deaths, being the fifth most common cause of cancer death overall and the second in developed regions. Geographic variation in incidence is the opposite of that of cervical cancer, being highest in Northern America and lowest in Eastern and Middle Africa, but mortality rates are relatively constant, resulting in a wide variance in case mortality, ranging from 25% in developed regions to 37% in developing regions, and with 62% of deaths occurring in developing countries.

Cervical cancer

Globally, cervical cancer is the fourth commonest cancer amongst women, particularly those of lower socioeconomic status. Women in this group have reduced access to health care, high rates of child and forced marriage, parity, polygamy and exposure to STIs from multiple sexual contacts of male partners. All of these factors place them at higher risk.In developing countries, cervical cancer accounts for 12% of cancer cases amongst women and is the second leading cause of death, where about 85% of the global burden of over 500,000 cases and 250,000 deaths from this disease occurred in 2012.

The highest incidence occurs in Eastern Africa, where with Middle Africa, cervical cancer is the commonest cancer in women. The case fatality rate of 52% is also higher in developing countries than in developed countries (43%), and the mortality rate varies by 18-fold between regions of the world Cervical cancer is associated with human papillomavirus (HPV), which has also been implicated in cancers of the vulva, vagina, anus, and oropharynx. Almost 300 million women worldwide have been infected with HPV, one of the commoner sexually transmitted infections, and 5% of the 13 million new cases of cancer in the world have been attributed to HPV. In developed countries, screening for cervical cancer using the Pap test has identified pre-cancerous changes in the cervix, at least in those women with access to health care. Also an HPV vaccine programme is available in 45 countries. Screening and prevention programmes have limited availability in developing countries although inexpensive low technology programmes are being developed, but access to treatment is also limited. If applied globally, HPV vaccination at 70% coverage could save the lives of 4 million women from cervical cancer, since most cases occur in developing countries.

Ovarian cancer

By contrast, ovarian cancer, the leading cause of reproductive organ cancer deaths, and the fifth commonest cause of cancer deaths in women in the United States, lacks an effective screening programme, and is predominantly a disease of women in industrialised countries. Because it is largely asymptomatic in its earliest stages, more than 50% of women have stage III or higher cancer (spread beyond the ovaries) by the time they are diagnosed, with a consequent poor prognosis.

Mental health

Almost 25% of women will experience mental health issues over their lifetime. Women are at higher risk than men from anxiety, depression, and psychosomatic complaints.Globally, depression is the leading disease burden. In the United States, women have depression twice as often as men. The economic costs of depression in American women are estimated to be $20 billion every year. The risks of depression in women have been linked to changing hormonal environment that women experience, including puberty, menstruation, pregnancy, childbirth and the menopause. Women also metabolise drugs used to treat depression differently to men. Suicide rates are less in women than men (<1% vs. 2.4%), but are a leading cause of death for women under the age of 60. In the United Kingdom, the Women's Mental Health Taskforce was formed aiming to address differences in mental health experiences and needs between women and men.

Dementia

The prevalence of Alzheimer's Disease in the United States is estimated at 5.1 million, and of these two thirds are women. Furthermore, women are far more likely to be the primary caregivers of adult family members with depression, so that they bear both the risks and burdens of this disease. The lifetime risk for a woman of developing Alzheimer's disease is twice that of men. Part of this difference may be due to life expectancy, but changing hormonal status over their lifetime may also play a par as may differences in gene expression. Deaths due to dementia are higher in women than men (4.5% of deaths vs. 2.0%).

Bone health

Osteoporosis ranks sixth amongst chronic diseases of women in the United States, with an overall prevalence of 18%, and a much higher rate involving the femur, neck or lumbar spine amongst women (16%) than men (4%), over the age of 50 (Gronowski and Schindler, Table IV). Osteoporosis is a risk factor for bone fracture and about 20% of senior citizens who sustain a hip fracture die within a year. The gender gap is largely the result of the reduction of estrogen levels

Violence

Women experience structural and personal violence differently than men. The United Nations has defined violence against women as; " any act of gender-based violence that results in, or is likely to result in, physical, sexual or mental harm or suffering to women, including threats of such acts, coercion or arbitrary deprivation of liberty, whether occurring in public or in private life." (United Nations, Declaration on the Elimination of Violence against Women, 1993) Violence against women may take many forms, including physical, sexual, emotional and psychological and may occur throughout the life-course. Structural violence may be embedded in legislation or policy, or be systematic misogyny by organisations against groups of women. Perpetrators of personal violence include state actors, strangers, acquaintances, relatives and intimate partners and manifests itself across a spectrum from discrimination, through harassment, sexual assault and rape, and physical harm to murder (femicide). It may also include cultural practices such as female genital cutting. Non-fatal violence against women has severe implications for women's physical, mental and reproductive health, and is seen as not simply isolated events but rather a systematic pattern of behaviour that both violates their rights but also limits their role in society and requires a systematic approach.

The World Health Organization (WHO) estimates that 35% of women in the world have experienced physical or sexual violence over their lifetime and that the commonest situation is intimate partner violence. 30% of women in relationships report such experience, and 38% of murders of women are due to intimate partners. These figures may be as high as 70% in some regions. Risk factors include low educational achievement, a parental experience of violence, childhood abuse, gender inequality and cultural attitudes that allow violence to be considered more acceptable.

Violence was declared a global health priority by the WHO at its assembly in 1996, drawing on both the United Nations Declaration on the elimination of violence against women(1993) and the recommendations of both the International Conference on Population and Development (Cairo, 1994) and the Fourth World Conference on Women (Beijing, 1995) This was followed by its 2002 World Report on Violence and Health, which focusses on intimate partner and sexual violence. Meanwhile, the UN embedded these in an action plan when its General Assembly passed the Millennium Declaration in September 2000, which resolved inter alia "to combat all forms of violence against women and to implement the Convention on the Elimination of All Forms of Discrimination against Women". One of the Millennium Goals (MDG 3) was the promotion of gender equality and the empowerment of women, which sought to eliminate all forms of violence against women as well as implementing CEDAW. This recognised that eliminating violence, including discrimination was a prerequisite to achieving all other goals of improving women's health. However it was later criticised for not including violence as an explicit target, the "missing target". In the evaluation of MDG 3, violence remained a major barrier to achieving the goals. In the successor Sustainable Development Goals, which also explicitly list the related issues of discrimination, child marriage and genital cutting, one target is listed as "Eliminate all forms of violence against all women and girls in the public and private spheres" by 2030.

UN Women believe that violence against women "is rooted in gender-based discrimination and social norms and gender stereotypes that perpetuate such violence", and advocate moving from supporting victims to prevention, through addressing root and structural causes. They recommend programmes that start early in life and are directed towards both genders to promote respect and equality, an area often overlooked in public policy. This strategy, which involves broad educational and cultural change, also involves implementing the recommendations of the 57th session of the UN Commission on the Status of Women (2013To that end the 2014 UN International Day of the Girl Child was dedicated to ending the cycle of violence. In 2016, the World Health Assembly also adopted a plan of action to combat violence against women, globally.

Women in health research

Changes in the way research ethics was visualised in the wake of the Nuremberg Trials (1946), led to an atmosphere of protectionism of groups deemed to be vulnerable that was often legislated or regulated. This resulted in the relative underrepresentation of women in clinical trials. The position of women in research was further compromised in 1977, when in response to the tragedies resulting from thalidomide and diethylstilbestrol (DES), the United States Food and Drug Administration (FDA) prohibited women of child-bearing years from participation in early stage clinical trials. In practice this ban was often applied very widely to exclude all women. Women, at least those in the child-bearing years, were also deemed unsuitable research subjects due to their fluctuating hormonal levels during the menstrual cycle. However, research has demonstrated significant biological differences between the sexes in rates of susceptibility, symptoms and response to treatment in many major areas of health, including heart disease and some cancers. These exclusions pose a threat to the application of evidence-based medicine to women, and compromise to care offered to both women and men.

The increasing focus on Women's Rights in the United States during the 1980s focused attention on the fact that many drugs being prescribed for women had never actually been tested in women of child-bearing potential, and that there was a relative paucity of basic research into women's health. In response to this the National Institutes of Health (NIH) created the Office of Research on Women's Health (ORWH) in 1990 to address these inequities. In 1993 the National Institutes of Health Revitalisation Act officially reversed US policy by requiring NIH funded phase III clinical trials to include women.

This resulted in an increase in women recruited into research studies. The next phase was the specific funding of large scale epidemiology studies and clinical trials focussing on women's health such as the Women's Health Initiative(1991), the largest disease prevention study conducted in the US. Its role was to study the major causes of death, disability and frailty in older women. Despite this apparent progress, women remain underepresented. In 2006 women accounted for less than 25% of clinical trials published in 2004, A follow up study by the same authors five years later found little evidence of improvement. Another study found between 10–47% of women in heart disease clinical trials, despite the prevalence of heart disease in women. Lung cancer is the leading cause of cancer death amongst women, but while the number of women enrolled in lung cancer studies is increasing, they are still far less likely to be enrolled than men.

One of the challenges in assessing progress in this area is the number of clinical studies that either do not report the gender of the subjects or lack the statistical power to detect gender differences. These were still issues in 2014, and further compounded by the fact that the majority of animal studies also exclude females or fail to account for differences in sex and gender. for instance despite the higher incidence of depression amongst women, less than half of the animal studies use female animals. Consequently, a number of funding agencies and scientific journals are asking researchers to explicitly address issues of sex and gender in their research.

A related issue is the inclusion of pregnant women in clinical studies. Since other illnesses can exist concurrently with pregnancy, information is needed on the response to and efficacy of interventions during pregnancy, but ethical issues relative to the fetus, make this more complex. This gender bias is partly offset by the initiation of large scale epidemiology studies of women, such as the Nurses' Health Study (1976), Women's Health Initiative and Black Women's Health Study.

Women have also been the subject of abuse in health care research, such as the situation revealed in the Cartwright Inquiry in New Zealand (1988), in which research by two feminist journalists revealed that women with cervical abnormalities were not receiving treatment, as part of an experiment. The women were not told of the abnormalities and several later died.

National and international initiatives

In addition to addressing gender inequity in research, a number of countries have made women's health the subject of national initiatives. For instance in 1991 in the United States, the Department of Health and Human Services established an Office on Women's Health (OWH) with the goal of improving the health of women in America, through coordinating the women's health agenda throughout the Department, and other agencies. In the twenty first century the Office has focussed on underserviced women. Also, in 1994 the Centers for Disease Control and Prevention (CDC) established its own Office of Women's Health (OWH), which was formally authorised by the 2010 Affordable Health Care Act (ACA).

Internationally, many United Nations agencies such as the World Health Organization (WHO), United Nations Population Fund (UNFPA)and UNICEF maintain specific programs on women's health, or maternal, sexual and reproductive health. In addition the United Nations global goals address many issues related to women's health, both directly and indirectly. These include the 2000 Millennium Development Goals (MDG) and their successor, the Sustainable Development Goals adopted in September 2015, following the report on progress towards the MDGs (The Millennium Development Goals Report 2015). For instance the eight MDG goals, eradicating extreme poverty and hunger, achieving universal primary education, promoting gender equality and empowering women, reducing child mortality rates, improving maternal health, combating HIV/AIDS malaria and other diseases, ensuring environmental sustainability, and developing a global partnership for development, all impact on women's health, as do all seventeen SDG goals, in addition to the specific SDG5: Achieve gender equality and empower all women and girls

Goals and challenges

Research is a priority in terms of improving women's health. Research needs include diseases unique to women, more serious in women and those that differ in risk factors between women and men. The balance of gender in research studies needs to be balanced appropriately to allow analysis that will detect interactions between gender and other factors. Gronowski and Schindler suggest that scientific journals make documentation of gender a requirement when reporting the results of animal studies, and that funding agencies require justification from investigators for any gender inequity in their grant proposals, giving preference to those that are inclusive. They also suggest it is the role of health organisations to encourage women to enroll in clinical research. However, there has been progress in terms of large scale studies such as the WHI, and in 2006 the Society for Women's Health Research founded the Organization for the Study of Sex Differences (OSSD) and the journal Biology of Sex Differences to further the study of sex differences.

Research findings can take some time before becoming routinely implemented into clinical practice. Clinical medicine needs to incorporate the information already available from research studies as to the different ways in which diseases affect women and men. Many "normal" laboratory values have not been properly established for the female population separately, and similarly the "normal" criteria for growth and development. Drug dosing needs to take gender differences in drug metabolism into account.

Globally, women's access to health care remains a challenge, both in developing and developed countries. In the United States, before the Affordable Health Care Act came into effect, 25% of women of child-bearing age lacked health insurance. In the absence of adequate insurance, women are likely to avoid important steps to self care such as routine physical examination, screening and prevention testing, and prenatal care. The situation is aggravated by the fact that women living below the poverty line are at greater risk of unplanned pregnancy, unplanned delivery and elective abortion. Added to the financial burden in this group are poor educational achievement, lack of transportation, inflexible work schedules and difficulty obtaining child care, all of which function to create barriers to accessing health care. These problems are much worse in developing countries. Under 50% of childbirths in these countries are assisted by healthcare providers (e.g. midwives, nurses, doctors) which accounts for higher rates of maternal death, up to 1:1,000 live births. This is despite the WHO setting standards, such as a minimum of four antenatal visits. A lack of healthcare providers, facilities, and resources such as formularies all contribute to high levels of morbidity amongst women from avoidable conditions such as obstetrical fistulae, sexually transmitted diseases and cervical cancer.

These challenges are included in the goals of the Office of Research on Women's Health, in the United States, as is the goal of facilitating women's access to careers in biomedicine. The ORWH believes that one of the best ways to advance research in women's health is to increase the proportion of women involved in healthcare and health research, as well as assuming leadership in government, centres of higher learning, and in the private sector. This goal acknowledges the glass ceiling that women face in careers in science and in obtaining resources from grant funding to salaries and laboratory space. The National Science Foundation in the United States states that women only gain half of the doctorates awarded in science and engineering, fill only 21% of full-time professor positions in science and 5% of those in engineering, while earning only 82% of the remuneration their male colleagues make. These figures are even lower in Europe.

CHAPTER - 7

TRAFFICKING PROTOCOL

The Protocol to Prevent, Suppress and Punish Trafficking in Persons, especially Women and Children (also referred to as the Trafficking Protocol or UN TIP Protocol) is a protocol to the Convention against Transnational Organised Crime. It is one of the three Palermo protocols. Its purpose is defined at Article 2. Statement of purpose as: "(a) To prevent and combat trafficking in persons, paying particular attention to women and children; (b) To protect and assist the victims of such trafficking, with full respect for their human rights; and (c) To promote cooperation among States Parties in order to meet those objectives." Content of the protocol

The protocol covers the following:

- Defining the crime of trafficking in human beings; To be considered trafficking in persons, a situation must meet three conditions: act (i.e., recruitment), means (i.e., through the use of force or deception) and purpose (i.e., for the purpose of forced labour)

"Trafficking in persons" shall mean the recruitment, transportation, transfer, harbouring or receipt of persons, by means of the threat or use of force or other forms of coercion, of abduction, of fraud, of deception, of the abuse of power or of a position of vulnerability or of the giving or receiving of payments or benefits to achieve the consent of a person having control over another person, for the purpose of exploitation. Exploitation shall include, at a minimum, the exploitation of the prostitution of others or other forms of sexual exploitation, forced labour or services, slavery or practices similar to slavery, servitude or the removal of organs... The consent of a victim of trafficking in persons to the intended exploitation set forth [above] shall be irrelevant where any of the means set forth [above] have been used.

- Facilitating the return and acceptance of children who have been victims of cross-border trafficking, with due regard to their safety

- Prohibiting the trafficking of children (which is defined as being a person under 18 years of age) for purposes of commercial sexual exploitation of children (CSEC), exploitative labour practices, or the removal of body parts
- Suspending parental rights of parents, caregivers, or any other persons who have parental rights in respect of a child should they be found to have trafficked a child
- Ensuring that definitions of trafficking reflect the need for special safeguards and care for children, including appropriate legal protection
- Ensuring that trafficked persons are not punished for any offences or activities related to their having been trafficked, such as prostitution and immigration violations
- Ensuring that victims of trafficking are protected from deportation or return where there are reasonable grounds to suspect that such return would represent a significant security risk to the trafficked person or their family
- Considering temporary or permanent residence in countries of transit or destination for trafficking victims in exchange for testimony against alleged traffickers, or on humanitarian and compassionate grounds
- Providing for proportional criminal penalties to be applied to persons found guilty of trafficking in aggravating circumstances, including offences involving trafficking in children or offences committed or involving complicity by state officials
- Providing for the confiscation of the instruments and proceeds of trafficking and related offences to be used for the benefit of trafficked persons

The convention and the protocol obligate ratifying states to introduce national trafficking legislation.

Regional action against trafficking in human beings

In Warsaw on 16 May 2005, the Council of Europe Convention on Action against Trafficking in Human Beings was opened for accession. The convention established a Group of Experts on Action against Trafficking in Human Beings (GRETA) which monitors the implementation of the convention through country reports. It has been ratified (as of January 2016) by 45 European states, while a further one state (Turkey) has signed but not yet ratified it. Complementary protection is ensured through the Council of Europe Convention on the Protection of Children against Sexual Exploitation and Sexual Abuse ,

International child abduction

The term international child abduction is generally synonymous with international parental kidnapping, child snatching, and child stealing. However, the more precise legal usage of international child abduction originates in private international law and refers to the illegal removal of children from their home by an acquaintance or family member to a foreign country. In this context, "illegal" is normally taken to mean "in breach of custodial rights" and "home" is defined as the child's habitual residence. As implied by the "breach of custodial rights," the phenomenon of international child abduction generally involves an illegal removal that creates a jurisdictional conflict of laws whereby multiple authorities and jurisdictions could conceivably arrive at seemingly reasonable and conflicting custodial decisions with geographically limited application. Such a result often strongly affects a child's access and connection to half their family and may cause the loss of their former language, culture, name and nationality, it violates numerous children's rights, and can cause severe psychological and emotional trauma to the child and family left behind.

There is a common misconception that because the abductor in these cases is usually not a stranger the children are not in danger.The harmful consequences for children and families have been shown in several studies and child abduction has been characterized as a form of parental alienation and child abuse. Adding international dimensions to the detrimental effects of child abduction significantly increases the detrimental effects on children and families. The modern day ease of international travel and corollary increase in international marriages is leading to a rapid rise in the number of international child abductions.

International child abduction occurs when one parent unlawfully takes (or retains) a minor child in a country other than the one the child has his/her habitual residence. If that country is a party to the Hague Convention on the Civil Aspects of International Child Abduction(applicable to children under 16), then the child will usually be returned to the country of origin. If there is a conflict of law between two countries, the guardian must follow the laws of the country where the child physically present. It is very common that a parent that has legal custody of the child in the country where the child physically present, is wanted for parental abduction in another country. In such cases the child cannot be removed from the country where the child physically present, before child custody ends at age 18, because otherwise the child will not be returned to the taking parent. This does not have any thing to do with children's rights or welfare, only parental rights. According to the law the left behind parent is legally the only victim if the child is not returned before child custody ends at age 18.

Origin of the term

What is today called "parental kidnapping," "international child abduction,", "parental child abduction" and "parental child trafficking" has existed as long as different legal jurisdictions and international borders have—though often under different names. None of these names achieved the modern day broad acceptance of terms like international child abduction. Lacking a common set of terminology or specifically designed laws to address the, at the time, poorly defined problem, researchers on the history of cross-border child abduction must search for terms like "custodial interference," "contempt of child custody orders," "legal kidnapping" or, in cases where children were viewed more as property than as individual subjects of rights, name variations on theft, child-maintenance debt and smuggling, among others.

Lawmakers struggled to typify and discuss international child abduction and discussions at the Hague Conference on Private International Law noted that, what some were referring to with variations on "legal kidnapping," was an oxymoron since that which is legal cannot be kidnapping and that which is kidnapping cannot be legal. The response to these concerns was the coining of the term "international child abduction." The terms first prominent use was in the title of the 1980 Hague Convention on the Civil Aspects of International Child Abduction. The term is not, however, used anywhere in the actual text of the convention itself in preference of the more technical terms "wrongful removal" or "wrongful retention" which were better suited for describing the mechanics of the Convention's system. The use of the term is now widespread in international law.

Internationalization of family law

In all family law disputes a determination must be made as to which legal systems and laws should be applied to the dispute. This question becomes much more complicated when aspects, or parties, of the case occur in, or hail from, multiple legal jurisdictions. Today's international family law norms were heavily influenced by the concepts of domicile and nationality. In Europe these ideas were refined during the nineteenth century by Italian politician, Pasquale Mancini, who believed matters of personal status were to be governed by the nationality of the person. During the same period in the US and Latin America the prevailing principle was that jurisdiction over personal matters was determined by domicile which, in the Americas, was acquired immediately upon moving to a foreign jurisdiction even if neither citizenship nor nationality were acquired.

Starting in the late eighteenth century until the early 1920s a number of efforts were made to develop a series of international treaties governing international conflicts of law in Europe. Treaties that favored nationality as the determining jurisdictional factor either never got of the ground, were not widely signed or had substantial practical problems with countries renouncing them after signing. At the same time the inter-American system in Latin America produced the Bustamante Code of 1928 and the Montevideo Conventions of 1939 and 1940. Of particular note in these later Conventions was the introduction of a definition of "domicile" that started with a reference to the "habitual residence" for civil status. Lessons learned in prior efforts to create successful multilateral treaties culminated in a number of successful treaties in the mid-1900s, such as the 1961 Convention on the Protection of Minors, the New York Convention of 1956 on the Recovery Abroad of Maintenance drafted under the auspices of the United Nations, and the Hague Convention of 1961 concerning the powers of authorities and the law applicable in respect of the protection of minors ("1961 Convention.")

The 1961 Convention brought an innovation in terminology by creating a compromise between advocates of "nationality" as the determining factor for jurisdiction and advocates for the modern fact-centric model of "habitual residence." It also included expanded language to encompass both judicial and administrative authorities in response to the Boll case, in which Sweden claimed its public administrative law was exempt from the 1902 Convention on the Guardianship of minors because it only governed domestic private judicial law and not public administrative law. The 1961 Convention also emphasized the concept of the "interests of the child" as a basis for authorities of the child's nationality to overrule the authorities of the child's habitual residence. Of particularly special note, the drafters of the 1961 Convention expressly considered a provision addressing the removal of a child from their habitual residence with an intent to evade rightful jurisdiction—primarily for child custody reasons. This first attempt to codify international child abduction failed due to an inability to agree on a definition or manner of describing the phenomenon, with a number of countries that adhered to the principle of nationality regulating personal child and family law unable to classify their nationals removing children from foreign countries to their home state as fraudulent evasion.

In actual cases of international child abduction, this lack of a specific provision on child abduction in the 1961 treaty resulted in countries regularly interpreting the "habitual residence" concept of the Convention in a manner that allowed parents to take children to a foreign country and immediately acquire "habitual residence." This allowed judicial forum shoppingand created perverse incentives for removing children from their homes to foreign jurisdictions in order to game the family law system and obtain a more favorable custodial outcome than could be gained in the jurisdiction of the child's home.

In the 1970s, dissatisfaction with these results led to efforts to create conventions on the foreign recognition and enforcement of judgments to make it harder for courts to favor a parent solely because that parent is a national suing in his or her home state. Canada also proposed that the Hague Conference work on a Convention to address what it termed "legal kidnapping." The Hague received Canada's request enthusiastically and, inspired by a Swiss proposal originally submitted at the Council of Europe in 1976 coined a new term in international family law – "international child abduction." Although the problem of international child abduction was well understood, finding a way to address the problem in practice was exceedingly difficult, but the Swiss proposal had a solution that was elegant in its simplicity. Why not simply restore the status quo ante?

The Hague Convention on the Civil Aspects of International Child Abduction In 1980 the Hague Conference drafted a convention to address the problem of international child abduction: the Hague Convention on the Civil Aspects of International Child Abduction – commonly referred to as the Abduction Convention. The Swiss idea of restoring the status quo ante after a "wrongful removal" or "wrongful retention" became a mainstay of the Abduction Convention. Under the convention, an application could be made for the return of a child who had been wrongfully removed or retained so long as the applicant possessed rights of custody, and provided that those rights were being "actually exercised" at the time of the abduction. The concept of "actually exercised" in reference to custodial rights itself was an innovation in terminology. Having met these requirements a child was to be returned "forthwith" except in exceptional circumstances.

Inspired by the Hague Evidence Convention and the Hague Service Convention's of 1965 and 1970, the Abduction Convention required the establishment of a single Central Authority in each country that would handle two-way communications with domestic courts, administrative agencies and foreign central authorities. Furthermore, each central authority was required to take "any and all actions" to secure the goals of the treaty and cooperate with other central authorities to do the same. All of these new obligations emphasized the need for international cooperation amongst state parties in achieving the objectives of the convention.

The United Nations Convention on the Rights of the Child

Established in 1989 the Convention on the Rights of the Child reflected the growing international consensus that children be viewed as a subject of rights and not merely as an object of rights or of protective action. The UNCRC roused an unprecedented response with 187 countries ratifying it within seven years forming an essential backdrop in international children's law. Article 11 of the Convention explicitly requires State Parties to combat the illicit transfer and retention of children and promote the conclusion of bilateral or multilateral agreements or accession to existing agreements that do so, Article 35 stipulates that "States Parties shall take all appropriate national, bilateral and multilateral measures to prevent the abduction, sale or traffic of children for any purpose or in any form." The Hague Convention on Jurisdiction, Applicable Law, Recognition, Enforcement and Cooperation The 1996 Convention on Jurisdiction, Applicable Law, Recognition, Enforcement and Co-operation in respect of Parental Responsibility and Measures is the third of the modern Hague Conventions on international family law, following in the footsteps of the Abduction Convention and the Adoption Convention. It is much broader in scope than the first two conventions and covers a wide range of civil measures related to the protection of children including: orders concerning parental responsibility and contact, public measures of protection or care, matters of legal representation and the protection of children's property.

The Convention has uniform rules determining which country's authorities are competent to take the necessary measures of protection. The Convention also determines which country's laws are to be applied and provides for the recognition and enforcement of measures taken in one Contracting State in all the other Contracting States. The co-operation provisions of the Convention provide the basic framework for the exchange of information and the necessary degree of collaboration between administrative authorities in the Contracting States. Reflecting an ever-increasing emphasis on the need for international cooperation as an essential element in the success of these measures the Convention has a full chapter on cooperation consisting of eleven articles. Although initially slow to gain support and plagued with political problems, the number of states acceding to it has begun to grow.

Impact on society, families and children

As the result of the harmful effects on children, parental kidnapping has been characterized as a form of child abuse and an extreme form of parental alienation. Abducted children suffer emotionally and sometimes physically at the hands of their abducting parents. Many are told the other parent is dead or has abandoned them. Uprooted from their entire life, home, family and friends, abducted children are often even given new names by their abductors and instructed to hide their real names or where they used to live. Generally the abductor avoids mentioning the victim parent and waits for time to erase difficult questions, such as "When can we see mom/dad again?". These children become hostages. It is beyond their comprehension that a parent who truly cares and loves them cannot discover their whereabouts. Childhood cannot be recaptured. Abductions rob a child of their sense of history, intimacy, values and morals, self-awareness, opportunity of knowing one's beginnings and the love and contact of extended family—a loss no child possesses the ability to protect themselves against. Huntington (1982) lists some of the deleterious effects of abduction on child victims:

1. Depression;
2. Loss of community;
3. Loss of stability, security, and trust;
4. Excessive fearfulness, even of ordinary occurrences;
5. Loneliness;
6. Anger;
7. Helplessness;
8. Disruption in identity formation; and
9. Fear of abandonment.

Many of these effects can be subsumed by the problems relevant to reactive attachment disorder, stress, fear of abandonment, learned helplessness, and guilt. The extended support systems of abducting and victim parents can also become part of the dispute. Believing primarily one side of the abduction story, family, friends, and professionals in each parents individual country may lose their objectivity. As a result, protective concerns expressed by the abandoned parent may be viewed as undue criticism, interference, and histrionics preventing the victim parent from effectively relieving the trauma imposed on their innocent child by the abduction.

Mediation in child abduction cases

Mediation is a process during which abductors and the left behind family, assisted by mediator(s), attempt to resolve conflicts independent of the judicial system. Mediators create a constructive atmosphere for discussions and ensure fair dealings between parents. The mediators do not make decisions; instead, they confine themselves to assisting the parties in working out for themselves a fair and sensible solution to their problems. More specifically, the mediation can address not only the child's primary residence, but also the child's contact with both parents, visitation arrangements, agreements concerning the child's maintenance, schooling, further education, bi-cultural and bi-lingual upbringing, necessary arrangements for financial support etc. Mediation can be helpful in international child abduction cases. In the context of mediation families can deal with the question of return and also find solutions to other issues relating to their children.

Legal justifications for abduction

International law has generally recognized that there may be extenuating circumstances where a child abduction may have been necessary or justifiable due to extenuating circumstances. The 1902 Convention on the Guardianship of minors limited such considerations to strictly emergency situations. Starting with the 1924 Declaration on the Rights of the Child and the 1959 United Nations Declaration on the Rights of the Child there was a growing recognition at the international level of the shift in nation's domestic laws away from parental authority and towards an emphasis on protecting the child, even from their own parents. This foreshadowed the 1989 UN Convention on the Rights of the Child and led to the establishment of exceptional circumstances in Article 13 of the Hague Abduction Convention where the removal of children would not be considered child abduction and allow the child to remain in their new country.

International adoption

International adoption (also referred to as intercountry adoption or transnational adoption) is a type of adoption in which an individual or couple becomes the legal and permanent parent(s) of a child who is a national of a different country. In general, prospective adoptive parents must meet the legal adoption requirements of their country of residence and those of the country whose nationality the child holds. International adoption is not the same thing as transcultural or interracial adoption. However, the fact is that a family will often become a transcultural or interracial family upon the adoption of a child internationally. The laws of countries vary in their willingness to allow international adoptions. Some countries have established rules and procedures for international adoptions, while other countries expressly forbid it. Various countries, notably many African nations, have extended residency requirements for adoptive parents that, in effect, rule out most international adoptions.

Process overview

The requirements necessary to begin the process of international adoption can vary depending on the country of the adoptive parent(s). For example, while most countries require prospective adoptive parents to first get approval to adopt, in some the approval can only be given afterwards. Often an "orphan" is a child whose living birth family has consented to an adoption. Some describe orphanages as "nurseries" or "children's homes" because in numerous instances children's parents have not consented to an adoption of their children. It is not uncommon for a parent to put a child in a "nursery" temporarily while they deal with poverty or work, or want to take advantage of the educational opportunities in the orphanage/nursery. Because orphanages/nurseries often provide education, they function more like subsidized boarding school.

Prospective parents of international adoptees wait to get a referral for a child, which often means waiting until one of these parents of the children in nurseries/orphanages consents to the adoption. Although bureaucracy is often blamed for the slow process of adopting a child, often what is to blame is that the demand for children in the less-developed world exceeds the supply. A senior advisor on child protection with UNICEF, Alexandria Yuster, argues that international adoption is now more about finding children for first world (developed world) parents than finding homes for children. Susan Bissell, also of UNICEF, said that she does not oppose international adoption, but believes that it is preferable for abandoned children to be taken back by their previous families and advises governments to provide small monetary incentives to families who are willing to do so.

In the United States, typically the first stage of the process is selecting a licensed adoption agency or attorney to work with. Each agency or attorney tends to work with a different set of countries, although some only focus on a single country. Pursuant to the rules of the Hague Adoption Convention (an international treaty related to adoption issues) the adoption agency or attorney must be accredited by the U.S. government if the child's country is also a participant in the Hague Convention. If the child's country is not a participant then the rules of the Hague do not apply, and the specific laws of the child's and adoptive parent(s)' countries must be followed. Even when the Hague does not apply, a home study and USCIS (United States Citizen and Immigration Services; formerly INS, Immigration and Naturalization Service) approval are requirements. The Hague is discussed below.

A dossier is prepared that contains a large amount of information about the prospective adoptive parents required by the child's country. Typically this includes financial information, a background check, fingerprints, a home study review by a social worker, report from the adoptive parents' doctor regarding their health, and other supporting information. Again, requirements will vary widely from country to country, and even region to region in large countries such as Russia. Once complete, the dossier is submitted to the appropriate authorities in the child's country for review.

After the dossier is reviewed and the prospective parents are approved to adopt, they are matched to an eligible child (except in some countries such as India, which does not allow "matching" of a child to (a) prospective parent(s)). The parent is usually sent information about the child, such as age, gender, health history, etc. This is generally called a referral. A travel date is typically provided at a later time in most adoptions. However, some countries might also provide a travel date at the time of referral, informing the parents when they may travel to meet the child and sign any additional paperwork required to accept the referral. Some countries, such as Kazakhstan, do not allow referrals until the prospective parent travels to the country on their first trip. This is called a "blind" referral Depending on the country, the parents may have to make more than one trip overseas to complete the legal process. Some countries allow a child to be escorted to the adoptive parents' home country and the adoptive parents are not required to travel to the country of their adopted child.

There are usually several requirements after this point, such as paperwork to make the child a legal citizen of the adopting parents' country or re-adopt them. In addition, one or more follow up (or "post placement") visits from a social worker may be required—either by the placing agency used by the adoptive parents or by the laws of the country from which the child was adopted. In the United States, citizenship is automatically granted to all foreign-born children when at least one adoptive parent is a U.S. citizen, in accordance with the Child Citizenship Act of 2000. Depending on the circumstances of the adoption, the grant of citizenship takes place upon the child's admission to the U.S. as an immigrant or the child's adoption in the parent's home jurisdiction.

Policies and requirements

Adoption policies for each country vary widely. Information such as the age of the adoptive parents, financial status, educational level, marital status and history, number of dependent children in the house, sexual orientation, weight, psychological health, and ancestry are used by countries to determine what parents are eligible to adopt from that countryInformation such as the age of the child, fees and expenses, and the amount of travel time required in the child's birth country can also vary widely from one country to another

Each country sets its own rules, timelines and requirements surrounding adoption, and there are also rules that vary within the United States for each state. Each country, and often each part of the country, sets its own rules about what will be shared and how it will be shared (e.g., a picture of the child, child's health). Reliability and verifiability of the information is variableMost countries require that a parent travel to bring the child home; however, some countries allow the child to be escorted to his or her new homeland The U.S. Department of State has designated two accrediting entities for organizations providing inter-country adoption services in the United States and work with sending countries that have ratified the Hague Convention on Protection of Children and Co-operation in Respect of Intercountry Adoption. They are the Council on Accreditation and the Colorado Department of Health and Human Services. The U.S. Department of State maintains a list of all accredited international adoption providers.

Major origin and receiving countries of children

Basic demographic data on origin and receiving countries since the 2000s have only recently been analyzed and summarized in a specialized publication.

Major origin countries of children

According to one recent study, 6 countries (China, Ethiopia, India, South Korea, Ukraine and Vietnam) were major origin countries for almost a decade in the period 2003-2011. Yet there has been slight change in other countries sending most children.

In 2017, the top sending countries for children adopted by US citizens were China, Ethiopia, South Korea, Haiti, India, Ukraine, Colombia and Nigeria.

Major receiving countries

Based on Selman's research, during the year of 1998 and 2007, the top 10 receiving countries of all 23 reported countries, (ranked from the large to small), are the United States, Spain, France, Italy, Canada, Netherlands, Sweden, Norway, Denmark, and Australia. Among these 10 countries, the top 5 accounts for more than 80% of overall adoption, and the US is responsible for around 50% of all cases. Although historically the United States has been among the leaders in adopting children via international adoption, this has changed dramatically over the last decade. In 2004, 22,884 children were adopted internationally, while only 5,648 were adopted in 2015. This is attributed to a combination of factors: increased bureaucracy due to implementation of the Hague Convention guidelines, legal changes in the countries from which the adoptions occur eliminating countries from which to adopt, increased cost, corruption in some foreign courts/orphanages, and the policy of many countries to only free child with significant special needs.

Adoption from Ethiopia has become an increasingly popular option for adoptive families in the U.S, but international adoption was banned in 2018 by Ethiopia. According to the statistics of U.S. Department of State, the number of adoptees from Ethiopia has grown sharply from 42 (in 1999) to 1568 (in 2012).

Sex ratio of children adopted (US)

Generally, the US adopts more girls than boys. From 1999 to 2012, around 62% of adoptees by US families were girls, and only 38% were boys. Yet this discrepancy between female and male adoptees has gradually declined. In other words, now the sex ratio of girls and boys adopted is more balanced. It used to be true that China had more girls available for adoption, due to the Chinese culture's preference for sons in combination with the official planned birth policy implemented in 1979. Until the early 2000s, around 90–95% of Chinese children adopted by American families were girls. For numerous reasons, including a recent amendment of the one child policy, the dwindling number of available females for marriage, and an increased prevalence of sex selective abortions, most orphanages in China now house only children with special needs, the majority of which are male. Because of the heavy preference for females in adopting families most waiting children in China are boys, as girls with the same needs are quickly matched with a long line of families seeking Chinese daughters. Although India also has a noticeable excess of girls available for adoption (around 70%), In contrast, South Korea, another East Asian country, has a relatively large excess of boys being adopted; about 60% are boys. Countries suspending/ or be suspended adoption by US families There have been several countries (including certain major sending countries) that are completely not or only partially accepting intercountry adoption request from US families for certain reasons.

- Russia: In December 2012, Russian President Vladimir Putin signed into law a measure, effective January 1, 2013, banning the adoption of Russian children by US families. The ban was seen as diplomatic retaliation for the passage of the Magnitsky Act in the US, while popular support in Russia focused on incidents of abuse to adoptees by US families. In January 2013 about 20,000 people marched against the law in Moscow.
- India (temporarily)

The US also suspended adoption relationship with selected countries, due to Hague Convention or other rationales.

- Vietnam, temporarily suspended due to allegations of corruption and baby-selling
- Guatemala, the adoption was shut down in 2007 for adoption after allegations of corruption, families being coerced and children kidnapped to feed U.S. demand. (See also: Adoption in Guatemala)
- Nepal: Although Nepal has not closed its doors for adoption, the United States government has suspended adoptions from Nepal. Documents that were presented documenting the abandonment of these children in Nepal have been found to be unreliable and circumstances of alleged abandonment cannot be verified because of obstacles in the investigation of individual cases.

International legal framework

At the international level, the main legal instrument on intercountry adoption is the Convention on Protection of Children and Co-operation in Respect of Intercountry Adoption (hereafter the Hague Adoption Convention, 1993). However other relevant international legal instruments exist to ensure that the best interest of the child and the concern for her/his welfare inform the practices of intercountry adoption.

For example, the United Nations Convention on the Rights of the Child (1989) contains some specific references to intercountry adoption. The Declaration on Social and Legal Principles relating to the Protection and Welfare of Children, with Special Reference to Foster Placement and Adoption Nationally and Internationally (1986) calls Member States to establish policy, legislation and effective supervision for the protection of children involved in intercountry adoption.

All those instruments have some common principles:

- The principle of subsidiarity according to which intercountry adoption should only take place when suitable adoptive parents cannot be identified in the country of origin of the child
- The best interest of the child should be the paramount consideration
- The placement of the child should be made through competent authorities or agencies with the same safeguards and standards as national adoptions
- In no case should an adoption result in improper financial gains for those involved.

According to the Convention of the Rights of the Child (art. 21), as well as to the UN Declaration on the Protection and Welfare of Children (art. 17) and the Hague Adoption Convention (Preamble and art. 4), international adoption should be considered as an option if other arrangements (with priority to kin and adoptive families) cannot satisfactorily be arranged for the child in her or his country of origin (principle of subsidiarity between national and international adoption). However the international community still disagrees on the point whether the option of being placed in a permanent family setting through international adoption should prevail on the alternative of the placement of children in domestic care institutions. The United Nations Optional Protocol to the Convention on the Rights of the Child on the Sale of Children, Child Prostitution and Child Pornography (2000) is an additional international instrument that calls on States parties to ensure that coercive adoption is criminalized under national law, regardless of whether the offence is committed domestically or transnationally, on an individual or organized basis.

UN Declaration Relating to the Welfare of Children (1986)

The UN Declaration on Social and Legal Principles relating to the Protection and Welfare of Children, with Special Reference to Foster Placement and Adoption Nationally and Internationally was adopted by General Assembly resolution 41/85 of 3 December 1986. The UN Declaration Relating to the Welfare of Children reaffirms principle 6 of the Declaration of the Rights of the Child, according to which, "The child shall, wherever possible, grow up in the care and under the responsibility of his parents and, in any case, in an atmosphere of affection and of moral and material security." Article 17 affirms the principle of subsidiarity in these terms: "If a child cannot be placed in a foster or an adoptive family or cannot in any suitable manner be cared for in the country of origin, intercountry adoption may be considered as an alternative means of providing the child with a family." Article 24 requires Member States to consider the child's cultural and religious background and interest. The Declaration encourages States not to hurry the adoptive process. Article 15 states, "Sufficient time and adequate counselling should be given to the child's own parents, the prospective adoptive parents and, as appropriate, the child in order to reach a decision on the child's future."

UN Convention on the Rights of the Child (1989)

The United Nations Convention on the Right of the Child marks a turning point in the international law of children's rights recognizing the child as an active subject of international law whose views must be taken into consideration when dealing with matters affecting her or him (art.12). The principle of the best interests of the child should be a primary consideration in all actions concerning children, whether undertaken by public or private social welfare institutions, courts of law, administrative authorities or legislative bodies (art, 3). This same principle shall be the paramount consideration also when States Parties recognize and/or permit the system of adoption. Particularly, article 21 requires that States Parties "ensure that the adoption of a child is authorized only by competent authorities who determine that the adoption is permissible in view of the child's status concerning parents, relatives and legal guardians and that, if required, the persons concerned have given their informed consent to the adoption. The placement of the child also should not result in improper financial gain for those involved in it (art. 21.d).

The Hague Adoption Convention (1993

Recognizing some of the difficulties and challenges associated with international adoption, and to protect those involved from the corruption, abuses, and exploitation that sometimes accompanies it, in 1993 the Hague Conference on Private International Law developed the Convention on Protection of Children and Co-operation in Respect of Intercountry Adoption. The Convention came into force on May 1995. As of December 2018, there were 99 states parties to the Convention. Korea, Nepal and the Russian Federation are signatories but have not ratified.

With respect to the previous multilateral instruments, which include some provisions regarding intercountry adoption, the Hague Adoption Convention is the major multilateral instrument regulating international adoption. It calls for coordination and direct cooperation between countries to ensure that appropriate safeguards promote the best interest of the child (Article 1) and prevent the abduction, sale, or trafficking of children.

The Convention also requires that all processes should be authorized by central adoption authorities designated by the contracting states. (Chapter III of the Convention outlines the roles and responsibilities of this authority.) If fully implemented at the national level, the Convention offers also a protective framework against the risks potentially implied in private adoption (when the adoptive parents set the terms of the adoption directly with the birth parents or with children's institutions placed in the country of origin, without recurring to accredited adoption service providers).

The Convention lets states decide which public agency is the central adoption authority (whose supervision and authorization is necessary to proceed with adoption (article 17) and which other bodies should be accredited as the provider of adoption services (Article 9). If fully implemented at the national level, the Convention offers also a protective framework against the risks potentially implied in private adoption (when the adoptive parents set the terms of the adoption directly with the birth parents, without recurring to accredited bodies). The Implementation and Operation of the 1993 Inter country Adoption Convention****: Guide to Good Practice provides a guidance for the Convention operation, use and interpretation. The Convention is crucial because it provides formal international and intergovernmental recognition of intercountry adoption, working to ensure that adoptions under the Convention are recognized in other party countries.

To comply with international standards, many changes have been introduced in national legislation enacting laws to criminalize the act of obtaining improper gains from intercountry adoptions. However instances of trafficking in and sale of children for the purpose of adoption continue to take place in many parts of the world. Especially during emergency situations, natural disasters or conflicts, has been found that children are adopted without following appropriate legal procedures and risk to be victims of trafficking and sale. It has been raised also the issue that an excessive bureaucratization of the adoption process – following the implementation of the Hague Adoption Convention – possibly establishes additional barriers to the placement of children.

The States Parties to the present Convention,

Considering that, in accordance with the principles proclaimed in the Charter of the United Nations, recognition of the inherent dignity and of the equal and inalienable rights of all members of the human family is the foundation of freedom, justice and peace in the world, Bearing in mind that the peoples of the United Nations have, in the Charter, reaffirmed their faith in fundamental human rights and in the dignity and worth of the human person, and have determined to promote social progress and better standards of life in larger freedom,

Recognizing that the United Nations has, in the Universal Declaration of Human Rights and in the International Covenants on Human Rights, proclaimed and agreed that everyone is entitled to all the rights and freedoms set forth therein, without distinction of any kind, such as race, colour, sex, language, religion, political or other opinion, national or social origin, property, birth or other status, Recalling that, in the Universal Declaration of Human Rights, the United Nations has proclaimed that childhood is entitled to special care and assistance, Convinced that the family, as the fundamental group of society and the natural environment for the growth and well-being of all its members and particularly children, should be afforded the necessary protection and assistance so that it can fully assume its responsibilities within the community, Recognizing that the child, for the full and harmonious development of his or her personality, should grow up in a family environment, in an atmosphere of happiness, love and understanding,

Considering that the child should be fully prepared to live an individual life in society, and brought up in the spirit of the ideals proclaimed in the Charter of the United Nations, and in particular in the spirit of peace, dignity, tolerance, freedom, equality and solidarity, Bearing in mind that the need to extend particular care to the child has been stated in the Geneva Declaration of the Rights of the Child of 1924 and in the Declaration of the Rights of the Child adopted by the General Assembly on 20 November 1959 and recognized in the Universal Declaration of Human Rights, in the International Covenant on Civil and Political Rights (in particular in articles 23 and 24), in the International Covenant on Economic, Social and Cultural Rights (in particular in article 10) and in the statutes and relevant instruments of specialized agencies and international organizations concerned with the welfare of children,

Bearing in mind that, as indicated in the Declaration of the Rights of the Child, "the child, by reason of his physical and mental immaturity, needs special safeguards and care, including appropriate legal protection, before as well as after birth", Recalling the provisions of the Declaration on Social and Legal Principles relating to the Protection and Welfare of Children, with Special Reference to Foster Placement and Adoption Nationally and Internationally; the United Nations Standard Minimum Rules for the Administration of Juvenile Justice (The Beijing Rules); and the Declaration on the Protection of Women and Children in Emergency and Armed Conflict, Recognizing that, in all countries in the world, there are children living in exceptionally difficult conditions, and that such children need special consideration, Taking due account of the importance of the traditions and cultural values of each people for the protection and harmonious development of the child, Recognizing the importance of international co-operation for improving the living conditions of children in every country, in particular in the developing countries,

Have agreed as follows:

Article 1

For the purposes of the present Convention, a child means every human being below the age of eighteen years unless under the law applicable to the child, majority is attained earlier.

Article 2

1. States Parties shall respect and ensure the rights set forth in the present Convention to each child within their jurisdiction without discrimination of any kind, irrespective of the child's or his or her parent's or legal guardian's race, colour, sex, language, religion, political or other opinion, national, ethnic or social origin, property, disability, birth or other status.
2. States Parties shall take all appropriate measures to ensure that the child is protected against all forms of discrimination or punishment on the basis of the status, activities, expressed opinions, or beliefs of the child's parents, legal guardians, or family members.

Article 3

1. In all actions concerning children, whether undertaken by public or private social welfare institutions, courts of law, administrative authorities or legislative bodies, the best interests of the child shall be a primary consideration.
2. States Parties undertake to ensure the child such protection and care as is necessary for his or her well-being, taking into account the rights and duties of his or her parents, legal guardians, or other individuals legally responsible for him or her, and, to this end, shall take all appropriate legislative and administrative measures.
3. States Parties shall ensure that the institutions, services and facilities responsible for the care or protection of children shall conform with the standards established by competent authorities, particularly in the areas of safety, health, in the number and suitability of their staff, as well as competent supervision.

Article 4

States Parties shall undertake all appropriate legislative, administrative, and other measures for the implementation of the rights recognized in the present Convention. With regard to economic, social and cultural rights, States Parties shall undertake such measures to the maximum extent of their available resources and, where needed, within the framework of international co-operation.

Article 5

States Parties shall respect the responsibilities, rights and duties of parents or, where applicable, the members of the extended family or community as provided for by local custom, legal guardians or other persons legally responsible for the child, to provide, in a manner consistent with the evolving capacities of the child, appropriate direction and guidance in the exercise by the child of the rights recognized in the present Convention.

Article 6

1. States Parties recognize that every child has the inherent right to life.
2. States Parties shall ensure to the maximum extent possible the survival and development of the child.

Article 7

1. The child shall be registered immediately after birth and shall have the right from birth to a name, the right to acquire a nationality and. as far as possible, the right to know and be cared for by his or her parents.
2. States Parties shall ensure the implementation of these rights in accordance with their national law and their obligations under the relevant international instruments in this field, in particular where the child would otherwise be stateless.

Article 8

1. States Parties undertake to respect the right of the child to preserve his or her identity, including nationality, name and family relations as recognized by law without unlawful interference.
2. Where a child is illegally deprived of some or all of the elements of his or her identity, States Parties shall provide appropriate assistance and protection, with a view to re-establishing speedily his or her identity.

Article 9

1. States Parties shall ensure that a child shall not be separated from his or her parents against their will, except when competent authorities subject to judicial review determine, in accordance with applicable law and procedures, that such separation is necessary for the best interests of the child. Such determination may be necessary in a particular case such as one involving abuse or neglect of the child by the parents, or one where the parents are living separately and a decision must be made as to the child's place of residence.
2. In any proceedings pursuant to paragraph 1 of the present article, all interested parties shall be given an opportunity to participate in the proceedings and make their views known.
3. States Parties shall respect the right of the child who is separated from one or both parents to maintain personal relations and direct contact with both parents on a regular basis, except if it is contrary to the child's best interests.
4. Where such separation results from any action initiated by a State Party, such as the detention, imprisonment, exile, deportation or death

(including death arising from any cause while the person is in the custody of the State) of one or both parents or of the child, that State Party shall, upon request, provide the parents, the child or, if appropriate, another member of the family with the essential information concerning the whereabouts of the absent member(s) of the family unless the provision of the information would be detrimental to the well-being of the child. States Parties shall further ensure that the submission of such a request shall of itself entail no adverse consequences for the person(s) concerned.

Article 10

1. In accordance with the obligation of States Parties under article 9, paragraph 1, applications by a child or his or her parents to enter or leave a State Party for the purpose of family reunification shall be dealt with by States Parties in a positive, humane and expeditious manner. States Parties shall further ensure that the submission of such a request shall entail no adverse consequences for the applicants and for the members of their family.
2. A child whose parents reside in different States shall have the right to maintain on a regular basis, save in exceptional circumstances personal relations and direct contacts with both parents. Towards that end and in accordance with the obligation of States Parties under article 9, paragraph 1, States Parties shall respect the right of the child and his or her parents to leave any country, including their own, and to enter their own country. The right to leave any country shall be subject only to such restrictions as are prescribed by law and which are necessary to protect the national security, public order (ordre public), public health or morals or the rights and freedoms of others and are consistent with the other rights recognized in the present Convention.

Article 11

1. States Parties shall take measures to combat the illicit transfer and non-return of children abroad.
2. To this end, States Parties shall promote the conclusion of bilateral or multilateral agreements or accession to existing agreements.

Article 12

1. States Parties shall assure to the child who is capable of forming his or her own views the right to express those views freely in all matters affecting the child, the views of the child being given due weight in accordance with the age and maturity of the child.
2. For this purpose, the child shall in particular be provided the opportunity to be heard in any judicial and administrative proceedings

affecting the child, either directly, or through a representative or an appropriate body, in a manner consistent with the procedural rules of national law.

Article 13

1. The child shall have the right to freedom of expression; this right shall include freedom to seek, receive and impart information and ideas of all kinds, regardless of frontiers, either orally, in writing or in print, in the form of art, or through any other media of the child's choice.
2. The exercise of this right may be subject to certain restrictions, but these shall only be such as are provided by law and are necessary:

(a) For respect of the rights or reputations of others; or

(b) For the protection of national security or of public order (ordre public), or of public health or morals.

Article 14

1. States Parties shall respect the right of the child to freedom of thought, conscience and religion.
2. States Parties shall respect the rights and duties of the parents and, when applicable, legal guardians, to provide direction to the child in the exercise of his or her right in a manner consistent with the evolving capacities of the child.
3. Freedom to manifest one's religion or beliefs may be subject only to such limitations as are prescribed by law and are necessary to protect public safety, order, health or morals, or the fundamental rights and freedoms of others.

Article 15

1. States Parties recognize the rights of the child to freedom of association and to freedom of peaceful assembly.
2. No restrictions may be placed on the exercise of these rights other than those imposed in conformity with the law and which are necessary in a democratic society in the interests of national security or public safety, public order (ordre public), the protection of public health or morals or the protection of the rights and freedoms of others.

Article 16

1. No child shall be subjected to arbitrary or unlawful interference with his or her privacy, family, home or correspondence, nor to unlawful attacks on his or her honour and reputation.

2. The child has the right to the protection of the law against such interference or attacks.

Article 17

States Parties recognize the important function performed by the mass media and shall ensure that the child has access to information and material from a diversity of national and international sources, especially those aimed at the promotion of his or her social, spiritual and moral well-being and physical and mental health.

To this end, States Parties shall:

(a) Encourage the mass media to disseminate information and material of social and cultural benefit to the child and in accordance with the spirit of article 29;

(b) Encourage international co-operation in the production, exchange and dissemination of such information and material from a diversity of cultural, national and international sources;

(c) Encourage the production and dissemination of children's books;

(d) Encourage the mass media to have particular regard to the linguistic needs of the child who belongs to a minority group or who is indigenous;

(e) Encourage the development of appropriate guidelines for the protection of the child from information and material injurious to his or her well-being, bearing in mind the provisions of articles 13 and 18.

Article 18

1. States Parties shall use their best efforts to ensure recognition of the principle that both parents have common responsibilities for the upbringing and development of the child. Parents or, as the case may be, legal guardians, have the primary responsibility for the upbringing and development of the child. The best interests of the child will be their basic concern.
2. For the purpose of guaranteeing and promoting the rights set forth in the present Convention, States Parties shall render appropriate assistance to parents and legal guardians in the performance of their child-rearing responsibilities and shall ensure the development of institutions, facilities and services for the care of children.
3. States Parties shall take all appropriate measures to ensure that children of working parents have the right to benefit from child-care services and facilities for which they are eligible.

Article 19

1. States Parties shall take all appropriate legislative, administrative, social

and educational measures to protect the child from all forms of physical or mental violence, injury or abuse, neglect or negligent treatment, maltreatment or exploitation, including sexual abuse, while in the care of parent(s), legal guardian(s) or any other person who has the care of the child.

2. Such protective measures should, as appropriate, include effective procedures for the establishment of social programmes to provide necessary support for the child and for those who have the care of the child, as well as for other forms of prevention and for identification, reporting, referral, investigation, treatment and follow-up of instances of child maltreatment described heretofore, and, as appropriate, for judicial involvement.

Article 20

1. A child temporarily or permanently deprived of his or her family environment, or in whose own best interests cannot be allowed to remain in that environment, shall be entitled to special protection and assistance provided by the State.
2. States Parties shall in accordance with their national laws ensure alternative care for such a child.
3. Such care could include, inter alia, foster placement, kafalah of Islamic law, adoption or if necessary placement in suitable institutions for the care of children. When considering solutions, due regard shall be paid to the desirability of continuity in a child's upbringing and to the child's ethnic, religious, cultural and linguistic background.

Article 21

States Parties that recognize and/or permit the system of adoption shall ensure that the best interests of the child shall be the paramount consideration and they shall:

(a) Ensure that the adoption of a child is authorized only by competent authorities who determine, in accordance with applicable law and procedures and on the basis of all pertinent and reliable information, that the adoption is permissible in view of the child's status concerning parents, relatives and legal guardians and that, if required, the persons concerned have given their informed consent to the adoption on the basis of such counselling as may be necessary;

(b) Recognize that inter-country adoption may be considered as an alternative means of child's care, if the child cannot be placed in a foster or an adoptive family or cannot in any suitable manner be cared for in the child's country of origin;

(c) Ensure that the child concerned by inter-country adoption enjoys safeguards and standards equivalent to those existing in the case of national adoption;

(d) Take all appropriate measures to ensure that, in inter-country adoption, the placement does not result in improper financial gain for those involved in it;

(e) Promote, where appropriate, the objectives of the present article by concluding bilateral or multilateral arrangements or agreements, and endeavour, within this framework, to ensure that the placement of the child in another country is carried out by competent authorities or organs.

Article 22

1. States Parties shall take appropriate measures to ensure that a child who is seeking refugee status or who is considered a refugee in accordance with applicable international or domestic law and procedures shall, whether unaccompanied or accompanied by his or her parents or by any other person, receive appropriate protection and humanitarian assistance in the enjoyment of applicable rights set forth in the present Convention and in other international human rights or humanitarian instruments to which the said States are Parties.
2. For this purpose, States Parties shall provide, as they consider appropriate, co-operation in any efforts by the United Nations and other competent intergovernmental organizations or non-governmental organizations co-operating with the United Nations to protect and assist such a child and to trace the parents or other members of the family of any refugee child in order to obtain information necessary for reunification with his or her family. In cases where no parents or other members of the family can be found, the child shall be accorded the same protection as any other child permanently or temporarily deprived of his or her family environment for any reason , as set forth in the present Convention.

Article 23

1. States Parties recognize that a mentally or physically disabled child should enjoy a full and decent life, in conditions which ensure dignity, promote self-reliance and facilitate the child's active participation in the community.
2. States Parties recognize the right of the disabled child to special care and shall encourage and ensure the extension, subject to available resources, to the eligible child and those responsible for his or her care, of assistance for which application is made and which is

appropriate to the child's condition and to the circumstances of the parents or others caring for the child.

3. Recognizing the special needs of a disabled child, assistance extended in accordance with paragraph 2 of the present article shall be provided free of charge, whenever possible, taking into account the financial resources of the parents or others caring for the child, and shall be designed to ensure that the disabled child has effective access to and receives education, training, health care services, rehabilitation services, preparation for employment and recreation opportunities in a manner conducive to the child's achieving the fullest possible social integration and individual development, including his or her cultural and spiritual development

4. States Parties shall promote, in the spirit of international cooperation, the exchange of appropriate information in the field of preventive health care and of medical, psychological and functional treatment of disabled children, including dissemination of and access to information concerning methods of rehabilitation, education and vocational services, with the aim of enabling States Parties to improve their capabilities and skills and to widen their experience in these areas. In this regard, particular account shall be taken of the needs of developing countries.

Article 24

1. States Parties recognize the right of the child to the enjoyment of the highest attainable standard of health and to facilities for the treatment of illness and rehabilitation of health. States Parties shall strive to ensure that no child is deprived of his or her right of access to such health care services.

2. States Parties shall pursue full implementation of this right and, in particular, shall take appropriate measures:

(a) To diminish infant and child mortality;

(b) To ensure the provision of necessary medical assistance and health care to all children with emphasis on the development of primary health care;

(c) To combat disease and malnutrition, including within the framework of primary health care, through, inter alia, the application of readily available technology and through the provision of adequate nutritious foods and clean drinking-water, taking into consideration the dangers and risks of environmental pollution;

(d) To ensure appropriate pre-natal and post-natal health care for mothers;

(e) To ensure that all segments of society, in particular parents and children, are informed, have access to education and are supported in the use of basic knowledge of child health and nutrition, the advantages of breastfeeding, hygiene and environmental sanitation and the prevention of accidents;

(f) To develop preventive health care, guidance for parents and family planning education and services.

3. States Parties shall take all effective and appropriate measures with a view to abolishing traditional practices prejudicial to the health of children.

4. States Parties undertake to promote and encourage international co-operation with a view to achieving progressively the full realization of the right recognized in the present article. In this regard, particular account shall be taken of the needs of developing countries.

Article 25

States Parties recognize the right of a child who has been placed by the competent authorities for the purposes of care, protection or treatment of his or her physical or mental health, to a periodic review of the treatment provided to the child and all other circumstances relevant to his or her placement.

Article 26

1. States Parties shall recognize for every child the right to benefit from social security, including social insurance, and shall take the necessary measures to achieve the full realization of this right in accordance with their national law.

2. The benefits should, where appropriate, be granted, taking into account the resources and the circumstances of the child and persons having responsibility for the maintenance of the child, as well as any other consideration relevant to an application for benefits made by or on behalf of the child.

Article 27

1. States Parties recognize the right of every child to a standard of living adequate for the child's physical, mental, spiritual, moral and social development.

2. The parent(s) or others responsible for the child have the primary responsibility to secure, within their abilities and financial capacities, the conditions of living necessary for the child's development.

3. States Parties, in accordance with national conditions and within their means, shall take appropriate measures to assist parents and others responsible for the child to implement this right and shall in case of need provide material assistance and support programmes, particularly with regard to nutrition, clothing and housing.

4. States Parties shall take all appropriate measures to secure the recovery of maintenance for the child from the parents or other persons having financial responsibility for the child, both within the State Party and from abroad. In particular, where the person having financial responsibility for the child lives in a State different from that of the child, States Parties shall promote the accession to international agreements or the conclusion of such agreements, as well as the making of other appropriate arrangements.

Article 28

1. States Parties recognize the right of the child to education, and with a view to achieving this right progressively and on the basis of equal opportunity, they shall, in particular:

(a) Make primary education compulsory and available free to all;

(b) Encourage the development of different forms of secondary education, including general and vocational education, make them available and accessible to every child, and take appropriate measures such as the introduction of free education and offering financial assistance in case of need;

(c) Make higher education accessible to all on the basis of capacity by every appropriate means;

(d) Make educational and vocational information and guidance available and accessible to all children;

(e) Take measures to encourage regular attendance at schools and the reduction of drop-out rates.

2. States Parties shall take all appropriate measures to ensure that school discipline is administered in a manner consistent with the child's human dignity and in conformity with the present Convention.

3. States Parties shall promote and encourage international cooperation in matters relating to education, in particular with a view to contributing to the elimination of ignorance and illiteracy throughout the world and facilitating access to scientific and technical knowledge and modern teaching methods. In this regard, particular account shall be taken of the needs of developing countries.

Article 29

1. States Parties agree that the education of the child shall be directed to:

(a) The development of the child's personality, talents and mental and physical abilities to their fullest potential;

(b) The development of respect for human rights and fundamental freedoms, and for the principles enshrined in the Charter of the United Nations;

(c) The development of respect for the child's parents, his or her own cultural identity, language and values, for the national values of the country in which the child is living, the country from which he or she may originate, and for civilizations different from his or her own;

(d) The preparation of the child for responsible life in a free society, in the spirit of understanding, peace, tolerance, equality of sexes, and friendship among all peoples, ethnic, national and religious groups and persons of indigenous origin;

(e) The development of respect for the natural environment.

2. No part of the present article or article 28 shall be construed so as to interfere with the liberty of individuals and bodies to establish and direct educational institutions, subject always to the observance of the principle set forth in paragraph 1 of the present article and to the requirements that the education given in such institutions shall conform to such minimum standards as may be laid down by the State.

Article 30

In those States in which ethnic, religious or linguistic minorities or persons of indigenous origin exist, a child belonging to such a minority or who is indigenous shall not be denied the right, in community with other members of his or her group, to enjoy his or her own culture, to profess and practise his or her own religion, or to use his or her own language.

Article 31

1. States Parties recognize the right of the child to rest and leisure, to engage in play and recreational activities appropriate to the age of the child and to participate freely in cultural life and the arts.

2. States Parties shall respect and promote the right of the child to participate fully in cultural and artistic life and shall encourage the provision of appropriate and equal opportunities for cultural, artistic, recreational and leisure activity.

Article 32

1. States Parties recognize the right of the child to be protected from economic exploitation and from performing any work that is likely to be hazardous or to interfere with the child's education, or to be harmful to the child's health or physical, mental, spiritual, moral or social development.

2. States Parties shall take legislative, administrative, social and educational measures to ensure the implementation of the present article. To this end, and having regard to the relevant provisions of other international instruments, States Parties shall in particular:

(a) Provide for a minimum age or minimum ages for admission to employment;

(b) Provide for appropriate regulation of the hours and conditions of employment;

(c) Provide for appropriate penalties or other sanctions to ensure the effective enforcement of the present article.

Article 33

States Parties shall take all appropriate measures, including legislative, administrative, social and educational measures, to protect children from the illicit use of narcotic drugs and psychotropic substances as defined in the relevant international treaties, and to prevent the use of children in the illicit production and trafficking of such substances.

Article 34

States Parties undertake to protect the child from all forms of sexual exploitation and sexual abuse. For these purposes, States Parties shall in particular take all appropriate national, bilateral and multilateral measures to prevent:

(a) The inducement or coercion of a child to engage in any unlawful sexual activity;

(b) The exploitative use of children in prostitution or other unlawful sexual practices;

(c) The exploitative use of children in pornographic performances and materials.

Article 35

States Parties shall take all appropriate national, bilateral and multilateral measures to prevent the abduction of, the sale of or traffic in children for any purpose or in any form.

Article 36

States Parties shall protect the child against all other forms of exploitation prejudicial to any aspects of the child's welfare.

Article 37

States Parties shall ensure that:

(a) No child shall be subjected to torture or other cruel, inhuman or degrading treatment or punishment. Neither capital punishment nor life imprisonment without possibility of release shall be imposed for offences committed by persons below eighteen years of age;

(b) No child shall be deprived of his or her liberty unlawfully or arbitrarily. The arrest, detention or imprisonment of a child shall be in conformity with the law and shall be used only as a measure of last resort and for the shortest appropriate period of time;

(c) Every child deprived of liberty shall be treated with humanity and respect for the inherent dignity of the human person, and in a manner which takes into account the needs of persons of his or her age. In particular, every child deprived of liberty shall be separated from adults unless it is considered in the child's best interest not to do so and shall have the right to maintain contact with his or her family through correspondence and visits, save in exceptional circumstances;

(d) Every child deprived of his or her liberty shall have the right to prompt access to legal and other appropriate assistance, as well as the right to challenge the legality of the deprivation of his or her liberty before a court or other competent, independent and impartial authority, and to a prompt decision on any such action.

Article 38

1. States Parties undertake to respect and to ensure respect for rules of international humanitarian law applicable to them in armed conflicts which are relevant to the child.
2. States Parties shall take all feasible measures to ensure that persons who have not attained the age of fifteen years do not take a direct part in hostilities.
3. States Parties shall refrain from recruiting any person who has not attained the age of fifteen years into their armed forces. In recruiting among those persons who have attained the age of fifteen years but who have not attained the age of eighteen years, States Parties shall endeavour to give priority to those who are oldest.
4. In accordance with their obligations under international humanitarian law to protect the civilian population in armed conflicts, States Parties shall take all feasible measures to ensure protection and care of children who are affected by an armed conflict.

Article 39

States Parties shall take all appropriate measures to promote physical and psychological recovery and social reintegration of a child victim of: any form of neglect, exploitation, or abuse; torture or any other form of cruel, inhuman or degrading treatment or punishment; or armed conflicts. Such recovery and reintegration shall take place in an environment which fosters the health, self-respect and dignity of the child.

Article 40

1. States Parties recognize the right of every child alleged as, accused of, or recognized as having infringed the penal law to be treated in a manner consistent with the promotion of the child's sense of dignity and worth, which reinforces the child's respect for the human rights and fundamental freedoms of others and which takes into account the child's age and the desirability of promoting the child's reintegration and the child's assuming a constructive role in society.
2. To this end, and having regard to the relevant provisions of international instruments, States Parties shall, in particular, ensure that:

(a) No child shall be alleged as, be accused of, or recognized as having infringed the penal law by reason of acts or omissions that were not prohibited by national or international law at the time they were committed;

(b) Every child alleged as or accused of having infringed the penal law has at least the following guarantees:

(i) To be presumed innocent until proven guilty according to law;

(ii) To be informed promptly and directly of the charges against him or her, and, if appropriate, through his or her parents or legal guardians, and to have legal or other appropriate assistance in the preparation and presentation of his or her defence;

(iii) To have the matter determined without delay by a competent, independent and impartial authority or judicial body in a fair hearing according to law, in the presence of legal or other appropriate assistance and, unless it is considered not to be in the best interest of the child, in particular, taking into account his or her age or situation, his or her parents or legal guardians;

(iv) Not to be compelled to give testimony or to confess guilt; to examine or have examined adverse witnesses and to obtain the participation and examination of witnesses on his or her behalf under conditions of equality;

(v) If considered to have infringed the penal law, to have this decision and any measures imposed in consequence thereof reviewed by a higher competent, independent and impartial authority or judicial body according to law;

(vi) To have the free assistance of an interpreter if the child cannot understand or speak the language used;

(vii) To have his or her privacy fully respected at all stages of the proceedings.

3. States Parties shall seek to promote the establishment of laws, procedures, authorities and institutions specifically applicable to children alleged as, accused of, or recognized as having infringed the penal law, and, in particular:

(a) The establishment of a minimum age below which children shall be presumed not to have the capacity to infringe the penal law;

(b) Whenever appropriate and desirable, measures for dealing with such children without resorting to judicial proceedings, providing that human rights and legal safeguards are fully respected. 4. A variety of dispositions, such as care, guidance and supervision orders; counselling; probation; foster care; education and vocational training programmes and other alternatives to institutional care shall be available to ensure that children are dealt with in a manner appropriate to their well-being and proportionate both to their circumstances and the offence.

Article 41

Nothing in the present Convention shall affect any provisions which are more conducive to the realization of the rights of the child and which may be contained in:

(a) The law of a State party; or

(b) International law in force for that State.

Article 42

States Parties undertake to make the principles and provisions of the Convention widely known, by appropriate and active means, to adults and children alike.

Article 43

1. For the purpose of examining the progress made by States Parties in achieving the realization of the obligations undertaken in the present Convention, there shall be established a Committee on the Rights of the Child, which shall carry out the functions hereinafter provided.
2. The Committee shall consist of eighteen experts of high moral standing and recognized competence in the field covered by this Convention.1/ The members of the Committee shall be elected by States Parties from among their nationals and shall serve in their personal capacity, consideration being given to equitable geographical distribution, as well as to the principal legal systems.
3. The members of the Committee shall be elected by secret ballot from a list of persons nominated by States Parties. Each State Party may nominate one person from among its own nationals.

4. The initial election to the Committee shall be held no later than six months after the date of the entry into force of the present Convention and thereafter every second year. At least four months before the date of each election, the Secretary-General of the United Nations shall address a letter to States Parties inviting them to submit their nominations within two months. The Secretary-General shall subsequently prepare a list in alphabetical order of all persons thus nominated, indicating States Parties which have nominated them, and shall submit it to the States Parties to the present Convention.

5. The elections shall be held at meetings of States Parties convened by the Secretary-General at United Nations Headquarters. At those meetings, for which two thirds of States Parties shall constitute a quorum, the persons elected to the Committee shall be those who obtain the largest number of votes and an absolute majority of the votes of the representatives of States Parties present and voting.

6. The members of the Committee shall be elected for a term of four years. They shall be eligible for re-election if renominated. The term of five of the members elected at the first election shall expire at the end of two years; immediately after the first election, the names of these five members shall be chosen by lot by the Chairman of the meeting.

7. If a member of the Committee dies or resigns or declares that for any other cause he or she can no longer perform the duties of the Committee, the State Party which nominated the member shall appoint another expert from among its nationals to serve for the remainder of the term, subject to the approval of the Committee.

8. The Committee shall establish its own rules of procedure.

9. The Committee shall elect its officers for a period of two years.

10. The meetings of the Committee shall normally be held at United Nations Headquarters or at any other convenient place as determined by the Committee. The Committee shall normally meet annually. The duration of the meetings of the Committee shall be determined, and reviewed, if necessary, by a meeting of the States Parties to the present Convention, subject to the approval of the General Assembly.

11. The Secretary-General of the United Nations shall provide the necessary staff and facilities for the effective performance of the functions of the Committee under the present Convention.

12. With the approval of the General Assembly, the members of the Committee established under the present Convention shall receive emoluments from United Nations resources on such terms and conditions as the Assembly may decide.

Article 44

1. States Parties undertake to submit to the Committee, through the Secretary-General of the United Nations, reports on the measures they have adopted which give effect to the rights recognized herein and on the progress made on the enjoyment of those rights

(a) Within two years of the entry into force of the Convention for the State Party concerned;

(b) Thereafter every five years.

2. Reports made under the present article shall indicate factors and difficulties, if any, affecting the degree of fulfilment of the obligations under the present Convention. Reports shall also contain sufficient information to provide the Committee with a comprehensive understanding of the implementation of the Convention in the country concerned.

3. A State Party which has submitted a comprehensive initial report to the Committee need not, in its subsequent reports submitted in accordance with paragraph 1 (b) of the present article, repeat basic information previously provided.

4. The Committee may request from States Parties further information relevant to the implementation of the Convention.

5. The Committee shall submit to the General Assembly, through the Economic and Social Council, every two years, reports on its activities.

6. States Parties shall make their reports widely available to the public in their own countries.

Article 45

In order to foster the effective implementation of the Convention and to encourage international co-operation in the field covered by the Convention:

(a) The specialized agencies, the United Nations Children's Fund, and other United Nations organs shall be entitled to be represented at the consideration of the implementation of such provisions of the present Convention as fall within the scope of their mandate. The Committee may invite the specialized agencies, the United Nations Children's Fund and other competent bodies as it may consider appropriate to provide expert advice on the implementation of the Convention in areas falling within the scope of their respective mandates. The Committee may invite the specialized agencies, the United Nations Children's Fund, and other United Nations organs to submit reports on the implementation of the Convention in areas falling within the scope of their activities;

(b) The Committee shall transmit, as it may consider appropriate, to the specialized agencies, the United Nations Children's Fund and other competent bodies, any reports from States Parties that contain a request, or indicate a need, for technical advice or assistance, along with the Committee's observations and suggestions, if any, on these requests or indications;

(c) The Committee may recommend to the General Assembly to request the Secretary-General to undertake on its behalf studies on specific issues relating to the rights of the child;

(d) The Committee may make suggestions and general recommendations based on information received pursuant to articles 44 and 45 of the present Convention. Such suggestions and general recommendations shall be transmitted to any State Party concerned and reported to the General Assembly, together with comments, if any, from States Parties.

Article 46

The present Convention shall be open for signature by all States.

Article 47

The present Convention is subject to ratification. Instruments of ratification shall be deposited with the Secretary-General of the United Nations.

Article 48

The present Convention shall remain open for accession by any State. The instruments of accession shall be deposited with the Secretary-General of the United Nations.

Article 49

1. The present Convention shall enter into force on the thirtieth day following the date of deposit with the Secretary-General of the United Nations of the twentieth instrument of ratification or accession.
2. For each State ratifying or acceding to the Convention after the deposit of the twentieth instrument of ratification or accession, the Convention shall enter into force on the thirtieth day after the deposit by such State of its instrument of ratification or accession.

Article 50

1. Any State Party may propose an amendment and file it with the Secretary-General of the United Nations. The Secretary-General shall thereupon communicate the proposed amendment to States Parties, with a request that they indicate whether they favour a conference of States Parties for the purpose of considering and voting upon the proposals. In the event

that, within four months from the date of such communication, at least one third of the States Parties favour such a conference, the Secretary-General shall convene the conference under the auspices of the United Nations. Any amendment adopted by a majority of States Parties present and voting at the conference shall be submitted to the General Assembly for approval.

2. An amendment adopted in accordance with paragraph 1 of the present article shall enter into force when it has been approved by the General Assembly of the United Nations and accepted by a two-thirds majority of States Parties.
3. When an amendment enters into force, it shall be binding on those States Parties which have accepted it, other States Parties still being bound by the provisions of the present Convention and any earlier amendments which they have accepted.

Article 51

1. The Secretary-General of the United Nations shall receive and circulate to all States the text of reservations made by States at the time of ratification or accession.
2. A reservation incompatible with the object and purpose of the present Convention shall not be permitted.
3. Reservations may be withdrawn at any time by notification to that effect addressed to the Secretary-General of the United Nations, who shall then inform all States. Such notification shall take effect on the date on which it is received by the Secretary-General

Article 52

A State Party may denounce the present Convention by written notification to the Secretary-General of the United Nations. Denunciation becomes effective one year after the date of receipt of the notification by the Secretary-General.

Article 53

The Secretary-General of the United Nations is designated as the depositary of the present Convention.

Article 54

The original of the present Convention, of which the Arabic, Chinese, English, French, Russian and Spanish texts are equally authentic, shall be deposited with the Secretary-General of the United Nations. In witness thereof the undersigned plenipotentiaries, being duly authorized thereto by their respective Governments, have signed the present Convention.

Regional and Domestic legal orders

Africa

Much interest is shown for cases of international adoption in Africa especially after highly publicized stories of adoption of African children by celebrities like Madonna and Angelina Jolie. Legal frameworks on adoption in general and on international adoption in particular are available across Africa and may vary from one country to another. The following overview of legal provisions put into place by African countries reflects a diverse but not a comprehensive view on how the question of international adoption is dealt with on the African continent. The focus is on countries for which bibliographical resources were immediately accessible.

The Democratic Republic of Congo (DRC)

On September 25, 2013, the government of the Democratic Republic of Congo enacted a suspension of exit permits for Congolese adoptive children that prevents adoptive children from being allowed to depart the country with their adoptive parents. Although Congolese courts continue to issue new adoption decrees, these are not currently recognized by the Congolese immigration service, the Direction Generale de Migration (DGM), which controls the points of entry. Congolese officials have said the suspension will remain in place until the parliament enacts new legislation reforming the adoption process. Because of the suspension, the U.S Department of State announced on October 6, 2014, that it strongly recommends against adopting from the DRC at this time.

According to the DRC Family Code, an adopted holds the same rights as a biological child in the adopting family. Links with original family are preserved. This regime is applied to simple adoption. As far as international adoption is concerned, the DRC Law does not provide a definition specifically; but the judicial practice authorizes the adoption of Congolese children by foreign parents. Fundamental principles for any child adoption are defined by Law No. 09/001 from 10 January 2009 relating child protection, as follow:

All children are entitled to adoption

The adoption of a child by a foreigner can only happen when competent authorities from the origin state:

1. Have verified, after having examined the social conditions in the origin state that the adoption is to be done in the best interest of the child.
2. Have made sure that:
1. The consent for adoption is not given in exchange with payment or any kind of compensation and that this consent was not later retrieved.
2. The Child's wishes and opinions have been taken into account in

accordance with their age and level of maturity

3. The consent expressed by the child for their adoption, when it is required, is freely expressed in ways required by the law, and that this consent is given or recorded in a written form

As for conditions to be met in the host state for a valid international adoption, article 19 of the Child Protection Code explains that the host state should certify that:

- The future parents are qualified and are capable of adopting children
- The adopted child is authorized to enter and reside permanently in the host country

However, even though international adoption is allowed under fulfillment of the above-mentioned conditions, article 20 of the DRC Child Protection Code denies the right to adoption to homosexuals, pedophiles and mentally-ill people.

Ethiopia

I n 2018, Ethiopia banned the adoption of children by foreigners. Existing data shows that, in Africa, Ethiopia has the highest number of adoptions into US families. It is one of the biggest source countries for international adoptions by US citizens, accounting for about 20% of the total.

Asia

According to recent research, certain Asian countries have been top origins of intercountry adoption, namely China, India, The Republic of Korea (South Korea), Vietnam etc. Yet Asian countries have different legal framework towards intercountry adoption.

China and Hong Kong

China and Hong Kong Special Administrative Region (SAR) have been party to the Hague Adoption Convention since 1 January 2006. All adoptions in China from another country must meet these requirements as well as Chinese domestic law. On the international level, China also has bilateral agreements with certain countries, including Australia (The Family Law (Bilateral Agreements - Intercountry Adoption) Regulations 1998) etc. Domestically, China has two major legislations directly responsible for international adoption affairs.

- Adoption Law of the People's Republic of China (Revised), which deals with general adoption issue. Its Article 21 is specifically linked to international adoption.
- Measures for Registration of Adoption of Children by Foreigners in the People's Republic of China, solely addressing international adoption issues.

Other pertinent documents include

- Article 26 in Marriage Law of the People's Republic of China, also defines adoption in China in a general manner.
- Measures of China Center of Adoption Affairs for Authorizing Foreign Adoption Organizations to Seek Adoptive Families for Children of Special Needs

Legally, the China Centre for Children's Welfare and Adoptions (CCCWA) (which is different from the China Center of Adoption Affairs (CCAA) is the only agency authorized by the Chinese government to regulate and process all inter-country adoptions from China. And China requires all inter-country adoption be handled through government approval instead of any individual application.

Taiwan

Having been one of the major sources of adoptive children, yet Taiwan is not party to the Hague Convention on Protection of Children and Co-operation in Respect of Intercountry Adoption (Hague Adoption Convention). Domestically, Taiwan has enforced The Protection of Children and Youths Welfare and Rights Act since May 30, 2012. And according to the Act, all the adoption cases in Taiwan shall consider the national adopter as priority. Besides, all the international adoption cases shall be matched via the legal adoption matching services agency. Except almost the same peer within six degrees of kinship of relatives and five degrees of kinship of relatives by marriage, or one of the couple adopts the other party's children. Taiwan organizations that provide international adoption service work with foreign agency or governmental authority instead of individuals.

The Republic of Korea (South Korea)

The Republic of Korea (South Korea) is not party to Hague Adoption Convention. South Korea's law requires the use of an adoption agency for the overseas adoption of all Korean orphans, and requires that such agencies are authorized by The Ministry for Health, Welfare and Family Affairs. On May 24, 2013, it signed the Convention on Protection of Children and Co-operation in Respect of Intercountry Adoption (the Convention). This is the first step for South Korea in becoming a Convention partner. Adoptions between the United States and South Korea, however, are not yet subject to the requirements of the Convention and relevant implementing laws and regulations. According to the Ministry of Health and Welfare, which will be designated as South Korea's Central Authority, there is no set date when South Korea will deliver its instrument of ratification or when the Convention will enter into force with respect to South Korea. Domestically, the Republic of Korea (ROK) Special Adoption Act, which governs intercountry adoptions from South Korea, went into effect on August 5, 2012. This law prioritizes domestic adoptions and endeavors to reduce the number of South Korean children adopted abroad. Under the Special Adoption Act, each inter country adoption requires the approval of the ROK Family Court.

India

India is party to the Hague Convention on Protection of Children and Co-operation in Respect of Intercountry Adoption (Hague Adoption Convention). In January 2011, India implemented new procedures to provide more centralized processing of intercountry adoptions. In addition to the new guidelines, prospective adoptive parents should be aware of all Indian laws that apply to inter country adoption. A child can be legally placed with the prospective adoptive parents under the Hindu Adoption and Maintenance Act of 1956 (HAMA), the Guardians and Wards Act of 1890 (GAWA), or the Juvenile Justice (Care and Protection of Children) Act of 2000 (JJA).

Vietnam

Vietnam is party to the Hague Convention on Protection of Children and Co-operation in Respect of Intercountry Adoption (Hague Adoption Convention). Domestically, Vietnam Government has promulgated the Law on Adoption and it took effect from January 1, 2011. It contains 53 Articles, and addresses both domestic and intercountry adoption. Article 14 of the Vietnamese law outlines the requirements for adopters, which is also applicable to foreign adoptive parents.

Europe

Since the 1970s, European countries such as Spain, France, Italy, and several Scandinavian countries have experienced a considerable increase in the demand for adopted children from non-European countries as a result of a scarce numbers of national children available for adoptions. Gender studies have also suggested that this is the result of the modern trend in the Global North of delaying conception of the first child, which increases the risk of reduced fertility and the demand for adoption. However, recent data show a stabilization or even a decrease in the inter-country adoptions. From one side it has been argued that this is the result of a decrease in the causes of abandonment, implementation of social policies in favour of families, less stigmatization of unmarried mothers, economic development and an increase in the national adoptions in the main source countries.

From the other side it has been considered also the result of new regulations and policies adopted by some countries of origin (e.g. Romania) aiming at regulating the outflow of children and preventing child trafficking. The trend however differs from country to country. Between 2000 and 2005, for example Spain, France and Italy have experienced an increase in international adoptions of 70%, while in Switzerland and in Germany they have decreased and in Norway have remained stable.

Council of Europe

The enactment and enforcement of international standards and laws regulating adoption depends on how the competent authorities in each contracting state interpret international instruments and implement their provisions. European regulation and practices on the matter vary from country to country. An attempt to harmonize adoption laws among Member States of the Council of Europe was made with the European Convention on the Adoption of Children (1967), which entered into force in April 1968. In 2008 a revised version of the European Convention on the Adoption of Children was prepared by a Working Party of the Committee of Experts on Family Law under the authority of the European Committee on Legal Cooperation within the framework of the Council of Europe. The Convention was opened for signature on 27 November 2008. As of November 2013, the 1967 Convention has been ratified by 18 of the 46 Member States of the Council of Europe, while 3 Member States are signatories but have not yet ratified. As for the revised Convention, 16 countries have ratified, while another 3 have only signed. The European Convention establishes common principles that should govern adoption. The Convention establishes procedures affecting adoption and its legal consequences to reduce the difficulties in promoting the welfare of the adopted children caused by the differences in legislation and practices among the European States. Among its essential provisions, the Convention stipulates that the adoption must be granted by a competent judicial or administrative authority (art. 4), that birth parents must freely consent to the adoption (art.5) and that the adoption must be in the best interest of the child (art.8). Any improper financial advantages arising from the adoption of a child are prohibited (art.15).

European Union

Within the European Union regulation, reference to intercountry adoption is made in article 4 of the Council Directive 2003/86/EC of 22 September 2003 on the right to family reunification. The article regulates the immigration of adoptive third-country-national children provided that the parents are established third country nationals within the European Union. EU Member States authorized the entry and residence of children adopted in accordance with a decision taken by the competent authority of the Member State concerned. Entry can also be authorized by a decision that is automatically enforceable due to international obligations of the Member State or must be recognized in accordance with international obligations (art. 4 (b)). With the ratification and adoption of the Hague Adoption Convention, European countries have developed training for social workers in charge of providing international adoption-related services. They have appointed competent specialists and created a centralized system of control (e.g. Italy and Germany). In Switzerland, on the other hand, the bureaucratization of the procedures has been considered to have slowed down the process resulting in a decrease of the number of children adopted. Traditionally in Spain, France and Switzerland, the adopting parents can choose between two paths to carry out international adoption: referring to the intermediation of an accredited body - most of the time a private organization - and with the supervision of the central adoption authority designated by the state, or opting for a private adoption without the referral to the intermediary. In Italy and Norway the second option, considered as "private adoption", is forbidden. In Italy for example all international adoptions must be arranged by competent bodies accredited by national law. The only exception is granted to prospective adoptive couples where one spouse is a native of the country the child comes from, or for Italian families who have lived for a long time in the country and have a significant relation with its culture. In these two cases their demand for international adoption can be sent to the International Social Service, an international not-for-profit organization active in more than 100 countries through a network of branches, affiliated bureaus, and correspondents, without recurring to the accredited national bodies. France and Germany recently adopted a third path, creating public bodies that simultaneously exercise a formal intermediary role and in practice perform the functions of a central adoption authority. Data show that in all European countries, both those that legally prohibit and allow for it, the practice of private adoption is widespread and has raised concerns most of all in relation to the risk of child trafficking. Many European countries have signed bilateral agreement with countries of origin of the adopted children (e.g. Spain with Philippines and Bolivia, France with Vietnam). Legally speaking, bilateral agreements cannot disregard the guarantees provided by the Convention of the Rights of the Child and by the Hague Adoption Convention.

North America

United States

The United States (US) is bound both by domestic and international laws regarding adoptions of children. The laws cover US families adopting children from abroad, and families abroad adopting US-born children. Many US children are adopted abroad. Families in the US adopted 8,668 children from abroad in 2012. There are several international treaties and conventions regulating the inter country adoption of children. When possible, the US prefers to enter into multilateral agreements over bilateral ones, because of the difficulty in getting the Senate to ratify international agreements.

Inter-American Convention on Conflict of Laws Concerning the Adoption of Minors, 1984 (US not signed or ratified) US bilateral agreement with Viet Nam on 1 Sept 2005United Nations General Assembly Declaration on Social and Legal Principles Relating to Adoption and Foster Placement of Children

Nationally and Internationally (adopted without vote) Hague Adoption Convention on the Protection of Children and Co-operation in Respect of Inter-Country Adoption (Hague Adoption Convention). The US has acceded to (signed) but the Senate has not ratified the Hague Convention. The US also made a declaration that this convention does not supersede Title 18, United States Code, Section 3190 relating to documents submitted to the United States Government in support of extradition requests. United Nations Convention on the Rights of the Child. The US signed (16 Feb 1995) but the Senate has not ratified because of states' rights to execute children (minors tried as adults). This was deemed unconstitutional by Supreme Court in 2005, but the Senate has not reversed its position.

The US Department of State lists the pertinent legal documents regarding adoptions. In particular, the Inter country Adoption Act of 2000 incorporates the Hague Convention into domestic law. The act stipulates requirements for US children being adopted internationally. Paragraph 97.3 (§97.3) stipulates the requirements for a US child being adopted internationally in a country that has also ratified the Hague Convention. A family' eligibility to adopt from another country is fairly similar to the requirements of domestic adoptions, with additions regarding citizenship, visas, and immigration. These are detailed in the booklet Intercountry Adoption from A to Z. The State Department provides interactive maps detailing US adoption rates since 1999 by several categories.

Reform efforts

Due to the appeal and otherwise obvious difficult issues presented by international adoption, the reform movement seeks to influence governments to adopt regulations that serve the best interest of the child and meet the interests of both the adoptive and biological family members. Significant advances have been made in increasing the regulation of international adoptions. Adopting families in general have a variety of motivations, including infertility, being a same-sex couple or single parent, and not wanting to contribute to human overpopulation. International adoptions can have additional motivations, including reducing the chance that a biological family member will later challenge the adoption or interfere in the child's life, rescuing a child from a life of poverty (seen by some as patronizing or even neo-colonialist), and "saving" a child in the religious sense of converting them to the family's religion (not necessarily considered beneficial by those of different religions or no religion). In particular, evangelical Christians have been urged to adopt internationally in addition to having large biological families. International adoption generates additional controversy where the children will be raised in a different culture or religion than they were born into, or by parents of a different ethnicity, especially where this will be visually apparent to others in the society (which may subject the child to stigmatization or discrimination). Some adoptions compensate for problematic attitudes or practices in the source country, such as abandonment of girls and children with disabilities or serious medical problems, or for economic or aesthetic reasons.

Considering adoption in the crude terms of a market, the global demand to adopt infants is higher than the naturally available supply; most children available for adoption are of school age. This mismatch encourages international adoption as domestic supply is exhausted, but also creates financial incentives to identify more young children for adoption, especially in developing countries and those with high levels of societal corruption or poor law enforcement. Certain aspects of international adoption make it easier for agencies and child recruiters to commit fraud, including distance, language barriers, difficulty enforcing laws across international boundaries, and adoption agency contracts disclaiming responsibility for incorrect biographical details. Abuses which impact adoption decisions that laws, treaties, and reform efforts are trying to stop include representing a child as an orphan when parents are still alive, representing an orphan child as without family when there are extended family members willing to adopt, representing a child as more impoverished than they actually are, falsely representing a child as having no siblings they would be leaving behind, representing to biological parents that a permanent adoption is actually a program to temporarily send their children to a developed country for educational opportunity, and not disclosing that biological parents were (probably illegally) paid to relinquish custody of their children.

After a disaster

Of special note to international adoption are campaigns for adoptions that occur after disasters such as hurricanes, tsunamis, and wars. There is often an outpouring of adoption proposals in such cases from foreigners who want to give homes to children left in need. While adoption may be a way to provide stable, loving families for children in need, it is also suggested that adoption in the immediate aftermath of trauma or upheaval may not be the best option. Moving children too quickly into new adoptive homes among strangers may be a mistake because it may turn out that the parents survived and were unable to find the children or there may be a relative or neighbor who can offer shelter and homes. Providing safety and emotional support may be better in those situations than immediate relocation to a new adoptive family. There is an increased risk, immediately following a disaster, that displaced and/or orphaned children may be more vulnerable to exploitation and child trafficking.

Effects of adoption

Adoption is a dynamic shift on both the adoptive parent(s) and the child. The adoption process is long and arduous to ensure that the living environment will be suitable for the child. However, it can be very overwhelming. According to Child Welfare Information Gateway, "The home study process can feel intrusive and may highlight issues that you have not fully addressed." The uncertainty of the whole process, including being able to even adopt a child can be overwhelming. However, the adoption of the child has countless beneficial effects on the child. Adopting a child can provide a stable foundation and family situation that is essential for growth and development, and can provide new opportunities and resources for an adoptive child. It can also give the adoptive parents a sense of purpose and completion. However, the Post-Adoption Period can be mentally and emotionally taxing for both parties. Child Welfare Information Gateway also states, "Parents may be unprepared for the issues that may come up throughout the lifelong adoption journey." Unidentified trauma from the adopted child can be hard to pinpoint and treat. Adopted children can also have a fear of rejection and abandonment, which make it hard the parent(s) to connect instantly with the child. This in turn can trigger senses

The principal purpose of the Abduction Convention is to cause the prompt return of a child to his or her "habitual residence." In certain exceptional cases under Article 13b, the court's mandatory return obligation is changed to a discretionary obligation, specifically, "the judicial or administrative authority of the requested State is not bound to order the return of the child if the person, institution or other body which opposes its return establishes that there is a grave risk that his or her return would expose the child to physical or psychological harm or otherwise place the child in an intolerable situation." It is important to note that the duty to return a child is not abrogated by a finding under Art. 13(b) but merely changes from mandatory to discretionary. Since the general intent of the Convention is to cause the return of a child to his or her "habitual residence," unless there are some powerful and compelling reasons otherwise the court is normally and routinely expected to exercise its discretion and return the child to his or her "habitual residence".

In the primary source of interpretation for the Convention, the Explanatory Report, Professor E. Perez-Vera noted the following: "it would seem necessary to underline the fact that the three types of exception to the rule concerning the return of the child must be applied only so far as they go and no further. This implies above all that they are to be interpreted in a restrictive fashion if the Convention is not to become a dead letter. In fact, the Convention as a whole rests upon the unanimous rejection of this phenomenon of illegal child removals and upon the conviction that the best way to combat them at an international level is to refuse to grant them legal recognition. The practical application of this principle requires that the signatory States be convinced that they belong, despite their differences, to the same legal community within which the authorities of each State acknowledge that the authorities of one of them - those of the child's habitual residence - are in principle best placed to decide upon questions of custody and access. As a result, a systematic invocation of the said exceptions, substituting the forum chosen by the abductor for that of the child's residence, would lead to the collapse of the whole structure of the Convention by depriving it of the spirit of mutual confidence which is its inspiration."

In spite of the spirit and intent of the Convention as conveyed by the Convention itself and further reinforced by the Perez-Vera report, Article 13b is frequently used by abductors as a vehicle to litigate the child's best interests or custody. Although Article 13(b) inquiries are not intended to deal with issues or factual questions appropriate for custody proceedings, many countries use article 13b to request psychological profiles, detailed evaluations of parental fitness, evidence concerning lifestyle and the nature and quality of relationships.These misinterpretations of the Abduction Convention's exceptions have rendered the Convention largely ineffective in accomplishing its objectives. The best interests of a child, which is explicitly never mentioned in the Convention, is an essentially subjective standard that judges often use to facilitate foreign nations' manipulation of the treaty and create a pretext for discretionary decisions. This discretion often takes the form of gender, cultural and national biases. The result is substantive non-compliance with the Abduction Convention.

Domestic violence

At the time the Hague Abduction Convention was drafted domestic violence was never explicitly considered as an affirmative defense for child abduction, although it may be brought as a defense under Article 13, if "there is a grave risk that his or her return would expose the child to physical or psychological harm or otherwise place the child in an intolerable situation." Article 13 supposed that the child's primary caretaker would abduct the child to escape the domestic violence of a non-custodial parent. At the time of the Conventions drafting, joint custody laws were rare. One parent was usually both the custodial parent and primary caretaker while the other, non-custodial parent had rights of access. The move towards joint custody laws conferred both the parent who acted as the primary caretaker and their ex-partner with custodial rights and, by extension, a right to request the return of children wrongfully removed from their place of habitual residence. In addition to not accounting for a shift in child custody law towards shared parentingand joint custody, according to Weiner, the framers of the Convention also did little to account for the motivation for abducting a child, generally assuming that all abductions were harmful to children; however, the child's primary caretaker may be fleeing with a child to protect himself or herself from a dangerous domestic situation.

Global Missing Children's Network

Launched in 1998 as a joint venture of the International Centre for Missing & Exploited Children (ICMEC) and the US National Center for Missing and Exploited Children, the Global Missing Children's Network (GMCN) is a network of countries that connect, share best practices, and disseminate information and images of missing children to improve the effectiveness of missing children investigations. The Network has 22 member countries: Albania, Argentina, Australia, Belarus, Belgium, Brazil, Canada, Germany, Greece, Ireland, Italy, Mexico, the Netherlands, New Zealand, Poland, Romania, Russia, Serbia, South Africa, South Korea, Spain, the United Kingdom, and the US.

CHAPTER - 8

CHILD WELFARE

THE LAWS OF NEGLIGENCE AND CONTRACT

As can be seen from the above provisions, which all follow the principles of the Children and Young Peoples Act 1933, child protection is concerned with the child's exposure to, and consumption of, potentially hazardous products of all description. The act followed Donoghue v Stevenson [1932] UKHL 100 to reflect the new law of negligence and demolition of the privily barrier in the law of contract. The new law recognised that the product manufacturer may be many parties removed from the ultimate product consumer and that the product may contain potentially hazardous but un-examinable content. This may be either through ingredient or packaging. Food intolerances are a simple example. The purchaser will be unaware of potentiality allergic content unless clearly advised by the producer.

The purchaser, or more generally 'procurer' (person who obtains), of product may not be the ultimate consumer. A parent procures for a child who is, potentially, the most vulnerable consumer. Section 1(1) of the Children and Young Peoples Act 1933 makes it a criminal offence of child cruelty for the person responsible for a child to expose him/her "in a mannerlikely to cause him unnecessary suffering or injury to health" (emphasis supplied). The approach is no different to employment health and safety, but for the consumer rather than the employee.

It is the "manner" of acting that is important: is this activity being carried out safely after an appropriate risk assessment to meet the duty of care in the law of negligence established by Donoghue. The person responsible for a child should know the child's food allergies and check any product content for potential food intolerances before allowing the child to consume the product.

Safeguarding the welfare of the child

Child safeguarding follows directly from these principles. Safeguarding means taking the necessary protective measures for the child's safe consumption of any product, stair-gates, seatbelts, protective footwear, glasses, basic hygiene, etc. The list is both endless and, to the most part, obvious common sense. Failure by the responsible person is an offence of child cruelty on the grounds of failing to protect the child in circumstances consistent with the provision of safe and effective care .

A parent, person with parental responsibility for a child, has an express liability, whoever is responsible for the child at the time (s.17 of the act). Just as in employment health and safety, the powers of parenthood can be delegated but not the duties. Parents should make arrangements for suitable and properly informed others to have responsibility for their children (see also s.2(9)-(11) Children Act 1989).

Proper consent or agreement

For the product to be safely consumed by a child means that the responsible person must fully understand the product's safe use for its intended purpose. Miss-selling in the law of contract, suggesting the product does something it doesn't or selling products to those that do not fully understand what they are getting is potentially hazardous to the child as the ultimate consumer. Health and medical treatment may involve some form of physical contact in which case lack of proper consent is a potential battery, or even assault, of the person. The procurer must be placed in a position to assess any potential risk to the child in the reliable use of the product

Welfare, risk assessment and the calculus of negligence

Just as in all of life, the likely benefits of a procured product come with possible non-beneficial qualities. Procurement is a careful activity attempting to achieve the best value for money. The benefits of the product must be satisfactorily delivered as specified for performance in the law of contract. Just as in food intolerances and consent to examination and treatment, the procurer must be made aware of any potential hazards in their circumstances of a product that performs reliably.

Welfare defines the process by which proper consent or agreement is given when procuring products that will be beneficial and safe in the procurer's particular circumstances. If a child is the ultimate consumer of a procured product then the child's welfare (health, safety and happiness) is the paramount consideration when coming to the decision A balance must be struck between the obligations of the producer and the obligations of the procurer for the child's safe consumption of the product. The calculus of negligence is a legal approach, in the spirit of procurement efficiency, that attempts to strike that balance on economic grounds. This is most easily understood in terms of insurance liability. Should a car driver have a duty of care towards until cyclists at night or should the cyclist have a duty of care to properly illuminate his bicycle at night? The costs of bicycle illumination are considerably less than the cost of driving with a duty of care to unlit cyclists.

Promoting the welfare of the child and the CAF Assessment

A parent must also procure (obtain) all necessary products, environments, accommodation, goods and services to be provided for the child's safe consumption. Failure to do so is, again, an offence of child cruelty under s.1(2) of the act on the grounds of physical neglect and failing to prevent harm as impairment of health and development in Working Together to Safeguard Children (see, Part 2 B, 24, sentencing guidance, Overarching Principles: Overarching Principles: Assaults on children Assaults on children and Cruelty to a child; and Introduction, Working Together to Safeguard Children (HMG 2015) the governmental child protection guidance). The procurement process for integrated provision is called a Children and Family Assessment, CAF Assessment, for integrated provision. The outcome is a CAF Action Plan to safeguard and promote the child's welfare with the specified outcomes of the services that best serve the child's needs to be delivered under the terms of proper consent

In the Family Justice System the CAF Assessment is conducted by the Children and Family Court Advisory and Supervisory Service (CAFCASS) to safeguard and promote the welfare of children involved in family court proceedings. In the Youth Justice System and Special Education Needs the CAF Assessment is conducted by local council parental responsibility units following Schedule 2 of the Special Educational Needs Regulations (Consolidated) 2001.

The best interests of the child

Decision making

Decisions made on all the necessary products: environments, accommodation, goods and services procured to be provided for the child's safe consumption must be in the best interests of the child. A child is a person, not an object of concern who simply lacks the capacity to give consent on her own behalf until Gillick Competent to do so. He/she must still be involved in the decision making processes for the products that best serve his/her needs in accordance with the best interests determination of s.4 Mental Capacity Act 2005. Failure of the responsible person to so is an offence on the grounds of emotional neglect (see, Part 2 B, 24, sentencing guidance, Overarching Principles: Overarching Principles: Assaults on children Assaults on children and Cruelty to a child; and Introduction, Working Together to Safeguard Children (HMG 2015) the governmental child protection guidance).

The welfare checklist

Working Together to Safeguard Children extends mental capacity to parental capacity for a person with parental responsibility and the best interests consideration under s.1(3)(a)-(f) the, so-called, [welfare checklist of family law http://www.legislation.gov.uk/ukpga/1989/41/section/1 Children Act 1989]. This is the UK implementation of Article 3 UN Convention on the Rights of the Child Best Interests of the Child. s.1(3)(a) the wishes and feelings of the child in light of his age and experience; are the child's involvement in the decision making process (see also s.17(4A) and s.47(4A) Children Act 1989) s.1(3)(b) the child's physical, emotional and educational needs; are for physical and emotional neglect to be prevented and to receive a proper education (s.36 Children Act 1989) in accordance with his/her aptitudes, abilities and any special needs he may have (s.7 Education Act 1996). s.1(3)(c) the likely effect of the change of circumstances are the likely outcomes for the child of the products as environment, accommodation, goods and services procured to be provided for him/her. s.1(3)(d) the age, sex, background, and other relevant characteristics of the child specifies the child's current condition for which the provision is required to address. s.1(3)(e) harm the child has suffered, or is at risk of suffering; specifies the harm, as ill-treatment or impairment of health and development the child has suffered or the hazards in his/her circumstances from which she is at risk of suffering harm. Just as in employment health and safety, these are the risks of the present care environment. s.1(3)(f) capability of the parents, or anybody else considered relevant, of meeting the child's needs; is the ability and responsibility of the parents for procuring the necessary products as environments, accommodation, goods and services to promote the child's welfare to be safely provided to him/her in safeguarding his/her welfare.

Decision making and legal disability

There is both a business and social imperative to give all the opportunity for safely and satisfactorily consuming the offerings of producers. Some, may not have the capacity to be capable of giving proper consent or agreement for the products that best serve their needs to use those products safely. In the case of parents, their children's needs to keep their children safe. This is called Legal Disability.

Disability is the difference between capacity and capability. In the case of parents parental capacity of Working Together and parental capability of s.1(3)(f) of the Children Act 1989. Disability is defined as a mental or physical impairment with and adverse effect on normal day-to-day activities. A person without the use of their legs lacks the physical capacity to walk. They are not capable of carrying out the normal day-to-day activity of, say, shopping without some corrective measure such as a mobility scooter (see s.6 Equality Act 2010and Guidance on Matters to be Taken into Account when Assessing

Disability). Mental capacity is the ability to make decisions in a best interests determination on a particular issue so as to be mentally capable of giving proper consent or agreement. Determining mental capacity requires the information on which the decision to be made to safeguard the person's welfare. A lack of mental capacity to process the information and make decisions is a legal disability leaving the person incapable of instructing a solicitor (s.3 Mental Capacity Act 2006, 26 Explanatory Notes to the Mental Capacity Act (2005); 1.6 Family Law Protocol (Law Society 2010)). Physical, moral and emotional health, the mental faculties of decision making

Physical and moral health refer to the faculties of the mind used in making decisions. Physical health is the mental capacity to understand the effects of matter and energy on both self and others. That is, to understand how a person may be physically harmed which is called causality in the law of negligence. Moral health is the mental capacity to recognise the persons and environment that may be damaged by the acts and omissions in the law of negligence, the neighbour and neighbourhood. Part 1 of the Children and Young Peoples Act 1933 is headed "Prevention of Cruelty to Children and Exposure to Physical and Moral Danger". The offence of child cruelty under s.1(1) includes "...exposure in a manner likely to cause an unnecessary injury to health...". Again, the manner of the exposure endangers the child's physical and moral health as faculties of the mind. It means nothing more than setting a bad example in either behaviour towards others (moral health) or carelessness with potentially dangerous items, e.g. speeding in a motor car.

Emotional health is firstly intellectual health, the capacity to reason based on the understandings of physical and moral health when making decisions so as not harm a neighbour or neighbourhood. It is secondly the competencies to engage in social relationships, personal or business, under the terms of proper consent or agreement following that reasoning and decision making. Thirdly, it is the likely capability of applying those competencies to take opportunities in the cause of growth and well-being and then to perform reliably.

Child development and parental responsibility

The Department of Health Introduction to the Children Act 1989 described new notion of parental responsibility as "the authorities conferred by parental responsibility exist only for raising the child to physical, emotional and moral health". Lord McKay of the Clasfern, the Lord Chancellor when introducing the act to Parliament said "...the overwhelming task of parenthood and the all the rights it brings are for raising the child to be a properly developed adult, both physically and morally.". The child's physical and moral health are developed as physical development and behavioural (moral) development of physical and moral capacities; the child's emotional health is developed as intellectual development for the capacity to reason based on those understandings when making decisions; social development as the competencies to enter into social relationships, both personal and business; and emotional development of likely capability to take opportunities in the cause of growth and well-being and perform reliably (see s.17(11) Children Act 1989).

A child is a person not an object of concern

Lady Elizabeth Butler Sloss made this oft quoted remark in her inquiry into the Cleveland child abuse scandal. As a medical discipline, child welfare under s.1 and s.44 of the Children and Young Peoples Act 1933 is only distinguished from animal welfare under s.9 Animal Welfare Act 2006 by consideration of the child's wishes and feelings when making decisions in her best interests following s.4 Mental Capacity Act 2005 extended to parental capacity by Working Together to Safeguard Children and s.1(3)(a)-(f) of the Children Act 1989. An animal is a possession whilst a child is a person and this distinction was a central intention of the Children Act 1989. Lord McKay also said when introducing the act, "The days when a child was regarded as a possession of his family, indeed to sue on their loss, are today buried forever". The child is socially and emotionally developed, whilst he lacks capacity, by full involvement in the decision making process in his best interests until he becomes competent as Gillick Competent.

Disability, parental disability and social inclusion

The Department of Work and Pensions disability assessment is a measure of physical and mental capacities under clinical or controlled conditions from occupational health in respect to employment performance. The test for disability is capability as "the mental or physical impairment with an adverse effect on day-to-day activities" as social performance. The assessment of capacity is used in a home based disability assessment under s.47 NHS and Community Care Act 1990. For a parent, a parental disability is the mental or physical impairment with the adverse effect on the day-to-day activity of giving the child the care it would be reasonable to expect a parent to give a similar child (s.31 Children Act 1989). Whatever their mental or physical impairments parents should be given the necessary disability support to care for their children to maintain a reasonable standard of health and development. (s.17(10) Children Act 1989).

For those with parental responsibility mental capacity to make decisions in own best interests is extended to parental capacity to make decisions in the best interests of the child by Working Together to Safeguard Children. The s.47 disability assessment is extended by Part III and s.8 Part 1 Schedule 2 Children Act 1989. Part III Children Act 1989 includes s.17 and the local authority duty to safeguard and promote the welfare of children by the provision of services for the families of children in need. The services include advocacy services for advice and assistance in decision making when exercising the authorities of parental responsibility. This was another clear intention of the act described in the Department of Health Introduction as "...the belief that children are best brought up in the family with both parents playing a full part...the local authority duty to provide support for children and families..."

The MARAC Process and risk assessment

The s.47 disability assessment is to support mental health care in the community and is conducted with a view to a possible deprivation of liberty for those who lack the capability to care for themselves in the community under Schedule A1 Mental Capacity Act 2005. The decision is made after a Multi Agency Risk Assessment Conference known as MARAC. In the case a parent who is not capable of meeting the child's needs then the local authority can intervene with a court order under s.31(2) Children Act 1989. To do so they must meet the public law thresholds that the child is suffering, or likely to suffer, significant harm attributable to the care it would be reasonable to expect a parent to give, the same criteria as for parental disability support.

State intervention

It is assumed that the parent has been given the necessary support for any parental disability under the terms of proper consent, that the welfare of the child has been safeguarded and the risk to the child is parental negligence. The test of parental negligence is, following Donoghue later called the Bolam Test, the same test as for professional negligence. If a care order is made the local authority acquires parental responsibility under s.33 of the act as the, so-called, corporate parent. These thresholds are highly controversial and poorly understood. A number of esoteric legal principles are involved and most easily understood in terms of employment performance and health and safety. A parent, just like the CEO of a corporate body, must be, and be seen to be a fit and responsible person. If called into question the court will firstly examine the facts. In employment health and safety there are the facts of accidents, the accident record book of harm suffered, and the facts of the employment environment, harm likely to be suffered, say, from a trip hazard.

The facts are found to the civil standard of proof, the balance of probabilities, 'Did the facts of the alleged trip hazard occur?", this is called 'The Trier of Fact'. If so, do these found facts amount to a trip hazard?, this is called the Question of Law. This conforms that the alleged events occurred and were unlawful but that is not enough there is next the issue of culpability or State of Mind. Negligence is a state of mind. This notion comes from the criminal law and the offence of child cruelty under s.1 Children and Young Peoples Act 1933. What was the motivation, carelessness or malice? There is a defence of diminished responsibility, the offence occurred but was not voluntary or reasonably foreseeable by an impaired or incapacitated defendant. The offence of child cruelty allows a defence of parental incapacity on a wide range of grounds (see sentencing guidance, Overarching Principles: Overarching Principles: Assaults on children Assaults on children and Cruelty to a child). The employment health and safety approach is again helpful in understanding this complexity. To summarise so far, as a matter of fact found on the balance of probabilities, the child has suffered harm or been exposed to an unsafe environment. The person responsible for the child was in, at least, a negligent state of mind in failing to protect the child to safeguarding or promote his/her welfare. This is all based in the present and the final finding is as a fit and proper person to hold this responsibility into the future. Is there a track record of such irresponsible behaviour?

Preventing child neglect and abuse

The offence of child cruelty can be prosecuted concurrently with any assault on the child. If a child is assaulted, sexually or physically, then both the assailant and the person responsible for keeping the child safe from the assault are culpable for the harm suffered as physical abuse or sexual abuse. This completes the definitions of child neglect and abuse in Annex A of Working Together (see also Preventing child maltreatment: a guide to taking action and generating evidence (WHO 2006)).

The offence of child cruelty is the UK implementation of Article 19(1) UN Convention on the Rights of the Child Protection of Children From Violence. Article 19(2) requires social programmes to for preventing violence to children and these are to be found under s.4 Part 1 Schedule 2 Children Act 1989 and include services to children and families under Part III of the same enactment in meeting the local authority duty to safeguard and promote the welfare of children.

Child protection assessment

A key part of child protection work is assessment.

A particular challenge arises where child protection professionals are assessing families where neglect is occurring. Professionals conducting assessments of families where neglect is taking place are said to sometimes make the following errors:

- Failure to ask the right types of question, including
- Whether neglect is occurring?
- Why neglect is occurring?
- What the situation is like for the child?
- Whether improvement in the family are likely to be sustained?
- What needs to be done to ensure the long-term safety of the child?

Odisha State Child Protection Society

Odisha State Child Protection Society (OSCPS) is the technical, fundamental and functional unit of Women & Child Development Department, Government of Odisha, for implementation of Integrated Child Protection Scheme (ICPS). OSCPS has been registered in the year 2009 under Society Registration Act. District Child Protection Units (DCPUs) as the extended bodies of OSCPS, have been constituted to carry out the activities of ICPS at district and sub-district level.

Genesis

Women and Child development Department has signed a MoU with Ministry of Women and Child Development, GoI to implement Integrated Child Protection Scheme (ICPS) in the state of Odisha through Government and Civil Society Partnership. The aim of ICPS is focused on institutionalizing child protection mechanism and services, effective functioning of existing stake holders and regular capacity building and monitoring of child protection programme & activities. For creating a safety net for children and to ensure an efficient Juvenile Justice system in the state of Odisha, OSCPS through Integrated Child Protection Scheme lay special emphasis upon the children at most difficult situations such as Child in Need of Care and Protection, Juvenile in Conflict Law, Juvenile in Contact with Law and Other Vulnerable Children. Care and Protection of Vulnerable Children are being catered through various protection measures under this scheme. Separate units were set up comprising dedicated and skilled professionals for effective implementation of the scheme.

Objectives

To facilitate and operate in an additional and technical capacity to the W & CD Deptt., Govt. of Odisha for the implementation of Integrated Child Protection Scheme(ICPS) in the State.

- To set up DCPUs in all the districts
- To establish and strengthen a continuum of services for Emergency Outreach, Institutional Care, Family and Community based Care, Counseling and Support services.
- To strengthen necessary structures and mechanisms for effective implementation of the scheme at the state and district level.
- Define and set standards of all services including the functioning of statutory bodies.
- Build capacities of all functionaries including, administrators and service providers, at all levels by establishing partnerships with relevant State and National Agencies.

- Ensure that members of allied systems including, local bodies, police, judiciary and other concerned departments of State Governments are sensitized and trained to undertake desired responsibilities towards protection of child rights.
- Create mechanisms for a Child Protection Data Management System including MIS, Resource Directory and Child Tracking System at the district and state level for effective implementation and monitoring of child protection services in the state.

Functions

Contribution to the effective implementation of child protection legislation, schemes and achievement of child protection goals laid out in the National Plan of Action for Children. In doing so, OSCPS follows national and state priorities, rules and guidelines.

- Implementation, supervision and monitoring of ICPS and all other child protection scheme/programs and agencies/institutions at State level and district level.
- Setting up and monitoring District Child Protection Unit (DCPU). Providing financial support to DCPU for carrying out district level activities.
- Ensuring effective implementation of the Juvenile Justice (Care and Protection of Children) Act, 2000 and its subsequent amendments and Odisha Juvenile Justice (Care and Protection of Children) Rules.
- Ensuring of effective implementation of other legislations and policies for child protection in the State viz. Hindu Adoption and Maintenance Act (HAMA) 1956, Child Labour (Prohibition and Regulation) Act 1986, Child Marriage Prohibition Act 2006, and Immoral Traffic Prevention Act 1986, Pre-Conception and Pre-Natal Diagnostic Techniques (Prohibition of Sex Selection) Act 1994, Commissions for Protection of Child Rights Act 2005, Protection of Children from Sexual Offence Act 2012, etc. and any other Act that comes into force for protecting child rights.
- Networking and coordinating with all government departments to build inter-sectoral linkages on child protection issues, including Departments of Health, Education, Social Welfare, Urban Basic Services, Backward Classes & Minorities, Youth Services, Police, Judiciary, Labour, State AIDS Control Society, voluntary and civil organizations working in the field of child rights and protection.
- Carrying out need-based research and documentation activities at state-level for assessing the number of children in difficult circumstances and creating State-specific databases to monitor trends and patterns.

- Training and capacity development of all personnel (Government and Nongovernment) working under child protection system.
- Providing quarterly progress report to MWCD on Program implementation.
- Liaisoning with MWCD and State Child Protection Societies of other States/UTs.
- Providing secretarial support to the State Level Committees related Child Protection.
- Maintaining a state level database of all children in institutional care and family based non-institutional care and update it on a quarterly basis.
- Undertake need based innovative projects aimed at bringing efficiency in child protection mechanism in the state of Odisha.
- Conceptualize and develop materials for creating informed citizenship and child sensitive environment at all levels through awareness generation and raising concerns.

Operation Smile

Operation Smile & Muskaan To locate, track and identify missing children of Odisha, OSCPS in W&CD Department collaborate with CID-Crime Branch in Odisha Police to execute joint operations within and outside the state twice every year. Children rescued during the operation get repatriated and rehabilitated to their families after rescue with due legal procedure.

Rainbow Festival

Rainbow is a benchmark festival of Odisha State Child Protection Society, observed at state level every year followed by observance of its district chapters. Rainbow creates a platform of inclusive growth for children living in child care institutions and special need children, where the children showcase their innate abilities. This two-day-long residential festival involves a series of workshops, competitions, events, etc. where children get an opportunity for their creative reflection.War Child (charity) War Child is a non-governmental organisation founded in the UK in 1993 which provides assistance to children in areas experiencing conflict and the aftermath of conflict. The establishment of War Child UK was soon followed by organisations in Canada and the Netherlands.

War Child UK

War Child UK aims to support and rehabilitate child victims of war, by working with local communities, their organisations and local authorities in both conflict and post-conflict areas to support children and the people they depend upon. War Child UK currently works in Democratic Republic of

Congo, Central African Republic, Uganda, Afghanistan, Iraq and with Syrian refugees in Jordan.

War Child Canada

Founded by medical doctors Samantha Nutt and Eric Hoskins, War Child Canada has active partnerships in Darfur, the Democratic Republic of Congo, Uganda, South Sudan, Afghanistan, and with Syrian refugees in Jordan.

War Child Netherlands

War Child Netherlands was founded in 1994 by Willemijn Verloop as a reaction to the war in Bosnia. Today it is the largest War Child office with a yearly expenditure of 12.6 million Euros in 2010, and has specialised in helping the psychosocial needs of children who have suffered from war and conflict situations, using creative arts. The organisation grew from a one-man office in 1994, to 40 employees in the Netherlands and 600 abroad in 2007. War Child runs music, creative, and sports activities for war-affected children. In 2005 War Child Netherlands introduced a new measurement system for the programmes in 14 countries. In the first results it was shown that the projects reach more than 650,000 children worldwide. War Child Netherlands currently works in Afghanistan, Colombia, Democratic Republic of Congo, Israel, the Palestinian territories, Lebanon. Sierra Leone, Sri Lanka. Sudan, and Uganda. It also has special projects for refugees in the Netherlands. Previous projects have included Chechnya, Ingushetia, Georgia, and Kosovo.

War Child USA

War Child USA is the newest member of the War Child family. It supports the programs managed by War Child Canada in its countries of operation by making grants to War Child Canada. War Child USA currently has offices in Los Angeles and New York City.

The founders

War Child was founded in 1993 by British filmmakers Bill Leeson and David Wilson, when they returned from filming in the war in former Yugoslavia. In 1993 the first War Child convoy with equipment, and food to run a mobile bakery travelled to former Yugoslavia. War Child Netherlands was founded shortly after in 1994 by Willemijn Verloop, when she met Music Therapy professor Nigel Osborne during the war in Bosnia; War Child Holland programmes have been concerned with provision of psychosocial aid. War Child Canada was founded in 1998 by Samantha Nutt and Eric Hoskins.

Stars, media, and music

During the war in the Balkan, War Child worked together with the media, music and entertainment industries to raise funds and public awareness of the daily struggle for survival facing children in war zones. Artists including Brian Eno, David Bowie, Bono, Luciano Pavarotti, and Tom Stoppard backed the War Child cause at the start-up of the organization. In 1995 the record-breaking release of The Help Albummade it possible for War Child to start major projects in the former Yugoslavia. Since 1993, artists including Paul McCartney, Paul Weller, Oasis and Radiohead have joined the War Child cause.

In 2005, to mark the 10th anniversary of The Help Album, War Child UK launched Help!: A Day in the Life. In addition to Radiohead and Manic Street Preachers, the new album featured artists such as Coldplay, Bloc Party, Gorillaz, Elbow, and Kaiser Chiefs, along with Keanewho are current patrons of War Child UK. Another compilation album, Heroes, was released in February 2009. In 2008 War Child helped realise the film "The Silent Army" which was an initiative of War Child ambassador Marco Borsato. The film attracted a lot of attention in the Netherlands and was selected for the 'Un Certain Regard' section of the Cannes film festival in 2009. On February 18, 2013, English alternative rock band Muse performed live, to a sold out crowd, at the O2 Shepherd's Bush Empire in honour of War Child's 20th year of existence.

The video game This War of Mine was released on November 14, 2014 by 11 bit studios in partnership with War Child as part of the "Real War is Not a Game" campaign. The goal of the campaign is to halt the perpetuation of war crimes, such as hostage taking or other breaches of the Geneva Conventions, in video games. On March 9, 2015, downloadable content for the game was released on Steam, titled "War Child Charity DLC", the proceeds of which were donated to War Child. A bundle of 12 games called HELP: THE GAME, also available on Steam, donates all of its proceeds to War Child as well. Released on July 28, 2016, this bundle is the result of various well-known game developers taking part in a 6-day-long game jam. Creative Assembly said it would donate 25 percent of pre-order profit from Total War Saga: Thrones of Britannia sales on Steam. In 2018 Lady Amelia Windsor donated twenty percent of the proceeds from her shoe line collaboration with Penelope Chilvers to War Child.

War Child programmes

Starting off with mobile bakeries from the UK and with both rebuilding and music programmes from Holland, War Child projects expanded rapidly during the years. War Child expanded programmes within the Balkan to other countries and regions, like Kosovo. In 1995 War Child UK was undertaking the establishment of a children's music centre in Mostar, later to be called The Pavarotti Music Centre. War Child Holland actively supporting the Music Therapy Programme in Bosnia, a direction they would later specialise in; using creative and psychosocial means to heal traumas of war. From 1995 the War Child Diabetic Programme restored the diabetic support system in Bosnia; and until 1998 War Child remained one of the main suppliers of diabetic medicines throughout Bosnia and Herzegovina.

Celebrity Patrons

War Child has historically been supported and endorsed by numerous influential patrons. However, it lost support from Luciana Pavarotti, Brian Eno, and three other celebrity patrons, along with 11 trustees, after it was discovered that in 1995 co-founder Bill Leeson took a bribe from contractors building a music centre in Bosnia. In 2001 when the story broke, War Child said that any financial mismanagement in the charity occurred "years ago" and they are "dealing properly with these historical charges". The UK Charity watchdog, the Charities Commission stated that they had been involved with the trustees regarding the matter since 1998. While the internal matter at War Child seems to have been rectified, David Wilson remains blacklisted in the aid world following his whistleblowing and Bill Leeson is now a director at GardenAfrica, a charity he co-founded in 2002.

Friends-International (FI) is an international social enterprise and registered non-governmental organization focusing on children's empowerment established in Cambodia in 1994. Its mission is "to build a future where all children are safe from all forms of abuse, are able to become productive citizens of their countries and contribute to a more equitable and sustainable world." FI works in Cambodia, Indonesia, Laos, Thailand and with almost 50 partners around the world, providing comprehensive social services to marginalized urban young people and their families. Since its inception, FI has supported the education, well-being, and sustainable reintegration of more than 300,000 marginalized children, youth, and caregivers.

FI pursues the empowerment and protection of children and youth through a variety of projects that fall into four programs: Friends Programs, ChildSafe Movement, ChildSafe Alliance, and Friends Social Business. In recognition of its impact, FI has received the following awards:

- The WTM Responsible Tourism Gold Award for best Responsible Tourism Campaign (2016)
- The Child10 Award (2014)
- The WildAsia Award for Most Inspiring Responsible Tourism Initiative (2014)
- The AGFund International Prize for Pioneering Human Development Project (2013)
- GlobalJournal Top 100 NGOs (2012,2013)
- The Schwab Foundation Award for Social Entrepreneurship (2009)

- The Isabelle Allende Foundation Espiritu Award (2008)
- The Skoll Award for Social Entrepreneurship (2007)
- The Gold Medal of the Cambodian Government for the Reconstruction of the Country (2005)
- The Silver Medal of the Sociétéd' Encouragement au Progrès (2003)
- The Order of Australia for Service to Humanity (2002)

Outreach[

FI's Outreach team (initiated in 1994) is central to the organization's child protection strategy and a critical first step in building the capacity of vulnerable children and youth to secure a higher quality of life. Outreach activities are carried out on the streets, in communities and in drop-in centers. Strong trust-based relationships are built with the children and their families over time, their needs assessed and alternatives to street life presented. The Outreach team, made up of trained social workers and medical staff, provides healthcare, medical services, hygiene facilities/materials, non-formal education (mobile schools and libraries to build children's affinity for school), life skills education and awareness raising (in reproductive health, drugs, hygiene, nutrition, street safety, early childhood care, child rights, safe migration), recreational activities (sports, games) and finally, referrals to other FI projects. In 2013, Outreach served 18,000 marginalized children, youth and caregivers.

Public school reintegration

FI's School Reintegration Project (initiated in 1996) aims to provide a path for out-of-school children to reintegrate into the public school system. Children who are able and willing to re-enter school are first enrolled in FI's remedial education project, where they are brought up to speed in literacy, mathematics, science, geography and history. At the start of the public school year, FI supports him/her to reintegrate into a local school and provides the necessities needed for class. After reintegration is achieved FI provides ongoing support for the child to stay in school through continuous follow-ups, support classes and by encouraging parents to become active participants in their child's education. In 2013, the project supported the reintegration of 4,000 children and provided remedial education to 400 children.

Vocational training and job placement

The Vocational Training Project (initiated in 1995) provides access to professional skills training in order to foster the future employment opportunities of marginalized youth. Depending on the country program, the project offers training in a range of different professions including: barbering/hairdressing, welding, hospitality/ cooking, electronic appliance repair, electronic circuitry, motor mechanics, sewing and beauty/manicure. The program also entails a full range of basic and social services, such as psycho-social counseling, literacy/numeracy education, life skills education and job readiness education. After graduation, FI social workers work together with graduates to help them find employment or start their own micro-enterprises. Periodic follows-up are organized for a minimum of one year to ensure sustained reintegration. In 2013, FI provided 900 youth with vocational training and placed 300 youth in employment/self-employment.

Transitional home

Transitional Homes are temporary shelters for marginalized children separated from their caregivers or in emergency situations. The purpose of the Transitional Home is to facilitate the transition from a state of emergency to a state of recovery and reintegration. Those who stay at the Transitional Homes are provided with a stabilizing environment consisting of hygiene facilities, medical treatment, daily meals and counseling from FI's social workers. Social workers work to reintegrate the resident into a family environment and, if applicable, offer them a place in FI's remedial education and vocational training projects. In 2013, 1,000 children and youth were provided shelter at the Transitional Homes.

Bibliography

- Novak, Matt (2016-11-03). "The Largest Bioterrorism Attack In US History Was An Attempt To Swing An Election". Gizmodo. Retrieved 2016-12-02.
- Parashar, Sachin (28 August 2009). "Kalam certifies Pokharan II, Santhanam stands his ground". The Times of India. Retrieved 31 August 2010.
- Past U.S. Incidents of Food Bioterrorism. In Bioterrorism: A Threat to National Security or Public Health Defining Issue, University of Wisconsin–Madison and the Wisconsin State Laboratory of Hygiene, MM&I 554, September 30, 2008[permanent dead link]
- Peter Williams; David Wallace (1989), Unit 731: Japan's Secret Biological Warfare in World War II, Free Press,1
- Pike, John. "Al-Qaida". Globalsecurity.org. Retrieved October 18, 2011.
- Richard J. Evans (2008). The Third Reich at War, 1939–1945. Penguin. p. 669. ISBN 978-1-59420-206-3. Retrieved January 13, 2013.
- Rothschild J.H. (1964), Tomorrow's Weapons: Chemical and Biological, New York, New York: McGraw-Hill.
- Ruffner KC (1995). Corona: America's first satellite program. [New York]: [Morgan James]. p. 185.
- S.k. Prasad (2009). Biological Agents, Volume 2. Discovery Publishing House. p. 36.
- Suspect CW Agent Production Plants, Dzerzhinsk, USSR, Changes Since 1962. CIA/NPIC. 1963.